The Earth Goddess

Celtic and Pagan Legacy of the Landscape

To Caeia
who shared the journey with me.

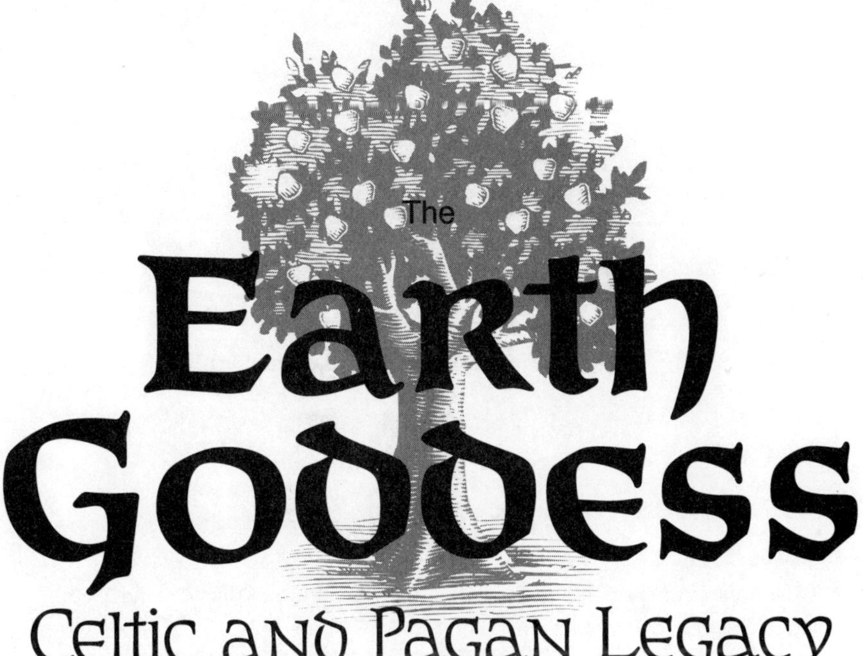

The Earth Goddess

Celtic and Pagan Legacy of the Landscape

Cheryl Straffon

BLANDFORD

A BLANDFORD BOOK
First published in the UK 1997 by Blandford
A Cassell Imprint
Cassell Plc, Wellington House,
125 Strand, London WC2R OBB

Distributed in the United States by Sterling Publishing Co., Inc.,
387 Park Avenue South, New York, NY 10016–8810

A Cataloguing-in-Publication Data entry for this title is available from the British Library

ISBN 0–7137–2644-X

Printed and bound in Great Britain by Hartnolls Limited, Bodmin, Cornwall.

Contents

Part 1: The Goddess

Part 2: The Gazetteer

Introduction

THE IDEA FOR THIS BOOK came to me one day a few years ago, when I was idly flicking through a book published in the 1860s on the legends and folklore of the island of Skye. I came across a whole section of mythology, handed down in oral tradition, that spoke of the belief in an ancient earth-creating Giantess of the land. I had just finished writing *Pagan Cornwall: Land of the Goddess*, in which I had tried to reclaim some of what I thought might have been the continuity of belief in a deity, which in prehistoric times had been visualized as a Goddess and under Christianity had metamorphosed into a saint or a legendary female supernatural being. I had found to my joy that, despite over 2,000 years of supression and denial, it was possible once again to get behind the 'establishment' view of religion and archaeology, and discover the roots of the native spirituality in my homeland of Cornwall. The book on Skye showed me that other places also had their stories and legends, and their special sites in the land whose meanings have been forgotten and associations lost. Indeed, the whole of Britain and Ireland could be looked at from this perspective and the long-forgotten past once again brought into the present.

Pagan Cornwall was to strike a chord with many readers, who wanted a view of history and prehistory which provided an alternative interpretation of our past that was not centred on battle, conquest and hierarchy, but equally was not based on fantasy and inaccurate information. I had become aware that ancient civilizations all over the world focused on, or incorporated into their belief structures, a recognition of the generative, nurturing and cyclical essence of the universe called the Goddess, and this pre-dated the later religions of Christianity, Judaism, Islam, Buddhism and Hinduism. I knew something of the history and development of these religions, having read for an English and Comparative Religion degree at university, and it seemed unlikely to me that Britain and Ireland would have been any different in this respect. Indeed, the extent and longevity of these Goddess religions is still being discovered and revealed by researchers. At a recent (1996) International Goddess Festival in San Francisco, Max Dashu showed some of the incredible 10,000 or so images of the Goddess she has found and investigated from civilizations all over the world, many little known even today.

At that same conference, Caeia March and I presented the research we had been doing on the Goddesses of Britain and Ireland, a personal odyssey that took us not only to the well-known sites but also to other, more obscure places, and had me delving into little-known legends and myths from all over the country. That research provides the matrix for this book – a book that attempts to peel away the obscuring layers to find the Goddess within, and to make this accessible so that everyone can go and see for themselves. This is the book I have always wanted to have with me when travelling around the country, for it tells me not just where the interesting places are (there are travel books and archaeological guides by the score to do that), but also about the places where the Earth Goddess was once celebrated – and can be again.

The book is divided into two parts. The first gives the contextual background to the continuity of Goddess belief. It tries to answer the questions about how and where she was celebrated, where she came from and what happened to her. It also draws together the threads of Goddess belief from different places all over Britain and Ireland, and tries to follow her story through 7,000 years of history. It will, I hope, provide a theoretical model for what I believe was the original spiritual belief of the British and Irish islands, although not everyone will necessarily accept my premise that Goddess belief slipped into folklore and tradition under Christianity.

The second part of the book is a country-by-country and county-by-county guide to sites that seem to have some link with Goddess(es) in Britain and Ireland. Some of these are obvious, others much less so. At some the Goddess link is clear, at others it has to be teased out. The selection of these sites has been difficult. I have no doubt that some readers will be unconvinced by some interpretations, while others may feel I have erred on the side of caution and not been imaginative enough. I leave it to each reader to decide for her or himself. At the end of the day, I wanted 'real Goddess', not the fey 'Goddess movement' that turns every stone into a grandmother crone and conjures up goddesses out of thin air. But at the same time I feel there is enough real Goddess out there for it not to be denied or dismissed as fictional folklore or reconstructed belief, as some reductionist historians and folklorists would like us to accept. Indeed, I was constantly amazed and delighted at what the research has thrown up: the sheer quantity and variety of Goddess places, Goddess names and Goddess stories. This is a book of a thousand Goddess tales, and they are all real and out there, waiting to be reclaimed.

Finally, a couple of points of explanation. Firstly, I have deliberately interpreted the term Earth Goddess in a very wide-ranging way. She proved to be impossible to box in or categorize, as she has changed and shape-shifted into different names and functions over the years. I take Earth Goddess to mean the original Earth Mother, whose body was the land and who later became the protectress of crops and cattle, and was celebrated in the agricultural wheel of the year. Later she became the guardian of the land, the home and the temple, and took on many names and forms. I also take her to mean the places in the land and on the earth where she may be discovered. Secondly, although I have tried to be as accurate as possible with my research into the source material, and have drawn widely on published ideas and interpretations (some of them well known, others less so), the final selection of material is my responsibility alone. Equally, although I have tried to present an accurate and up-to-date compendium of the location of sites and artefacts, with map directions, Ordnance Survey location finders and details of museum holdings, please remember that things do change all the time. For this reason, I have not attempted to give specific opening hours and days for places, but instead have included telephone numbers so that current information can be checked out.

There are some very good books on Goddess in Britain and Ireland, and I have drawn particularly on Miranda Green and Anne Ross (see Bibliography). There are also some very good guidebooks to ancient sites, and travel books that give museum details. But nowhere have I been able to find a book that will tell me where the sites are located that are particularly associated with Goddess, how to get to them, and where the Goddess figurines and artefacts from them have gone. I hope this book will fill that gap, and if it helps the traveller to find some of the wonderful spiritual places in our lands, see them perhaps with a new perspective, and go out and find some of our neglected and unacknowledged Goddess statues and images, then it will have been more than worthwhile.

Using this book

Dates are given in the non-denominational format, which seems appropriate for such a book: that is, BCE=Before Current/Common Era (equivalent to BC), and CE=Current/Common Era (equivalent to AD).

Arrangement Sites are organized geographically within their counties, rather than alphabetically, as neighbouring sites are often related in one way or another. Refer to the index in order to locate the descriptions of specific sites in which you are interested.

Map locations are those of the grid system of the Ordnance Survey maps of Britain and the Ordnance Survey of Ireland, which allow in those countries any site to be located precisely, no matter which scale of map is being used. For Britain, the 1:50,000 scale (2cm to 1km/1¼in to 1 mile) will be adequate for most sites, but the 1:25,000 (4cm to 1km/2½in to 1 mile) scale may be necessary for the more obscure places. For Ireland, existing maps are in a 1:126,720 scale (0.8cm to 1 km/½in to 1mile) but are gradually being replaced by 1:50,000 (2cm to 1km/1¼in to 1 mile), at present available mainly for the west of the country.

Directions are intended to help the visitor locate the site if travelling by car or train. There may also be local bus routes that pass near to the site. To avoid unnecessary repetition, compass-point directions are abbrevi-

ated: N=north, S=south, E=east, W=west.
Access Except in the case of churches, which unfortunately these days may not be open to the public at all times, there is access to the sites at all times unless otherwise specified (when opening hours and/or a contact telephone number are given). However, many of the locations are in open countryside, and therefore disabled access is difficult. If in doubt, call the local Tourist Information Office.
Telephone numbers are given with internal British and Irish area codes.
An asterisk (*) is used throughout the book to indicate Goddesses suggested by linguistic clues, for whom there is no written verification.

GOG MAGOG, WANDLEBURY, CAMBRIDGESHIRE
(ROUTLEDGE).
(SEE PAGE 119-120)

Acknowledgements

My primary acknowledgement is to Stuart Booth of Cassell, who believed in this book right from the beginning and helped to nurture it into being. Many other people have freely given me their time, help and information for the book, without which it would be a much poorer product. These include (in alphabetical order):

Jon Barker, Michael Bayley, Paul Beautyman, Tracey Brown, Aubrey Burl, David Clarke, Eamon Cody, Sally Cooper, Robin Ellis, Miranda Green, Bronwen Griffiths, Heather Henderson, Philip Heselton, Ruth Hirst, Patti Howe, Dave and Sue James, Chris Jenkins, Kelvin and Debbie Jones, Jules Kent, Thomas Lord, Calum MacIntosh, Gordon McLellan, Donald Macer-Wright, Terence Meaden, Jan Millington, Marian Nagahiro, Jo Pacsoo, Chesca Potter, Jack Roberts, Miceal Ross, Monica Sjöö, Brian Slade, Jill Smith, Amber Smithwhite, Pamela Soden, Arthur Straffon, Lynn Straffon, Rob Wilson.

My thanks go also to the many museum curators, county archaeologists and others who have provided information for the book. Special thanks are due to my colleagues in the Bibliographical Research Department of Cornwall County Libraries, and other library authorities, who have been unstintingly helpful in tracking down references and documents for me. Long may such an invaluable service continue!

The author and publishers would like specifically to acknowledge the permission given by Oxford University Press for the extract in Chapter 4 from *The Festival of Lughnasa* by Maire MacNeill, published in 1962; also the material reproduced from the many excellent small journals, often produced on a shoestring budget, that contain much original research and ideas not found elsewhere. Finally, my special thanks to Geraldine Andrew and Craig Chapman for their flexibility in putting up with my tight deadlines for all the artwork they have contributed to the book.

Part I:

The Goddess

The Goddess of the Stones:
the Prehistoric Sites

THE AGE IS ABOUT 5,000 YEARS AGO. The place is somewhere in the islands that were later to be named after the Goddess Britannia and the Goddess Eriu. The time is the darkest hour of the shortest day of the year. The night is cold, but the day has been warm and sunny, and the skies are clear as usual. Across the slopes of the hills, cleared quite recently from the forests that formerly covered them, weaves a serpentine line of people bearing flaming torches, and the sound of a low murmuring chant can be heard. They approach a large mound standing on the flank of the hill, its breast-like shape reflecting the curves of the slopes of the neighbouring hills and vales. It is covered in white quartz fragments that glisten and gleam by the light of the torches. The people stop at the entrance to the mound and form a circle.

A fire is lit from wood brought to the site earlier, and as the chanting becomes louder, the dancing around the fire begins. The chant is an invocation to she who rules the skies, gives them warmth and light, brings their crops to fruition in the summer, and now appears but briefly in this dark black, slumbering time of winter. This is her shortest day: the 'measurers' of the tribe have worked this out over the years, just as they have used their menstrual cycles to work out the times of the moon and her phases. The chanting builds higher and higher, the dancing becomes wilder and wilder, and at a pre-arranged signal, some step aside and begin to prise open a stone blocking part of the entrance to the mound.

Into the chamber goes the one whose turn it is to carry some of the bones of those who have died over the year since this ceremony was last performed. She has already ingested some plants that grow locally to the site and is in a state of heightened awareness and altered consciousness. She places the bones with others already in the chamber, and calls softly to the ancestors who dwell within the mound and watch over the day-to-day lives of the people as they till their newly created fields and milk their recently domesticated cattle. She asks the ancestors for their help and guidance, their knowledge and wisdom, to learn what must be done for the future well-being of the tribe. Her spirit seems to leave her body and she feels she is flying across the land, looking down at the stone circle that the tribe is beginning to build in the valley below for ceremonies to connect with the moon on her 18.6 year cycle. She feels at once exhilarated and at peace with herself.

Her spirit returns to her body and she becomes aware that the chanting outside has reached a crescendo, and in a dramatic moment of death and rebirth the first rays of the newly risen sun enter the dark space of the mound and illuminate a number of spiral carvings on the walls of the inner sanctum. The images seem to be moving around and standing out from the walls, pulsing with a life of their own. She feels a huge sense of joy, and the joy of the celebrants outside is also palpable. The Goddess is alive – they have felt her and seen her and acknowledged her presence in their lives and her protection for their tribe. She is in every stone, every blade of grass, every drop of water, every ancient hill. She flows through them and they through her. She *is* them and they are her. And so the wheel of the year has turned, and they are alive and thriving. And so they give thanks to her.

The foregoing reconstruction is just a fiction – anything from 5,000 years ago that has left no written record has, ultimately, to be a fiction – but it is a reconstruction based on everything we know from archaeology, climatology, prehistoric imagery, archaeo-botany and archaeo-astronomy. It is completely feasible that this is the kind of ceremony that would have happened at sacred places like this in the land, the remains of which can still be found today and which can speak to us over a period of 5,000 years.

The earliest evidence we have for occupation of these islands actually goes back even further than this. About 18,000 years ago, the Ice Age glaciers had retreated enough for early peoples to make their homes in the mouths of caves, which became places of safety and security from the many wild animals that still roamed freely. On the European continent these caves have yielded up amazing 'rock art' on the walls, including animals, shamans (priests and priestesses who connected with the spirit of the animal) and dancing women (from Cogus in Spain). In Britain and Ireland (which were then still attached to Europe) no rock art has been found, but remains in a cave on the Gower Peninsula in Wales revealed a body that had been painted red, the colour of the life blood. We can never be sure what was the faith or belief of these Paleolithic peoples, but it is perhaps legitimate to speculate that the caves may have been initiation chambers into the womb of the Goddess herself. Dating from this period, carvings of figures at the entrance of caves in Europe, such as those at Laussal and Lespugne, give credence to this theory.

By about 10000 BCE much of the ice had retreated from continental Europe, and the land was inhabited by small groups of hunter-gatherers called the Mesolithic (middle Stone Age) peoples. Around 6000–5000 BCE, rising sea levels from the melting ice had caused the land mass that was to become Britain and Ireland to separate from the rest of Europe, and by about 4000 BCE peoples following a different way of life began arriving by sea from the Continent. These Neolithic (New Stone Age) people had learned how to settle and farm, to grow crops and domesticate animals. They came originally from the Mediterranean and Eastern Europe, and from there we have evidence that they were Goddess-celebrating peoples. Some 30,000 miniature sculptures made of clay, marble, bone, copper and gold have been discovered in about 3,000 sites, including the amazing discoveries at Çatal Hüyük, in Turkey and of the Vinca culture in the former Yugoslavia. At Çatal Hüyük the central figure in one decorated shrine room after another was the Mother Goddess, and the archaeologist and excavator of the site, James Mellaart, has suggested that the religion may have been the creation of women, who elaborated a mythology where the birth-giving and nourishing capacity of the Goddess image was emphasized.

The other significant feature of the Neolithic peoples was pottery making, a domestic occupation probably created and practised originally by women. The pots which remain are covered with carvings such as chevrons, meanders and lozenges, as well as anthropomorphic images of birds, snakes, fish and so on, that have been interpreted as symbols of a Goddess culture. Some of these images can be found in the great mega-

KNOCKMANY DECORATED STONES (CRAIG CHAPMAN).

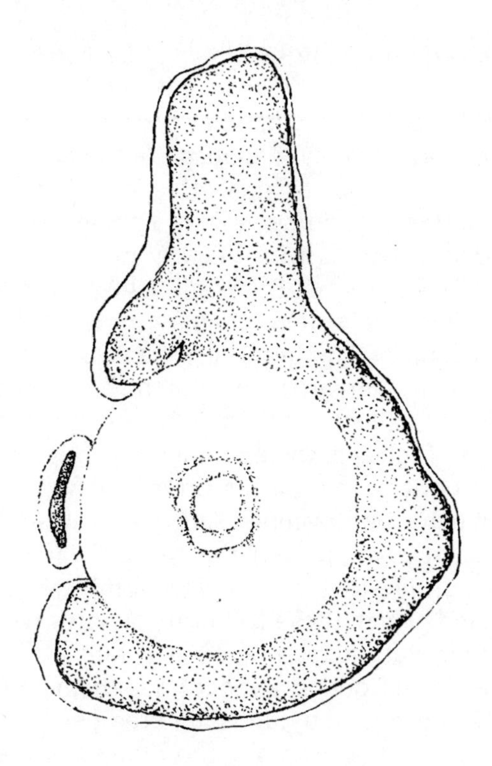

SILBURY GODDESS (CRAIG CHAPMAN).

lithic monuments that these people began to build once they had settled in an area: ceremonial sites like causewayed camps, henge monuments, long barrows and great mounds may be found all over Europe, Britain and Ireland. One of the oldest locations is Newgrange in Ireland, which contains many of the essential features of other such sites, but on a huge and very grand scale. It consists of a sizeable mound with an entrance passage and side chambers, surrounded by a ditch and a kerb. In this case, there is also a circle of standing stones around the outside, and it may be that the notion of such circles, which are indigenous to Britain and Ireland, developed from barrow mounds such as that at Newgrange. Many of the stones here are decorated with spiral and other motifs, and several of those inside the mound also bear spiral and lozenge patterns which, by analogy from other sites, have been interpreted as Goddess iconography. Such carvings can also be found at other important barrows, such as Barclodiad y Gawres on Anglesey and Knockmany in Ireland.

The entrance to the mound at Newgrange is aligned to the midwinter solstice sunrise, and time after time these Neolithic tombs have been found to be aligned in this way. Gavrinis in Brittany has a similar alignment, as does Stoney Littleton in the Cotswolds. Meas Howe on Orkney aligns to the midwinter solstice sunset, while Cairn T on Loughcrew in

Ireland faces the equinox sunrise, which illuminates a stone at the back of the tomb that is covered with circle and spiral motifs. These and many other sites combine a dramatic interplay of celestial symbolism with artistic imagery, that may be both a language of the cycles of the year and a celebration of the Goddess of life, death and rebirth.

The shapes of these monuments may also be suggestive of a perception of the land as a sacred, living deity. Many of the mounds are either breast shaped, such as that at Bryn-Celli-Dhu on Anglesey, in Wales, or appear to represent the swollen, pregnant body of the Mother, such as Silbury Hill in Wiltshire. The latter also has a special alignment to the *Lughnasad* or Lammas sunrise (the time of the harvest celebration), so the monument becomes a living symbol of a Goddess of nourishment and birth. The shapes of the chambered tombs also denote a symbolism that may imitate the body of the Earth Mother, Cotswold tombs like that at Stoney Littleton being one example. This type of symbolism is also apparent elsewhere, such as in the Neolithic temples of Malta.

We may thus surmise that these earliest tombs were built in a way that honoured the land, which these Neolithic peoples perceived literally as their Earth Mother. Natural features such as hills, valleys and rivers were the abode of the Earth Goddess, who formed them and sometimes dwelt in them, and the megalithic mounds imitated her form and distilled the essence of her being. For example, the mound of Freeborough Hill in Yorkshire was probably a naturally rounded outcrop, but is indistinguishable from the artificial Silbury Hill. Its shape and significance were noticed by the people, who built a cairn circle on the neighbouring Ainthorpe Rigg, from which this Goddess in the land could be viewed.

Many of these 'holy hills' may still be discernible in the landscape today as 'toot' mounds. The word can be traced back to its Indo-European root, where it probably meant 'to stick out', and words like 'teat' and 'tit'

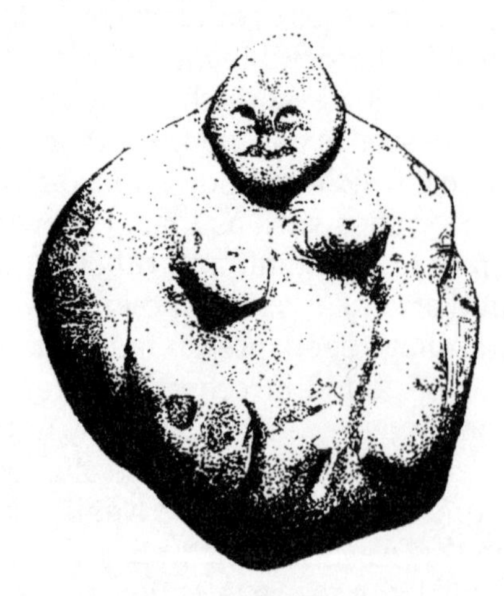

GRIMES GRAVES GODDESS (CRAIG CHAPMAN).

are derived from it. In old High German, *tutta* meant 'nipple', and the Old Norse *tutta* 'a teat-like prominence'. These toot mounds may thus have been seen in prehistoric times as the breasts of the Mother Goddess.

It is from this Neolithic period that a unique prehistoric Goddess figurine derives. Because of the time that has elapsed, and the overlaying by subsequent cultures, it is inevitable that much artefactual evidence from the period will have been lost. But deep within Mother Earth, protected from subsequent development, a chalk figure of a squatting goddess was found at the bottom of a flint mineshaft at Grimes Graves in Norfolk. She may have been left here as a means of placating the Earth Mother for digging deep into her body to extract the flints, or she may have been a way of thanking her for her gifts. She was found, together with two chalk balls, in a context suggestive of a shrine or some sort of sacred area, and is the earliest example in these islands of such an offering.

Another, lesser-known, wooden figurine was discovered beside the Bell Track in Somerset, and this appears to be an apotropaic carving of a goddess. The track, a wooden causeway that crossed the Somerset Levels, has been dated precisely to 2525 BCE, and it is possible that this goddess was made and given as a votive offering in recompense for cutting down the trees to make the causeway. From the same Neolithic period, a barrow at Folkton in Yorkshire has given up three small drums of shaped chalk from a child's grave, inscribed with the same kind of geometric designs that elsewhere have been interpreted as Goddess symbols[1]. At Black Burgh round barrow on the Sussex Downs north of Brighton, a pot was found with similar 'eyebrow' motifs; these may have symbolized a Goddess of fertility, who watched over the dead[2]. Various stone artifacts, which may represent Goddess heads and shapes, have also recently been discovered in Wessex (see Appendix 1).

Towards the end of the Neolithic period and into the Bronze Age (2500 BCE onwards), the so-called Beaker Folk moved into the British Isles. There is some debate as to whether they were a different kind of people – a more male-dominated hierarchy who worshipped a sun God rather than an earth and sun Goddess – or whether they were not really so different from the people already living in the islands. Certainly some of the practices changed around this time: communal long-barrow burials gave way to individual round-barrow burials with elaborate grave goods, but within this change of emphasis there was a tremendous variety of kinds of burial. Many of the high-status burials were of women as well as men, and as this is also the period of the great stone-circle construction, with its continuing focus on the cycles of the pastoral year and of the sun and the moon, it is perhaps wiser to think of it in terms of continuity of overall belief rather than radical change. The sacred places of the ancestors continued to be important, even if they were often remodelled or reused to reflect some changes in ritual practice, for example, at Stonehenge.

The stone circles continued the pattern of sacred sites aligned to significant landscape features at particular times of the year, including an increasing preoccupation with the moon and her 18.6 year cycle. Examples of this can be seen at Nine Stones Close in Derbyshire, which has a lunar alignment to a horned saddle hill, and the recumbent stone circles of Aberdeenshire in Scotland, many of which are aligned to significant phases in the moon's most southerly moonrise and moonset. However, the best example is perhaps Callanish stone circle on Lewis in the Western Isles of Scotland, from where at the major southern standstill (a lunar phenomenon that occurs once every 18.6 years) the full moon appears to rise out of the body of a hill in the shape of a sleeping woman and travel over her thighs and breasts before dropping down behind her head – one would be hard put not to accept the Goddess symbolism of a place such as this! On the nearby island of Jura in the Inner Hebrides, two prominent hills called the Paps of Jura (meaning 'breasts of Jura') are highlighted by the setting midsummer sun when viewed from some standing stones at Ballochroy on the mainland opposite. In all these cases there are significant hills associated with an Earth Mother or a Goddess, to which Bronze Age peoples deliberately aligned their ceremonial monuments at significant solar and lunar times, and this is firm evidence for the continuation of such ritual into the Bronze Age.

By about 1300 BCE the construction of these ritual megalithic monuments had all but ceased. It is interesting to speculate why – did the practice of religious belief change dramatically at this time, and if so, for what reason? One suggestion is that there was a deterioration in the climate: the warm, Mediterranean-type climate that prevailed in the Neolithic and early Bronze Ages and allowed settlement to take place on areas that are now quite bleak and inhospitable, such as Dartmoor and the North York Moors, was replaced by an altogether wetter, colder and harsher climate. In such circumstances it may well be that the old ways of celebrating the Goddess for her bounty and goodness were perceived to be outdated and ineffective. In addition, from about 700 BCE a continental Celtic culture began to move into the British Isles, and tribes such as the Belgae brought with them knowledge of iron, thus ushering in the Iron Age.

Hill forts now began to be built, or adapted from earlier Neolithic settlements, and while many of them may have been places of trade, commerce and ceremony, there is some indication that they also performed a defensive function. It is from this period that rich grave goods such as helmets, swords and shields are found, and these are indicative of some internecine rivalry between different tribes. At the same time, many of these deposits seem to have been made in a specifically ritual context. At Snettisham in Norfolk several hoards of Iron Age treasure have been found, many of the torques (neckbands) being decorated with intricate Celtic artwork and stylized faces that have been interpreted as possible Goddess representations. At Minster Abbey in Kent, a well shaft which may be from this period has yielded figurines of iron and wax formed in

GIGGLESWICK GODDESS (GERALDINE ANDREW).

the shape of a triple-headed goddess, although the finds are undated and could be earlier. At Giggleswick in Yorkshire a small lead figurine of a fertility Goddess was discovered in a context that may be connected with a sacred stream or holy well nearby, and at Ballachulish in the Highlands of Scotland an oak figure of a Mother Goddess has been discovered in a peat deposit, together with traces of a wicker basket, suggesting that she was placed in some kind of water shrine. There is also the enigmatic carving from Braunston in Rutland. Here a fierce Goddess figurine stands outside the rear of the church, and is quite unique in Britain and Ireland. It has been suggested that she dates from this period but this is by no means certain, and given the relatively good state of her preservation she may in fact be from a later time. If she is from the Iron Age, then she is one of a kind.

It may therefore be the case that visual representations of the Goddess were rare in Britain and Ireland from the Neolithic to the Iron Age, or it may be that any remaining icons have been ruthlessly destroyed by Christianity over the years, leaving only isolated examples in hidden places, such as the Grimes Graves and Bell Track goddesses from the

Neolithic period, the Minister Abbey goddess from the Bronze/Iron Age, and the Ballachulish and Giggleswick goddesses from the Iron Age. Perhaps these were unusual deposits, placed there because of some special significance of the site: two of the four examples above are from ritual pits, and two are associated with sacred waters. As we shall see, there are plenty of Goddess statues and friezes remaining from the Roman period, so perhaps prior to that celebration of the Goddess was made by means of ceremonial monuments in the landscape and/or perishable offerings, rather than permanent iconographic representations.

Some evidence for the religious significance of ceremonial monuments in the landscape continuing late into the Iron Age/Celtic period can be found in Cornwall. Here, a unique class of underground chambers called 'fogous' – Cornish for 'cave' – were built during this period (about 500 BCE to 500 CE). Although they bear some similarities to *souterrains* in Ireland, Scotland and Britanny, the suggested explanations for the use of the latter do not really apply to fogous. *Souterrains* often consist of many false entrances, traps and hidden passages, indicating that their primary function may have been for refuge, but fogous usually consist of a single curved passage, with perhaps a secondary passage leading to a dead end, and a small creep entrance. As places of refuge they would be disastrous, and as storage chambers quite ineffective except for dairy goods, for which purpose they seem ridiculously large. Researchers into Earth Mysteries have claimed for years that they were places of ritual and ceremony, and now archaeologists are coming to the same conclusion[3]. It has been shown that nearly all the structures are aligned to the midsummer solstice sunrise, except for two that are aligned to the midsummer solstice sunset. Corroboratory evidence for this theory comes from one site, Carn Euny in Cornwall, where the original beehive-hut circular chamber, which pre-dates the construction of the fogou, was aligned to the midwinter solstice sunrise. We know from other places that our ancestors revered their ancestors and would often build their religious monuments on sites that were already sacred, while at the same time having no compunction about altering the design. If fogous are astronomically aligned, and it seems very likely that they are, then we are seeing a very late continuation of megalith-

BALLACHULISH GODDESS (CRAIG CHAPMAN).

ic religious tradition. Given the relative isolation of Cornwall from the rest of England, it may well be that an indigenous tradition of symbolic orientation continued there much later than in other areas of Iron Age influence, where it had been abandoned.

There is evidence from other places[4] that to many ancient peoples the sun was a goddess who withdrew into a chamber or cave at solstice time and had to be lured out again by elaborate ritual and bonfires. There is some linguistic evidence for this from the period, where in the earliest recorded usage of the word 'sun' in Irish and Scots Gaelic (*griane/greine* or *tethin*) it is a feminine noun. A later Gaelic prayer refers to the sun as *mathair aigh nan reul* – 'glorious mother of the stars'. So, it seems likely that at the period in question the people were still referring to the sun as 'she', and the fogous in Cornwall may be an earthly embodiment of this.

We are now entering the historical period, where the nature of Goddess changes, because for the first time we have written evidence. The one Goddess of the Neolithic and Bronze Age, the giver of life, nurturer of the peoples, and watcher over the dead, has by now become fragmented into various goddesses and gods. These are still very important deities – goddesses of the tribe, or the land, or of the fertility of the earth and all her creatures, but for the first time we begin to know some of their names and attributions. Inscriptions are one source, stories and myths a second, and legends and folklore a third. Each of these comes with some difficulties and raises questions over interpretation and evidence, but the goddesses from here on in are more identifiable, and closer to us in time and distance.

And yet it is sometimes this earlier Goddess of the land who speaks most powerfully to us: in the hills and valleys, rivers and lakes, in the sunrise and sunset, the moon's cycle and the wheel of the year – she is there. In the tombs and mounds of our ancestors, in the Paleolithic caves and Iron Age fogous, in the burial deposits and offerings to the sacred streams, this prehistoric Goddess figure, unnamed and unknown, *was* the land, and the ancient sites were built to celebrate her imminence and her presence. She remains an enigmatic, distant and yet curiously ubiquitous presence in the landscape we have inherited thousands of years later.

Notes

[1] By Marija Gimbutas in *The Goddesses and Gods of Old Europe*, *Civilization of the Goddess* and *The Language of the Goddess*.

[2] Details in Aubrey Burl, *Rites of the Gods* page 151, and personal communication.

[3] See Ian Cooke, *Mother and Sun: the Cornish Fogou*, and Nick Johnson, Cornwall County Archaeologist on Boleigh fogou in *Time Team*, Channel 4 broadcast 7 January 1996, and reported in *Meyn Mamvro* No 30, May 1996.

[4] Details in Janet McCrickard, *Eclipse of the Sun*, pages 96–7.

The Goddess in the Temple:
the Romano-British Figurines

IN THE SPRING OF 43 CE, an army of 40,000 men of the Roman Legion landed at Richborough in Kent, and the Roman invasion of Britain had begun. The Roman era is a story of battles and skirmishes, conquest and domination – and yet it is also much more than this. The Romans had an elaborate and sophisticated religious pantheon of goddesses and gods, and one of the first things they did when they captured the first major town of Britain, Camulodunum (Colchester, in Essex), was to build a splendid temple to give thanks for their success.

History is always written through the eyes of the conquerer, and what the Roman history of Britain tells us is the names and places of their cities and towns, the locations of their temples and villas, and the dates and details of their victories and temporary setbacks. We have to peep between the lines of their straight roads and garrison forts to see the Celtic land beneath that was replaced with a Romanized way of thinking and being. Yet in many ways the Romans found themselves at home in Britain. It may have been cold and bleak compared with their homeland, but they would recognize in the native tribes a way of connecting with the spirits and goddesses and gods of the universe that was not dissimilar to their own. Time and again, when we dig below the surface layer of Roman shrines and temples, we find that they have been built on earlier sacred places. At Maiden Castle in Dorset, a fourth-century Roman temple was built on an earlier Neolithic and Iron Age hill fort; at Canterbury in Kent, the Celtic tribe of the Cantiaci had already established a settlement at the crossing of the River Stour when the Romans developed it in the third century; and at Bath, an elaborate Roman centre was built around a natural spring that was venerated in much earlier times.

At Bath we can see how the Romans took over not only the sacred sites of the Bronze Age, Iron Age and Celtic peoples, but their goddesses as well. The site was dedicated to the Goddess Sulis Minerva, a hybrid deity who assimilated into her being not only the Roman Goddess Minerva, the Goddess of wisdom and crafts, but also the native British Goddess Sulis, who presumably was the original Goddess of the site. The same thing must have happened at Coventina's Well on Hadrian's Wall in Northumberland: this was a powerful centre for healing by an important deity, but as Coventina is not known to be so celebrated anywhere else in the Roman world (except for three doubtful references to her in Spain and France), the suspicion must be that she was originally a native British Goddess given a convenient Roman name. On Nornour in the Isles of Scilly, the important Romano-British shrine to the Goddess *Sillina was established on a site previously occupied from the Bronze Age onwards. We can perhaps infer that it developed here precisely because it was already a sacred place dedicated to a marine goddess. At Littledean in Gloucestershire, too, the Romano-British temple, probably dedicated to the Goddess of the river, Sabraan, was built on a site occupied as far back as the Neolithic and Iron Ages.

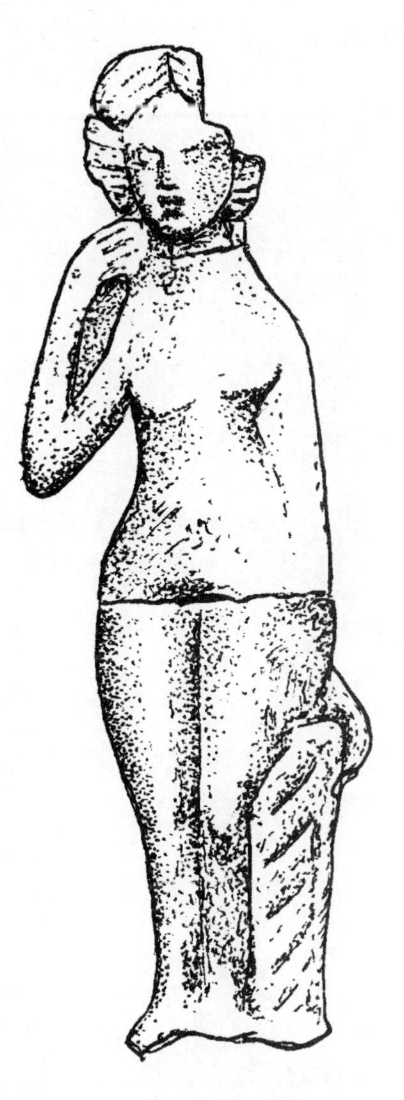

NORNOUR FIGURINE (GLEN LYON).

Another similar situation pertains to the Goddess Brigantia, the tribal deity of the Brigantes people who occupied most of northern England. Half a dozen altar inscriptions to her have been found, including at Greetland in Yorkshire, Corbridge in Northumberland on Hadrian's Wall, and at South Shields in Tyne and Wear. She is twice addressed as Victoria (the Roman Goddess of victory), once equated with Caelestis (a Syrian Goddess), and once described as a nymph. The principal depiction of her is from Birrens in Scotland, where she is shown winged like Victory, equipped with Minerva's spear, helmet and shield, wearing a mural crown and holding a globe in her left hand. She is clearly a very Romanized Goddess of victory, but the question remains as to what she represents. If she is a triumphal depiction of the Roman defeat of the Brigantes tribe, why is she shown as the personification of the hegemony of that tribe? It seems more likely that she is a Roman interpretation of the powerful Celtic deity of the land, who may have been visualized very differently by the Brigantes themselves. Other local Celtic Goddesses may have included ür-versions (earlier versions) of Setlocenia ('the long-lived one') from Maryport, Saitada ('grief Goddess')from the Tyne Valley, and

ILKLEY VERBIA
(CRAIG CHAPMAN).

THORNBOROUGH ISIS
(GERALDINE ANDREW).

Flidais ('woodland deity') from Ireland.

The Roman temples and shrines were often built at strategic river crossings that may well have existed already in pre-Roman times. At these places, the spirit of the waters would have been an important deity to be honoured and thanked for a successful passage. We know that these were thought of as liminal places that were at the threshold of this world and the world of the spirit, and several significant artifacts have been found at key sites. At Aust on the River Severn near Bristol in Avon, a beautiful Mediterranean-style Goddess figurine was found, which may have been imported and left as a thanksgiving for safe passage across the seas by traders. At Chedworth in Gloucestershire, a nymphaeum – a shrine to a water goddess – was discovered in a villa close to the River Colne. At East Stoke near Thorpe in Nottinghamshire, the Roman settlement of Ad Pontem lay at a crossing of the River Trent where a relief of a god and goddess was found. Her name, Nantosuelta, may mean 'meandering stream'. At Ribchester in Lancashire, the Roman fort of Bremetennacum stood beside the River Ribble at a major crossing point, and has yielded the statue of a god, Maponus, and two goddesses. At Ilkley in Yorkshire, at another Roman fort which stood at a crossing of the River Wharfe, an altar carving was found with an inscription to the Goddess Verbia, whose name may mean 'winding river'. And from Thornborough in Buckinghamshire, in a loop of Padbury Brook, a tributary of the River Ouse, a statue of the Goddess Isis, originally a goddess of the waters of the Nile in Egypt, was discovered.

Perhaps the most interesting of all these 'river-crossing' goddesses is one carved out of the natural rock face in Roman quarries to the south of the ancient crossing of the River Dee in Chester, in Cheshire. She is a depiction of Minerva and a shrine was made here by the Romans, who worked the quarries for the stone that was used to build the fortress in the city. The natural forces had to be honoured and placated, and even in these Roman times the goddesses were perceived as being in the land as well as in the temples of the land. Indeed, the Romans even had their own specific Earth Goddesses, the Ollototae, as evidenced by an altar inscription found at Chester.

Pre-Roman Britain had consisted of a number of Iron Age tribes, such as the Dumnonii in the south west, the Cantiaci in Kent, the Iceni in East Anglia, the Cornovii in the West Midlands, and the Brigantes in the north. Each of these had not only particular goddesses of sacred wells and springs, such as Sulis and the pre-Roman Coventina, and goddesses of rivers and river crossings, but also probable goddesses of sacred groves where, so Pliny the Roman historian tells us, the priestly caste of the Druids worshipped. These groves did not necessarily need permanent buildings or structures, but memory of them is hinted at in the Romanized names of some earlier Celtic places. A relief was found at Bath of the Goddess Nemetona, whose name literally means 'Goddess of the sacred

CHESTER MINERVA (GERALDINE ANDREW).

grove', and at Buxton in Derbyshire the Goddess Arnemetiae was worshipped, her name deriving from the same root and meaning 'in front of a sacred grove'. In London, the Walbrook stream was probably sacred in pre-Roman times, and many skulls found from the river attest to a sacrificial spot dedicated by the Iceni under Queen Boudica, who made her stand here against the Romans after she had been flogged mercilessly by them and her two daughters raped. Ironically, after her defeat the site continued in sacred use by the Romans, as the discovery there of many pipeclay figurines of Venus-style Goddesses shows. They also built a temple nearby, which not only was dedicated to the sun god Mithras but also contained a statue of the Mother Goddesses. Continuity of religious practice was as important to the Romans as it had been before.

Indeed, it was the Romans who left the greatest collection of nurturing Mother Goddesses in Britain. These Dea Nutrix were found in many Roman temples, shrines and dwellings, and demonstrate that the Romans continued to honour and worship a Goddess of nourishment and sustenance, as their British and Irish forebears had done in the sacred monuments of the land. Many of these Mother Goddess figurines are depicted in triple form, for reasons we do not fully understand. They do not seem to be three aspects of the Goddess (maiden, mother and crone) but usually consist of three similar figures, each holding some symbols of the fruits of the earth or showing slight variations on the theme of nourishment. The following examples all show the Goddess as fertile Earth Mother.

Firstly, a relief from Lincoln, found built into a wall in the lower part of the city, shows three seated Goddesses each in an arched niche. Each rests her right hand in her lap and with her left holds an object on her knee: one has a basket of fruit, the second a small animal or child, and the third a possible sheaf of corn. Each of these is a symbol of fertility and an aspect of an Earth Goddess. From nearby Ancaster (and now in Grantham Museum), a more formalized frieze shows the Three Matres (one now headless) who appear identical in pose, but once again each holds something different: the figure on the left has a *patera* – a dish for libations – in her right hand and a dish containing a small animal in her left; the central figure has a dish containing fruit in both hands; and the right-hand figure holds a large round loaf in her right hand, while her left is too badly damaged to tell.

From Cirencester in Gloucestershire come several reliefs of the Three Matres. In one they carry bowls or baskets, the one on the left with three long loaves, the central one with apples and the one on the right with four apples and three ears of corn; in another they are sitting on a bench and carry a baby, cakes and fruit. Also from the Cotswolds comes a rough carving of three Mother Goddesses sitting under a solar wheel – a rare identification of Goddesses as solar deities. From Carlisle in Cumbria comes a relief of three seated Matres, showing one holding a sacrificial knife or

CIRENCESTER MATRES (GERALDINE ANDREW).

loaf of bread across her chest, one a rounded object that may be a sacred cake, and the third a plant, all of which may be ceremonial offerings to the Goddess of the Earth. And from the abbey at Fort Augustus in Invernesshire comes a depiction of the Three Matres (one now headless), all identically dressed but each holding a different symbol of Mother Earth. The one on the left has a fruit and a wicker basket full of corn, the one on the right a fruit and a square basket, and the one in the centre a large bunch of grapes that spills over the edge of her lap and falls almost to her feet. These are all symbols of the fecundity and fertility of the Earth Goddess, who continued to be celebrated during this period.

As well as Mother Goddesses, there are depictions of three goddesses whose main attributes seem to be water rather than the fruits of the earth. These often occur in contexts where the representation of the water is of primary significance. For example, at Coventina's Well on Hadrian's Wall has come a relief of three water Goddesses, which have been interpreted as Coventina, the matron Goddess of the well, in triplicate. Nearby

HIGH ROCHESTER NYMPHS (GERALDINE ANDREW).

at High Rochester, a relief has been found depicting three naked Goddesses in a very animated and naturalistic pose. These three look much less identical than those in Coventina's relief, and probably depict a central Goddess, perhaps Venus, bathing with two attendant nymphs. At Maryport in Cumbria, an unusual frieze also shows three naked Goddesses, who do not appear to be nourishing or water Goddesses as they are not carrying or holding anything. Instead, they are differentiated by their hands being in different positions: the end two look as if their arms are folded, but the middle one has one arm pointing up and the other towards her pudenda. The latter seems to have more in common with the later sheela-na-gigs (see page 72–3), and if so she may be the earliest example of the genre and interesting proof of a fertility/sexual connotation.

The concept of the Three Matres is obviously a particularly Roman one as it has been found elsewhere in the Roman Empire, and yet it must have struck a chord in Romanized Britain. The Celtic peoples also had a great love of the concept of three, and although many of the figurines discovered would have been imported from Gaul, some seem to have a more native or Celtic feel to their execution. Very few statues or figurines of goddesses or even gods have been found that could be attributed directly to the pre-Roman period in Britain and Ireland, and yet we may suspect the hand of a native Celtic or British artist in some of the finds from a Roman context. For example, at Caerwent in South Wales a statuette of a seated Mother Goddess was found near the bottom of what may have been a ritual pit, a short distance to the east of the Romano-Celtic temple. Her large face is pear shaped, with round eyes and a wedge-shaped nose, and she has much more in common with an Earth Goddess than with the more formalized Roman matrons. From Drumburgh in Cumbria has come an unusual figure with a peasant-like appearance, a wreath, or even perhaps a grinding quern (stone), in one hand, and a staff or bowl in the other. She is not crudely or incompetently carved, but certainly shows a more 'earthy' appearance than some of the more formal Romanized sculptures. The altar depiction of the Goddess Verbia with snakes from Ilkley in Yorkshire (see page 24) has a similar local and unsophisticated feel to it. All these sculptures occur in areas where the Celtic influence was still strong in Roman times, and it may well be that the spirit of an older Earth Goddess still moved through these native artists who were carving for the Romans.

If this is the case, however, we have to ask why – with the possible exception of the Ballachulish figurine (see page 20) – no such depictions have been found from the Iron Age period prior to the Romans' arrival. It seems unlikely that they would all have been lost or destroyed, given the Romans' preference for conquest by assimilation rather than total destruction. The answer may well be that specific likenesses of the Goddess were relatively rare, and the Celtic tribes were still expressing their reverence for deity through sacred places in the land and intricate artwork. Support for this theory comes from Ireland, which (with the exception of a coastal settlement north of Dublin) the Romans never occupied and where no reliefs, friezes or figurines have been found. In Britain, when the Romans arrived with their already established pantheon of goddesses and gods the native Celtic/British peoples at first opposed them, then were conquered by them, and finally imitated them and copied their styles and practices. Thus some of the Goddess figurines were probably made locally by artists who expressed Roman formality through their own native informality. Their goddesses were the goddesses of the land used for worship in the temple.

The Roman Goddess statues, figurines and inscriptions that have been discovered are primarily those that would have been commissioned by the wealthy or relatively well-off higher echelons of Roman or Romano-British society. The Roman empire was built on slavery and privilege, and the ordinary peasant of Britain and Ireland would not have had the resources or opportunity to make or have made fine carvings of goddesses. There is, however, an interesting sub-class of figurines made from pipe-clay material, many of which were discovered in Kent, London, Carlisle, Bath, Sussex, York, Caerwent, Verulamium (St Albans), with a few in other places. One class of these depicts a Goddess who is generally called Venus, but who was probably venerated as a native water or fertility deity of unknown name[1]. The other class depicts a nursing mother called Dea Nutrix; although rarer than the Venus figurines, these probably represent a similar kind of native goddess equated with a Roman female deity of the same type[2]. These Goddess figurines may have been mass-produced, probably in Gaul, and made available to the poorer people to give as votive offerings. They may well be the localized version of the more formal and lavish Goddesses of fertility and the Très Matres that are found at Roman temples and shrines.

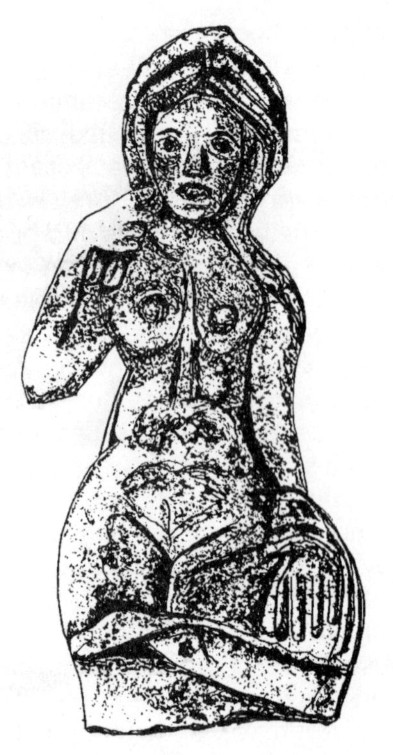

CHART SUTTON VENUS (GERALDINE ANDREW).

If the pipe-clay figurines lie at one end of the scale, then the temple goddesses lie at the other. Most of the goddesses that can be identified are Roman ones, but that is not to say that they are not also Romanized versions of native tribal goddesses, as in the case of Sulis Minerva in Bath. Minerva as a Goddess of war (Minerva Victrix) can be found in a relief carving of a head discovered at Corbridge in Northumberland that depicts the Goddess wearing a Corinthian helmet, and also in two heads from Cirencester in Gloucestershire, one showing her wearing a plumed helmet and the other a crested helmet. Other such heads have been found at Wall in Staffordshire and at Harlow in Essex; the latter may have been part of a cult statue that stood in a Romano-British temple. Warfare was about land and its ownership, so Minerva here was taking on the role of an Earth Goddess under patriarchal conflict.

But Minerva was not just a Goddess of war – she was also the Goddess of wisdom and crafts, with the owl as her totem symbol. This would have brought her much closer to the local Goddess of the birds, and an interesting statue found at Sibson in Cambridgeshire (now in Woburn Abbey, Bedfordshire) shows her holding an owl and wearing a gorgon's-head mask. Although executed in the Roman style, the statue came from a local quarry, and it has been suggested[3] that a vase also shown with a snake slithering up the back would indicate that this was a Goddess of crafts linked to the local pottery industry. Including as it does images of Goddess, owl, snake and pots, this may indeed be a depiction of a localized Earth Goddess given Roman form.

At Bath, Sulis Minerva is similarly depicted with an owl and a gorgon's-head mask with intertwining snakes. In her right hand she is carrying what has been interpreted as a spear, but in fact this looks much more like a staff, giving her the appearance of a Goddess connecting with the land and the sacred shrine of Aqua Sulis. Significantly, Bath was a place of healing waters, as was the site of Coventina's Well on Hadrian's Wall, where a relief of Minerva was discovered in the Roman fort nearby. On this relief she is carved with the figure of Aesculapius, and is associated with him in her capacity as a Goddess of healing. Minerva thus has a multi-faceted aspect and can be found not only as a Roman Goddess of war and territory, but also as a local Goddess of place.

The same kind of ambiguity applies to the Goddess Diana. She was the Roman huntress and lady of the beasts, and is often depicted with a wild animal at her side, a bow and arrow in her hand. At Housesteads in Northumberland, a relief from nearby Crow Hall Farm shows her with her bow and quiver, a stag standing behind her, while a fragment of a statue from Maiden Castle in Dorset shows a hound sitting close by. From Castle Combe in Wiltshire, a votive relief (now in the Ashmolean Museum in Oxford) shows a figure with a belt and what may be a bow. She may be drawing an arrow from a quiver, and is depicted with an animal that may be a dog or a doe. From Nettleton in Wiltshire comes an architectural relief (now in Bristol City Museum) showing a figure of Diana with a hound, and from Woodchester in Gloucestershire a headless statuette of Diana depicted with the head of a bull beside her right foot.

But Diana is also a lunar deity, and as such would have had a significant resonance with the indigenous Celtic peoples, who probably worshipped a Goddess of the moon. A child's grave recently discovered at Arrington in Cambridgeshire contained a carving of a Mother Goddess carrying a basket of apples or pomegranates. Around her neck hangs a crescent moon – the same symbol as was discovered in Leadenhall Street in London behind the head of a pipe-clay figurine. Nearby was found a bronze statuette depicting the horned huntress, with a *patera* in her right hand and a cornucopia – horn of plenty – in her left. A frieze from Bath also shows a lunar Goddess carrying a whip, who may be Diana in her embodiment as Luna. In all these cases Diana is associated with the moon and fertility, and by extension she has also been traditionally linked to the menstrual cycle and childbirth[4]. It seems likely that such a Goddess or Goddesses would already have existed among the native Celtic tribes, thus explaining the ready acceptance and popularity of Diana when she arrived.

A version of Diana is known from many other places, so she was clearly a universally loved Goddess. In Greece she was Artemis – 'the bow-bearing goddess who rides the moon or strides through the forest with her nymphs'[5]. In Italy she was Diana, the Goddess of the sun and moon, and was worshipped in the open air, where her realm was the skies above. Her feast day – 15 August – was assimilated into the Catholic faith to become the day of Mary's assumption into heaven. In Roman times, processions of women would journey to Aricia accompanied by hunting dogs, to give thanks at Diana's Grove. She was the Goddess of the divine hunt and the wild places, and of women and the moon, and she is remembered in Britain by the ancient Diana's Well, dedicated to her on Witton Fell in Yorkshire, and was still worshipped as late as the fourteenth century by monks from Frithelstock Priory in Devon. She was evidently a Goddess who exercised a powerful hold over the hearts and minds of the people.

ARRINGTON GODDESS
(GERALDINE ANDREW)

Much rarer than Diana figures and friezes are those that may be of the Celtic horse Goddess Epona. The best known is a bronze statuette now in the British Museum. Its provenance is unknown, but it may originally have come from Wiltshire[6]. Epona is depicted in a sitting position, with what has been interpreted variously as a cornucopia, a serpent or a yoke on her left arm. She is carrying a *patera* and large ears of corn, and is flanked by two small ponies. The corn links her with the Matres, but the ponies, represented as much smaller in proportion to the figure, emphasize her divine status and make it clear who she is. The name Epona derives from the Gaulish word *epos* meaning 'horse', and she was especially venerated in Gaul and the Rhineland. Many representations of her show her feeding her horses, or depict young ponies suckling the mare or sleeping beneath her. The iconography also shows her with a dog and a key, and it has been suggested[7] that she has other-world associations, representing a goddess who presides over the journey of the soul through life and into death and the next world. She thus seems to have been a Celtic Goddess of horses and the other world, whose original name and attributes persisted through into Roman times.

The Romans adopted Epona as they did many of the goddesses in the lands they conquered, their approach to religion being a somewhat eclectic one, and there was even a festival dedicated to her in Rome on 18 December. It is therefore perhaps somewhat surprising that we do not have more evidence of her iconography in Britain and Ireland, especially as horses and horse Goddesses (such as Macha and Rhiannon) feature so strongly in Irish and Welsh myth. From South Collingham in Nottinghamshire has come the cheekpiece of a helmet that depicts her standing in front of a horse and holding a cornucopia on her arm; from Colchester a fragment of a statue showing her sitting side-saddle on a horse; and from Winchester a statuette in wood depicting a Goddess holding a key in her right hand which may be a depiction of Epona in her chthonic aspect (pertaining to rites of the underworld or death). There are also a couple of dedications to her from Carvoran and from Auchendavy on the Antonione Wall. This quite meagre haul belies the importance of Epona in the Romano-Celtic world: she was a Goddess of fertility and fecundity, of land and prosperity, of life and death. She was of the earth, from the earth, and passed over the earth.

Finally, there are those Romanized goddesses who seem to perform a function relating to well-being, good fortune and success. There are many dedications to and representations of the Goddess Fortuna in Britain, particularly from Hadrian's Wall, Cirencester and Lincoln, all areas of strong Roman dominance. Her attributes include a cornucopia, a rudder and a globe or wheel, all symbolic of changes of fortune. She seems to have been not so much a Goddess of the land as an urbanized Goddess, one that today we might call 'lady luck'. However, a couple of depictions are interesting, for they show her associated with an Earth Goddess, namely Ceres, the Goddess of the harvest, a popular deity often portrayed on signet rings. This Earth Goddess was linked in the Roman world with Tellus: Tellus represented Mother Earth, Ceres the growth of plants in the earth. She was the Goddess of creation and the harvest, and her festival of Cerealia in June continued to be celebrated in parts of Britain right up to the nineteenth century.

From Corbridge on Hadrian's Wall comes a relief of Fortuna with a seated Goddess who has been tentatively identified as Ceres[8]. She is depicted holding a long, flaming torch in her left hand and what may be a cake or loaf in her right, both attributes of the Goddess. On a pedestal behind perches a cock, not normally associated with her but appropriate to her role as a chthonic deity (she also represents the death of the harvest in the whole cycle of life). Fortuna was also identified with the Greek Goddess Demeter. Moreover, her daughter Persephone was sometimes shown with a cock, and the distinction between mother and daughter often became blurred. There is a depiction from Cirencester showing the head of a Goddess who may be Ceres or Fortuna, and a relief of two Goddesses found at Housesteads on Hadrian's Wall (and subsequently destroyed in a fire) that has been interpreted as Ceres and Persephone, or perhaps Ceres with some other deity such as Cybele, the Great Mother – although Ceres was usually worshipped by the people and Cybele by the patricians.

In conclusion, we can see that the principal named Goddesses worshipped in Roman Britain were the Matres, Minerva, Diana, Epona and Fortuna/Ceres, all Goddesses who had probable Celtic antecedents which were assimilated into the Roman pantheon, and most of whom were Goddesses close to the concept of Mother Earth, her abundance and the prosperity of her people. These Goddesses are found mainly in the temples and shrines within the Roman spheres of influence, but they are often at key places in the land, such as strategic forts, river crossings and sacred springs. These places of Goddess were special places in the land that continued to be honoured and celebrated in Roman Britain.

Notes

[1] See Frank Jenkins, 'The Cult of the Pseudo-Venus in Kent', *Archaeologia Cantiana* vol LXXII, pages 60–76.

[2] See Frank Jenkins, 'The Cult of the Dea Nutrix in Kent', *Archaeologia Cantiana* vol LXXI, pages 38–46.

[3] By J.M.C. Toynbee in *Art in Roman Britain* No 27, plate 26.

[4] See Miranda Green, *Celtic Goddesses*, page 103.

[5] Patricia Monaghan, *The Book of Goddesses and Heroines*, page 96.

[6] See C.M. Johns, 'A Roman Bronze Statue of Epona', *British Museum Quarterly* vol 36, Part 1–2, pages 37–41.

[7] By Miranda Green, op cit, pages 184–7.

[8] By E.J. Phillips in *Corpus Signorum Imperii Romani*, vol 1, fasc 1, page 2.

The Goddess of the Land: the Celtic Myths

While the Romans were busy conquering England, the Scottish and Welsh borders, and the Irish coastal area, something quite different remained in the more inaccessible parts where the Celtic peoples continued to live, in particular in the Highlands and Islands of Scotland (Alba), the fastnesses of central and west Wales (Cymru), the remote countryside of Ireland (Eire), and the furthest reaches of Cornwall (Kernow). For people in these places, life carried on in much the same way as it had done for their forebears. They lived in fortified homesteads: *duns*, *brochs* and *crannogs* in Scotland, *duns*, *raths* and *cashels* in Ireland, and courtyard house settlements in Cornwall. They dwelt in circular timber-built houses, farmed the land, raided each other's territories, and fashioned fine gold, silver and bronze artwork. They spoke a common language with regional variations, which later became classified as the Goedelic (Q Celtic) branch, comprising Irish, Scots Gaelic and Manx, and the Brythonic (P Celtic) branch, including Welsh, Cornish and Breton. There were strong links between northern Ireland and southern Scotland, between Ireland and the Isle of Man, and between Ireland, Wales and Cornwall, and people sometimes moved across the western seaboard to settle in neighbouring lands. They thus shared a common culture, an epic mythic history, and a close similarity in religious belief and expression.

These beliefs would have included a mythology based on the sanctity of the land, and the old goddesses and gods who dwelt in and on the earth. Nothing of this original mythology remains, but fortunately some of the material was transmitted orally and later written down in the tenth and eleventh centuries in Ireland in the *Tales of the Ulster Cycle* and other books such as *Lebor na h Vidre* (*The Book of the Dun Cow*) and *Lebor Gabala Erenn* (*The Book of Invasions*). By this time the old goddesses and gods had been transformed into heroines and heroes from the Irish mythic sagas, but, making allowance for the Christian overlay and denial, we can often see the Celtic Earth Goddess coming through. In Wales the material was written down later, in the twelfth to fourteenth centuries, in such books as *The White Book of Rhydderch* and *The Red Book of Hergest*, containing the *Four Branches of the Mabinogi*, *The Book of Taliesen* and *The Tale of Culwch and Olwen*. By this time the goddesses have become queens or other-worldly beings, but nevertheless enough remains for us to see the Goddess lying within the queen. In Scotland, the Isle of Man and Cornwall we have to rely mainly on legend and local stories, an oral tradition sometimes not written down until the time of the folklore collectors of the eighteenth, nineteenth and early twentieth centuries. Any goddesses hidden in these stories have by this time become giantesses and witches.

According to the *Book of Invasions* there were five waves of invasion into Ireland: Cesair, Partholon, Nemed, the Fir Bolg and finally the Tuatha de Danaan. These were the earth shapers, forging order in the land from darkness and chaos. The Fir Bolg partitioned Ireland into five provinces, but were eventually driven out by the Tuatha de Danaan, the people of the Goddess Danu or Anu. She is thus a primal Earth Goddess of the people, and is still celebrated in the hills called the Paps of Anu in Munster. She was also synonymous with Ainé, an early sun Goddess who gave her name to Knock Aine in Munster, and Knockmany in Ulster, and eventually became Christianized into St Anne. She was also a powerful deity at Dunany in Leinster, where on the seashore a stone called Ana's Chair was supposed to relieve madness[1].

Other ancestor goddesses in Ireland are the three Goddesses of the land – Banbha, Eriu and Fodhla – whom the Milesians or Gaels first met when they arrived in Ireland. Their rulership depended on the favour of these Goddesses, and it was a condition of Eriu that her name should be given to the whole of Eire before she would grant sovereignty. Her focal place is the Hill of Uisnech in Leinster, in the centre of Ireland. Other early Goddesses were tutelary deities of their particular tribes: Macha of Emain Macha/Navan in Ulster, Boann of Newgrange and the River Boyne in Leinster, Mebd/Maeve of Knocknarea in Connacht, *Tea of Tara in Leinster and Tailtu of Teltown in Leinster. The sagas tell the stories of the adventures of these divine females, and contain within them some of the original attributes and meanings of the Goddesses.

The first of these is Macha, who in fact was three Goddesses in one. The first was the wife of Memedh, leader of the third invasion of Ireland; the second was the divine queen who ruled Emain Macha; and the third, often conflated with the other two, was a divine woman who married a mortal man, Crunnchu. In the story, he boasts that his wife can outrun the king's horses, and she is forced to take up the challenge although she is heavily pregnant. She wins the race, but dies giving birth to twins – *emhian* in Irish – and curses the Ulster men for forcing her on in her condition. The curse means that Ulster men will be 'as weak as women' for five days and four nights, which is ironic considering Macha's strength and power. Macha is thus a complex deity, and has been described as having 'three differing but interrelated manifestations, embodying concepts of war, rulership and fecundity'[2] and being a 'warrior, ruler, prophet, matriarch, guardian and benefactress of the land'[3].

Next, Boann features as the Goddess of the River Boyne, who was married at first to the God Nechtan, a water deity. She defied him by visiting a forbidden well and was turned into the water that now flows as the River Boyne, close to which stand the prehistoric tombs of Newgrange, Dowth and Knowth in Leinster. She was seduced by Daghda, the Father God, and to hide their union the sun stood still for nine months, so that the child was conceived and born on the same day. We have here a legend of a Goddess of river, fertility and time. Evidence for her latter role in relationship to the wheel of the year can be found in a story in which she gives birth to three sons, whose names can be linked with much earlier Indo-European names for the seasons of spring, summer and winter[4]. This would make her a Goddess of creation and the seasonal fertility cycle. Her name has also been translated[5] as 'she who has white cows', reinforcing her role as river and fertility Goddess of the Earth.

Mebd (Maeve) was the tutelary goddess of Connacht, a queen of the land. She ruled the army and was a war Goddess in the battles against the men of Ulster. She was in fact one of the five war Goddesses of the Gaels known collectively as the Babd (the other four being Fea the Hateful, Nemhain the Venomous, Badb the Fury and the Morrigan who was a multi-aspected deity of power and guardianship). Mebd's name is related to mead, the intoxicating honey drink that is still popular in some Celtic lands today, and the mead cup was often drunk before battle and at ritual gatherings of the tribe. No king could rule at the royal court of Tara in Leinster, unless he lay with her, so she was very much a Goddess of sovereignty (stewardship of the land), and the fertility of the earth. Her name is associated with many important sites, from Rothcroghan cave in Connacht where she was born, to Knocknarea, also in Connacht, where her tomb is situated. The ancient text *Táin Bó Cuailnge* (*The Cattle Raid of Cooley*) from *The Tales of the Ulster Cycle* tells of great furrows in the earth where the menstruating Mebd urinated, a story that undoubtedly harks back to the blood-mother motif of the earliest goddesses. Mebd was a shape-shifting Goddess who could change from old woman to young girl, a Goddess-queen who offered sexual favours but also brought about death, and was ruthless in her selection of the fittest ruler but protective in her guardianship of the land.

*Tea (Teamair) may have been the earliest name for the Goddess at the hill of Tara. She is a shadowy figure from the mythic period, much of whose story has been lost, but who was supposed to have died at the ancient sacred site and imbued the hill with its original sanctity[6]. Tailtu is another such ancient goddess, the foster mother of the sun God Lugh. Her role in the Lughnasad festival is a fascinating, and largely unknown, one: although the great harvest festival of the Celtic cross-quarter day of 1 August is known as Lughnasad and named after the God Lugh, early myth tells us that the deity honoured on this day was in fact Tailtu.

Tailtu was the wife of Eochaidh mac Erc, the last of the mythical Fir Bolg people, and after his defeat she married Eochaidh Garbh of the victorious Tuatha de Danaan. This makes her a Goddess of sovereignty, or well-being of the land. She came to the plains of Meath, cleared the forests and then died as a result of her labour. We may have here the memory of the coming of agriculture to the early peoples, with Tailtu as the Earth Mother, who died in August as the harvest was cut and thus inaugurated the festival of Lughnasad. Her foster son Lugh was later given the attributes of the harvest sacrificial victim, but this was only a patriarchal takeover from Tailtu herself. She may have been the original Goddess of the harvest, with her spirit remaining in the last sheaf of corn that was cut down annually at the Lammas festival. The place where this myth was originally enacted was named after her – Tailte/Teltown in Leinster – and became the origin of the whole Lughnasad ritual. The Great Games of Ireland took place here into medieval times, in memory of this Earth Goddess from the mists of Ireland's past.

There are other minor Goddesses/queens, children of the Goddess Danu, the Great Mother of all life. Examples include the Goddess Sinead, who gave her name to the River Shannon in Leinster; the Goddess of Glandore in Munster called Cliodna, whose domain was the happy other world and who can still be seen in the ninth wave of every series of waves; the Goddess Niau (or Niamh) of the golden hair, another other-world enchantress who dwelt in the land of Tir na N'og, the mythical land of perpetual youth; and the Goddess-maid Etain, a metamorphic entity who was spell-changed by Fuamncah, wife of the God Midhir, into a pool of water and then a purple fly. She fell into a goblet of wine and was swallowed by the wife of Edar, who conceived and bore a child who was the new Etain. A mysterious shape-shifting goddess, she appears in many places in Ireland including Beare Island, Slievenaman, Rathcroghan and Fremu (Frewin Hill). It has been suggested that she is either a sovereignty Goddess archetype[7] and/or a sun Goddess[8], following a national sun cycle around the holy hills of Ireland. All these Goddesses or Goddess archetypes are part of a rich pattern of ancient myth and legend from Ireland, Goddesses who shaped the earth and continued to be part of it in the sacred places of Eriu's land.

In Wales, the main source of information about Goddess archetypes comes from the *Four Branches of the Mabinogi*: Pwyll, Prince of Dyfed; Branwen, Daughter of Llyr; Manawyddan, Son of Llyr; and Math, Son of Mathonwy; plus *The Tale of Taliesen* and *The Tale of Culhwch and Olwen*. This material relates to the early Welsh period of around the fifth and sixth centuries, but was not written down until much later – probably between 1100 and 1250 – and is found in the manuscripts of *The White Book of Rhydderch* (c1300) and *The Red Book of Hergest* (c1400). By this time the Goddess had been banished by Christianity, but the power of the original deities that lie behind the stories of queens and princesses still shines through.

One of the Goddess archetypes is Rhiannon, wife of Pwyll, lord of

Dyfed. They first meet when Rhiannon appears riding past on a large white horse, dressed in a dazzling gold robe. However fast he rides, he cannot catch up with her. The same thing happens on the second day, but on the third she stops and admits that she has come to seek him. They make plans to marry in a year and a day, and Pwyll goes to the court of her father, where he wins her from her already betrothed lover, Gwawl, by trickery. Rhiannon is thus first introduced as a mysterious, almost otherworldly being whose dress (dazzling gold) and transport (large white horse) hint of a sun and horse Goddess identification. She may thus be a local version of the Irish Macha and the Gaulish Epona.

Another episode in her story has a strange, unearthly ring to it. After a wait of three years (note the 'magic' number again) she conceives, but her newborn son is spirited away by supernatural means on the evening of 1 May, the Celtic Beltane festival, when the space between this world and the other is open. In a stable, the boy is given to Teyrnon and his wife who, not realizing his origins, foster him. Meanwhile, Rhiannon is accused of infanticide and as penance is forced to sit outside the palace by a horse block, tell her story to anyone who comes by, and offer to carry them to the court on her back. This curious episode reinforces Rhiannon's role as a horse Goddess. Eventually son is restored to mother, and Rhiannon is reinstated as queen of the court.

In the Third Branch of the *Mabinogi* Rhiannon remarries after Pwyll's death, but the land of Dyfed becomes a wasteland and everything disappears – except Rhiannon, her new husband Manawydan, her son Pryderi and his wife Cigfa. Episodes of enchantment and magic follow, and the matter is resolved only by the appearance of Llwyd, a magician, who reveals that it was all his doing in retaliation for Pwyll's original trickery of Gwawl. Rhiannon here seems in some way to be connected with the prosperity of the land, and there may be faint echoes of an earlier role as Goddess of sovereignty.

We have in these tales some complex symbolism. The motif of the horse runs through the stories: Rhiannon on a horse that none could outrun; Pryderi appearing in a stable at the time of Teyrnon's mare foaling; and Rhiannon carrying visitors to the castle on her back. Although she has often been compared with Epona, perhaps her closest link is with the Irish Goddesses Macha, who outran the king's horses, and Aine, who assumed the form of a red mare, again a horse that none could outrun.

In addition, there are elements of other Goddess motifs in Rhiannon's story. Her sorrow at the abduction of her child makes her a 'grieving mother' Goddess, parallel to the Demeter and Persephone story from Greek myth, and links to a mother-and-son theme (Modron and Mabon) running through many Celtic stories. Also, in *The Tale of Culhwch and Olwen*, Rhiannon possesses three magic birds whose sweet singing can wake the dead and lull the living to sleep. This links her strongly with the Irish Goddess Cliodna, who dwelt in the other world, where she too possessed three magic birds who could lull humans to sleep with their song. These parallels indicate a strong link between the maritime cultures of Ireland and Wales at this time.

There are hints, too, of Rhiannon's role as an ancestor Goddess (Pryderi goes on to carry forward the line of Pwyll); as a vegetation Goddess, embodying as she does complex interrelated motifs of fertility (her own) fecundity (of the land) and barrenness (her own and the land); and as a Goddess of sovereignty, choosing the king to be her mate at a ritual place – the Mound of Arberth – which was a magical spot where kings were installed and experienced visions. Through concepts such as these, she is linked closely to the land as an Earth Goddess, upon whom its well-being depends.

Branwen, who appears in the Second Branch of the *Mabinogi*, has some similarities to Rhiannon. Both are 'foreign' wives of whom the people disapprove, and both are exiled from their native lands in the course of their stories. Branwen was sister to Brân, whose name was given to several places in Cornwall. As king of Harlech, in North Wales, he was asked by Matholwch, king of Ireland, for his sister's hand in marriage. He agreed, but his brother Efnissien was insulted and mutilated Matholwch's horses. As recompense, Brân gave him the Cauldron of Rebirth, which originally came from an Irish lake and could resurrect the dead. Branwen and Matholwch returned to Ireland where Branwen bore a son, but the Irish court did not take to their new queen and were still aggrieved at the horse episode. Branwen was banished to the kitchen and boxed on the ears every day by the butcher. She was forbidden any contact with Wales, but she taught a starling to carry a message to Brân at Caer Seint. He set sail for Ireland to rescue her, and the Irish sued for peace. However, trickery ensued and war broke out. Brân won, but lost his life, and only seven of his warriors survived: they cut off his head and returned to Wales, but the head continued to speak for many years afterwards. Branwen, however, died of despair at the destruction wrought in her name.

Branwen appears to be a passive instrument in all this in-fighting between Celtic tribes, but curiously she is described as one of the three chief ancestresses of the island of Britain. It has been suggested[9] that an earlier version of her name was Bronwen, in which form it appears in *The White Book of Rhydderch*, and she is described as an ancestress. She is commemorated in the mountain name of Cadair Bronwen in Powys, North Wales, which may make her a territorial Goddess. It has also been suggested[10] that Branwen is an aspect of sovereignty, confirming Matholwch's royal status, and is thus defended by Efnissien. She has a certain other-worldly aspect to her, being able to communicate with a starling, and at one point in the story is called upon to interpret the apparent mystery of a forest and mountain moving across the sea, which turn out to be her brother Brân and his ships: she thus takes on the role of oracle or interpreter of augury. Her death has some similarities with that of

Finnebair, daughter of Medb, the Goddess-queen of Connacht, as they both die of broken hearts resulting from being the cause of disaster and death. Branwen thus has echoes of other goddess figures and divine motifs.

Arianrhod appears in the Fourth Branch of the *Mabinogi* as the daughter of Don, who may be derived from the Irish Tuatha de Dannon – children of the Goddess Danu, the descendants of whom match those of Don almost exactly. She was neice of Math, lord of Gwynedd, and applied for the job as virgin lap-girl to Math – whose 'fate' it was always to have his feet resting in the lap of a virgin. As a test of her virginity, she had to step over Math's magic wand, but as she did so she gave birth to two boys. She is thus a virgin Goddess in the ancient sense of the word – one who is complete unto herself and who needs no man to impregnate her. This strange episode may be the memory of a much more ancient primal goddess figure who reproduced by a form of parthenogenesis, a theme that was carried over into the miraculous birth of Jesus in the Christian story.

One of Arianrhod's sons was called Dylan, who became a sea God. The other had three geises, or prohibitions, laid on him by his mother: that he would have no name unless she named him, that he would bear no arms unless she armed him, and that he would have no human wife. She was thus exercising her power as divine matriarch, although she was subsequently tricked into naming him Llew and arming him. As for the third taboo, this was circumvented by Math and Gwydion (Arianrhod's brother), who fashioned a magical wife made of flowers, called Blodeuwedd.

The name Arianrhod has been translated as 'silver wheel', so she may be a Goddess of the seasonal cycle or the lunar year. She dwelt in Caer Arianrhod – a mythical island that also has a physical counterpart off the coast of west Wales – with her attendant three priestesses or Druidesses, the land eventually being inundated with a flood of water. She seems to be an independent Goddess figure, somewhat akin to Artemis-Diana in the Hellenic/Roman pantheon. Like Branwen, she may also have an ancestor Goddess aspect to her: she is described in one of the *Triads* as one of the three fair maidens, the other two probably being Branwen and Rhiannon. Her son Llew is a Welsh version of the Irish sun God Lugh, so if Llew is divine then his mother was a Goddess.

There are many elements in Arianrhod's story that hint of her otherworldly and divine status, and even though the creation of the flower girl Blodeuwedd by magical means as wife for Llew is not by Arianrhod herself, it still reinforces the idea of vegetation or seasonal Goddess archetype linked to the wheel of the year. Blodeuwedd is portrayed as faithless, plotting with her lover to kill her husband; they fail and she is turned into an owl, whose symbolism links her to Minerva. It has been suggested[11] that both Arianrhod and Blodeuwedd were female rebels against masculine domination, and/or a mythic telling of the conflict between ancient Goddess belief and the patriarchal/God usurpation of that. Whatever the

ARIANRHOD OF THE SILVER WHEEL
(GERALDINE ANDREW)

precise truth, they remain fascinating Goddess archetypes, their stories filled with magic and mystery.

The final important earth goddess in the Welsh mythic literature is Cerridwen, who takes centre stage in *The Tale of Taliesen*. Here she is keeper of the Cauldron of Inspiration, which she keeps boiling for a year and a day and into which she prepares herbs and plants that bestow the gift of prophetic insight and secret knowledge. Cerridwen has two children: a daughter Crearwy (meaning 'light' or 'beautiful') and a son Morfran/Afagddu ('dark' or 'ugly'). She sets a young lad, Gwion, to watch over the cauldron, but three drops fall out of it on to his finger – in licking it, he receives the gift of inspiration intended for Afagddu. In her rage, Cerridwen chases Gwion, who changes into a hare to escape her. She then metamorphoses into a greyhound and he becomes a fish; she turns into an otter and he becomes a bird; she changes into a hawk and he becomes a grain of wheat. Finally, she becomes a hen and swallows him, but nine months later gives birth to him again. This time she is swayed by his extreme beauty, so instead of killing him she sets him adrift on a coracle, from where he is saved by a nobleman, Elphin, who names him Taliesen, meaning 'radiant brow'. Taliesen later becomes a visionary poet and Druid, who claims he was present at the birth of Mabon, the Great Mother herself.

We can see here many of the elements that we have noted in the other Goddess-archetype stories. The foster-parenting of the son of the Goddess was found in the Rhiannon story, and the birth-generating ability of the Goddess was seen in the Arianhod story. Cerridwen is variously described as a hag, the 'old one', a witch and a crone, which links her to the great Cailleach Goddess archetype, which is explored in the next chapter. She is the wise woman who knows the secrets of the magic spells and potions; she is also a Goddess of the two great seasons of the year, symbolized in her two children 'light' and 'dark', and her story contains many magical transformations of time, particularly with regard to Taliesen. She has the ability to shape-shift in her pursuit of Gwion, and it has been suggested[12] that the transformations they both undergo are part of an initiatory sequence in which Cerridwen takes Gwion through various degrees of shaministic insight until he reaches the primal essence of life. She then becomes a Goddess of rebirth and regeneration.

The cauldron that Cerridwen possesses also symbolizes this aspect of her divinity, especially in comparison with the Cauldron of Rebirth in Branwen's tale. In a sense, Cerridwen was the cauldron, swallowing Gwion and causing his rebirth, and the symbolism of the grain of corn eaten by the hen can be seen as an allegory of the seed buried in the womb of the earth for regeneration[13]. Relevant to the cauldron motif is her supposed dwelling place below the surface of Lake Bala in Powys, North Wales. The Irish Cauldron of Rebirth in Branwen's tale also came from a lake, and it is known from archaeological evidence that cauldrons and other ritual objects were deposited in lakes during the Iron Age and Celtic periods, especially in Llyn Cerrig Bach, the sacred lake on the island of Anglesey in North Wales. The Goddess Aine in Ireland also made her home below a lake (Lough Gur in Munster), from where ritual objects have been recovered.

Cerridwen is a Goddess who lives between the worlds of earth and water, death and rebirth, light and dark, above and below. She is a Goddess of transformation, and the cauldron is her womb-symbol of renewal. She is particularly remembered at Pentre Ifan burial chamber in Pembrokeshire, South Wales, again a place of initiation and actually called 'the womb of Ceridewen'. The 'old hag' motif that she embodies can also be found widely in the Cailleach Bhur of Ireland and Scotland, but we are now entering the realm of folklore and legend rather than transmitted myth. However, it is to this area that we now turn in our search for traces of the Earth Goddess in the land.

NOTES

1 See Patrick Logan, *The Holy Wells of Ireland*, page 72.
2 Miranda Green, *Celtic Goddesses*, page 40.
3 Ibid, page 71.
4 See Emily Lyle in Fradenburg (ed) *Women in Sovereignty*, pages 276–88.
5 By Anne Ross in *Pagan Celtic Britain*, page 279.
6 See Michael Dames, *Mythic Ireland*, page 225.
7 By Miranda Green, op cit, pages 123–4.
8 By Michael Dames, op cit, pages 233–4.
9 By Miranda Green, op cit, page 55.
10 By Caitlin Matthews in *Mabon and the Mysteries of Britain*, pages 37–48.
11 By Miranda Green, op cit, pages 57–61.
12 By Caitlin Matthews, op cit, pages 118.
13 See Miranda Green, op cit, page 69.

The Goddess in the Legends: the Earth-shaping Crone

The most prominent landmark in South Armagh is Slieve Gullion, a mountain... rich in mythological associations. A quarter of a mile from its south-eastern base there is a rocky hillock, called the Spellick, in a grove of trees. Here people used to go to pick bilberries on Blaeberry Sundays. On the hillock there is a rocky formation called the Cailleach Bearea's Chair, and in it everyone who took part in the Blaeberry outing used to sit. As an Adavoyle man said 'They'd all have to sit in the Cailleach Bearea's Chair. Oh, just to have it to say they sat there I suppose. Anyway, everyone would sit in it'. The Cailleach Bearea is of course the Cailleach Bhéara, the famous old woman of Irish mythology. In the tradition of South Armagh she is specially associated with Slieve Gullion and is said to live in a deep chamber beneath the cairn which crowns the mountain and which is known to the peasantry as her house. It is not surprising then to find a seat named for her in the hilly grove near the foot of her mountain.

Maire MacNeill, *The Festival of Lughnasa*

THE CAILLEACH BEAREA, the Old Woman of the Mountains, can be found in the folklore and legend of many places in Ireland and Scotland and, as we shall see, perhaps England as well. But who is she, where does she come from, and what does she represent?

Firstly, the name Cailleach Bearea is widely used but little understood. Cailleach means old woman, crone or hag, but Bearea is a placename, the Bhéara or Beara Peninsula in Munster. Why does the Cailleach come originally from here? Máiré Ni Dhonnchada of the Dublin Institute for Advanced Studies has suggested[1] that it could be because of the many associations on the Beara Peninsula with the arrival of early settlers in Ireland. If so, the Cailleach is indeed very old, for if legends have any grain of historical truth in them, then the earliest immigrants into Ireland – perhaps one of the Indo-European peoples – may have brought the notion of the old wise woman of the hills and mountains with them. It has been suggested[2] that the name Beara may also be cognate with the word Boand, the great cow-Goddess of the Boyne.

There is a memory of the presence of the Cailleach as Goddess in the Beara Peninsula in a metamorphic rock that stands overlooking Coulagh Bay, at the western end of the peninsula. This rock is said to be the Cailleach herself incarnate, the Earth Goddess in the earth. There were also two other Cailleachs associated with the two other peninsulas in south-west Ireland: the Cailleach Bholais of the Inveragh Peninsula, and the Cailleach Daingin of the Dingle Peninsula, making a triple Goddess manifestation.

Much of our knowledge of the Cailleach is through legend and folklore, but there are also a couple of written references. In the ninth-century *Lament of the Old Woman of Beare* she appears as an old crone speaking with nostalgia for her youth and beauty in contrast to her present old age. She also appears in the folk tale *Cailleach an Teampuill* (*The Hag of the Temple*), where her four sons appear as cranes. They can only escape an enchantment by obtaining a drop of blood from the Connra bull, a legendary beast owned by the Cailleach Bheara. All this may be a garbled memory of ancient bull or crane initiatory rites to the Goddess, known about from Crete and other places.

Márié Ni Dhonnchada suggests that the Cailleach was originally the Goddess of the land and nature. Her associations in Ireland are all with high mountain peaks and hilltops. For example, at Loughcrew in Leinster, the mountain is known as Slieve na Calliagh (the Hill of the Cailleach) and the many prehistoric cairns that litter it are supposed to have been dropped from her apron, a motif that we shall come across again. This is in all probability a metaphor for giving birth, and an indication of one of the aspects of the Cailleach, the Goddess who gives birth to the land and/or the ancient sites in the land. At Loughcrew she has her seat as well, only this one is on the side of the largest cairn, Cairn T, where she was supposed to sit and smoke her pipe and survey the land all around her! Even as late as the 1830s she was still thought of as a living presence[3], and it was known in the neighbourhood that she had performed a great magic feat on the hill with her apronful of stones. The same story is told of her at Newgrange overlooking the River Boyne in Leinster[4].

The Cailleach is also known at Slieve Daeane in Connacht, where a passage tomb at the summit of the mountain is called Cailleach Bhearra's House, and at Croag Skearda in Munster, where there is a cluster of Cailleach sites: Bothán na Caillighe (the Hag's Cabin), Cró na Caillighe (the Hag's Fold or Cave), and Fothrach na Caillighe (the Hag's Ruin). Here, two crones were supposed to have lived in the cave, one from Munster (Cailleach Dhuibhneach) and an interloper from Leinster (Cailleach Laighneach), which may be an indication that every region had its own version of the Old Crone. In this legend, the two hags live together, then quarrel, and finally one of them throws the other over the cliff. The Cailleachs are here enacting a geomythic memory of the formation of the land, and the role that other-worldly deities were thought of as playing in that process. Finally from Ireland, there is the tale of the Old Woman of the Glen, at the Hag's Glen (Coom Callee) in Munster. Here the role of the Cailleach as Mother Goddess – an unusual aspect of her symbolism – is emphasized, for it was thought she lived in the Glen with a young child whom she looked after.

The other aspect of the Cailleach was as the harvest Goddess, which makes her a sister to Tailtu. She is the veiled one (Caille), who appears at the end of the harvest in the last sheaf of corn. In 1944, an old man from Ballymoyer recalled: 'I saw the Cailleach cut by the scythe only. It was afterwards taken into the house and put around the woman of the house'[5]. Sometimes the sheaf was fed to the cattle or shaken over the land – both acts of sympathetic magic – and sometimes the sheaf was taken indoors, formed into a corn dolly and hung up over the hearth for the winter. We shall meet this aspect of the Cailleach when we look at her springtime transformation in the next chapter.

From Ireland, the Cailleach was taken to Scotland and Wales. In Wales she probably became Cerridwen, who is called 'old woman' and 'hag' as an epithet, but in Scotland she retains the name of Cailleach Bhur or Cailleach Beinne Bric. With one major exception (see page 48), she is found principally in the Highlands and in the islands of the Inner and Outer Hebrides, where the Irish migrants would have landed first. Between the islands of Jura and Mull is a whirlpool called the Corryvreckan, where the Cailleach is supposed to wash her clothes. This links her to the 'washer at the ford' motif found in many Celtic tales and legends, for example *Triad* 70 from the Welsh text *Trioedd Ynys Prydein*. These tales invariably include two themes: one is an encounter with an old woman washing her clothes at a ford, and the other involves a magical transformation from an old crone into a beautiful young woman. The first motif is a representation of the Cailleach as the dark Goddess Hecate, the Goddess of death – she whom men fear to meet because she is washing the bloody garments of those destined to die in battle. The second motif is more complex, and we shall return to it shortly.

The 'apronful of stones' theme also reappears at the Corryvreckan, for the Cailleach is carrying a creel of rocks on her back, and as she walks through the Sound of Mull the strap breaks and the rocks fall to form islets in the sea. Here she clearly represents an ancestral Goddess, shaping the land and forming its structures. On the island of Skye she performs the same function. Here she was known to dwell on the lonely plains when the world was young, and the mountain of Ben-na-Cailleach is still named after her. She was in conflict with spring, and this is the first clear indication we have of her other major aspect as the Goddess of winter. The old legend tells how the sun God threw his spear at her but missed, and instead formed the Cuchullin/Cuillin mountain range. We are dealing here with a legend that must have remained in the oral tradition for a very long time, telling as it does of the creation of the land. This is the

CAILLEACH OR CRONE WOMAN (JILL SMITH)

nearest thing we have anywhere in Britain to a pre-Christian creation myth.

In the Western Isles, on North Uist the Cailleach takes on the manifestation of Dubha (black), a probable reference to her aspect as Goddess of winter. On the islet of Vallay there are some Bronze Age standing stones called Leac nan Cailleacha Dubha (the Stones of the Old Black Crone), and on Boreray a cairn with three stones is known as Cailleach Dubha. On Lewis a former building was called Tigh nan Cailleachan Dubh (the House of the Old Black Crone), indicating that this epithet was widely attributed to the Cailleach in the Outer Hebrides. Other prehistoric sites named after her include Sithean nan Cailleach (Fairy House of the Old Woman) formerly on the island of Eigg; Carn Tigh na Cailleach (the Cairn of the Hag's House) at Kildonin in Sutherland; and Uaigh na Caillich (the Old Woman's Grave) at East Tarbert Bay on Gigha. The Old Crone was thus seen not only to be responsible for shaping the land, but also to dwell in the ancient ceremonial sites of the ancestors.

Finally in Scotland, an amazing remnant of Cailleach continuity can still be found in a glen leading off Glen Lyon on Tayside, in Perthshire and Kinross. Here the Cailleach/Cailliche is not only known in legend as the Goddess of the seasons, but can actually be seen and visited in her house in the land. This remote glen has maintained a living pagan tradition which must stretch back far into the past. Every year at the old Celtic festival time of Beltane (May Day), a shepherd would be responsible for taking a number of stones from inside a small stone 'house' and setting them up on the burnside. These stones, which came from the river nearby, were known as the Cailliche and her family, and their function was to watch over the glen and the well-being of the cattle. Then every year at the Celtic festival of Samhain (at the beginning of November) the stones would be replaced in the small stone house made for them. The house was formerly thatched, and it was part of the ritual to re-thatch it every year. The glen is called Glen Cailliche, and the house Tigh nam Cailliche or Tig nam Bodich (House of the Old Woman or Man).

The fascinating thing about this ancient ritual is that the Cailleach is not the Goddess of winter but the Goddess of spring and summer. On Skye she was in conflict with spring, but in another legend from that island she puts on her plaid and becomes the fairest maid in the land, the youthful personification of spring. This legend finds a parallel with other Celtic myths, such as the *Tale of the Nine Hostages*, where the hero encounters a 'loathsome old hag', who then metamorphoses into a beautiful young woman. In Ireland we saw that she could also be the Goddess of summer's end and the harvest, so her meaning is more complex than might at first appear. It could be said that she was a fertility/vegetation Goddess, whose significance varied according to the time of year in the different places she was celebrated. Perhaps she was the original Goddess of the wheel of the year for the prehistoric peoples, whose lives depended on a successful pastoral and agricultural cycle. If so, this would make her much more ancient than the Celts and take her back even to the Neolithic and Bronze Age peoples.

These interweaving threads of the Cailleach's mythology can also be found personified in other legends in different places, where they are not directly named as functions of the Cailleach but may refer back to her to a lesser or greater extent. The main strand is that of 'the Giantess' Apron', and we can now examine the legends of an earth-shaping, creation-making Goddess.

The legend of a Giantess striding across the land and dropping stones from her apron to make the mountains and hills, peaks and tors, cairns and mounds of the land is found widely in Britain and Ireland. We have already examined the examples from Ireland and Scotland, so it is now the turn of England and Wales. It has been suggested[6] that these traditions travelled from Ireland into North Wales, Scotland and northern England along well-established routes. From the Cailleach dropping her stones at Loughcrew in Ireland, we can trace the legend into North Wales, where the megalithic tomb Barclodiad-y-Gawres on Anglesey means 'the Giantess' apronful'. A similar legend pertains to a cairn about 80km (50 miles) to the east near the pass of Y Ddeufaen, beside the Roman road in Denbighshire. Here the legend tells of the Giantess and her husband, who were walking to Anglesey and dropped their load when they discovered how far they had to walk. Further east at Llanfyndd in Flintshire, a destroyed cairn was known as Arffedogaid-y-Wrack, which means 'the apronful of the hag', making the Cailleach link even clearer.

From North Wales, we can trace the legend to a cluster of sites in northern England, particularly in Yorkshire and Cumbria. A round cairn at Thornton-in-Lonsdale is called the Apronful of Stones, and the site of a barrow near Bradfield in the Don Valley has the same name. On Rombald's Moor in Yorkshire there are two cairns, called the Skirtful of Stones and the Little Skirtful of Stones. In this case the Giantess has been localized and turned into the wife of the Giant Rombald. They had a quarrel, and she filled her apron with stones with which to pelt her husband, but she overloaded it and the apron-strings broke, marking the two cairns. Sometimes the legend is attached to other mythological beings such as the Devil or Sampson, but predominantly this is a Giantess legend.

In other places the 'apronful of stones' motif has gone, but the notion of an old woman shaping the land remains. This has given rise to a number of Old Wives sites, particularly in the Yorkshire area. There are the Old Wife's Howes, a group of three round barrows near Fylingdales; the Old Wives' Hill near Thirsk; and the Old Wives' Ridge on Nidderdale. The name was even applied to much smaller structures than the hills, ridges and mounds, as the Old Wife's Well near Stape and the Old Wife's Neck standing stone near Sneaton Corner bear witness. Once again, as in the case of Rombald, the Old Wife is given a local name: here she is known as Bel, the wife of the Giant Wade, who himself was no mean earth shaper, building the causeway or old Roman road that runs across the Moors.

In other places, this ancient Goddess of the hills, mountains and rocks takes on additional local names. In Cornwall, she was the Giantess Cormelian who, together with her husband Cormoran, endlessly reshaped the landscape with a giant hammer and huge boulders; in Herefordshire, she was known as Mol Walbee and she dropped the stones that now remain of Hay-on-Wye castle; in Leicestershire, she was known as Black Annis on the Dane Hills, where she may have been a version of the Goddess Anu; in the High Peak of Derbyshire, she was called Biddy and was visualized as a shapeless form who sometimes appeared in the guise of a dark horse and foal; in Worcestershire, she was known as Old Mother Darky and was thought to live on Bredon Hill, with wolves who were young children in disguise; in South Wales, she was the nameless old woman of Llanhilleth mountain, haunting the hills and leading travellers astray (she even had an apron thrown across her shoulder); and on the Isle of Man, she was known as Berrey Dhone, who dwelt on North Barrule mountain. This brings us full circle back to the Cailleach, for her name may be a corruption of the Cailleach Bheur, brought to Man from Ireland.

In some of these examples, the earth-shaping qualities of the Goddess overlap with a land-guarding theme. This is close to a related motif – the Goddess of the protection of the land, or sovereignty. These tutelary Goddesses may be later versions of the Cailleach: once the land has been formed, there must be a Goddess to keep it fertile and ensure its prosperity. We have already met many of these Goddesses in Chapter 3, but others exist only in the legends and oral tradition. For example, on Skye, home to an ancient Cailleach earth-shaping legend (see pages 47–48), there is also a second Goddess of the land, Skiach/Sgathach, who gave her name to the island. She was a warrior woman who dwelt on the mountains and fought a battle with Cuchullin, the hero of Ulster, in which neither won and both agreed to make peace. Cuchullin returned to Ireland, and Skiach and her daughter remained on the island. This could be a mythologized account of the invasion of Skye from Ireland and the eventual repelling of the Irish migrants, or it could be a memory of the conflict between one set of beliefs and another. Either way, it seems that Skye has retained the knowledge of one of its ancestral Goddesses in its legends and folklore.

In some places, this ancestral Goddess of the land, or sovereignty, was known to have special places where the kings and rulers had to stand or place their feet before they could be legitimized. In Ireland, that special place was Tara in Leinster, and a granite stone – the Stone of Destiny – marks the spot. On this hill, the kings of Ireland were required to mate symbolically with the Goddess of the land, who was known as Mebd/Maeve. In legend, she cohabited with nine kings of Ireland and would not allow any king at Tara who did not mate with her, which was symbolized by her giving the king a goblet of red wine, perhaps representing her menstrual blood. A memory of this symbolic mating is retained in the legend recounted by Giraldus Cambrensis of a royal initiation ceremony, in which the king had to couple with a white mare (cf the Goddess Epona/Macha), which was then sacrificed. The king, then sitting in a bath prepared from the broth, had to eat the horse's flesh and drink the broth from the bath. Also in Ireland, a legend of the eponymous Goddess Eriu, mother of all Ireland, tells how she gave her mate a golden cup of wine, representing her power to bestow the gift of the land.

In Scotland, the inauguration stones were at Dunadd on the Mull of Kintyre, where a footprint is carved out of the rock and used for inauguration ceremonies for the kings of Dalriada; on Islay in the Inner Hebrides, at the Stone of the Footmarks on Eilean Mor in Loch Finnigan; in Caithness at Halkirk near Port-an-Eilean, where Clach na Lvirg is the stone of the footmark; at South Ronaldsway on Orkney, where a grey whinstone outside the Church of St Mary's Burwick has a pair of footprints cut into it; and at Clickhimin on Shetland. In all these places, the local kings could not rule unless they gained their authority from the land, who in earlier times would have been the Goddess of sovereignty.

Faint echoes of this custom can be found in Arthurian legend. At Tintagel in Cornwall, there is a similar footprint cut into a high rock above the castle which is known as King Arthur's Footprint. It has been suggested[7] that this, too, was a place where kings would have to stand to gain their power from the sovereignty of the land. There may be a memory of this enshrined in the Arthurian legends, where the boy Arthur draws the sword Excalibur from the stone and returns it to the lake (identified as Dozmary Pool on Bodmin Moor in Cornwall). This may be a late memory of the power of kingship and right to rule over the land being taken from and given back to the sovereignty Goddess, symbolized at Dozmary Pool as the Lady of the Lake, whose hand reaches out from beneath the water to take the sword.

It may seem that we have come a long way from the Cailleach Bearea sitting on her rock at Loughcrew, or dwelling on the mountain at Slieve Gullion – but in reality we have simply come full circle. It is the same places in the land that are known to be sacred to the Earth Goddess, whether they are the Old Crone's armchair at Spellick and Carnbane East, or the footprints of the kings in areas as far apart as Shetland and Cornwall. All over the country in Britain and Ireland the geomythic Cailleach has strode, dropping stones from her apron and making the ancient hills and sacred sites; all over the country her successor, the Goddess of sovereignty, lives in stones and rocks, offering well-being and prosperity in exchange for good management and rulership of the land; and all over the country her sisters, the hag-crone-witches, stalk the hills and tors, leading mere mortals astray and demanding respect and reverence. The Cailleach is perhaps the most ancient Goddess of all, and the most contemporary as well. She has been in, on and under the land for thousands of years, and still lives on in the folk memory and just below the level of our conscious mind today.

Notes

[1] Lecture *Who was the Cailleach of Beare?* given at the Dublin Institute of Advanced Studies, March 1996.
[2] By Jack Roberts in *The Sacred Mythological Centres of Ireland*, page 47.
[3] See Michael Dames, *Mythic Ireland*, page 220.
[4] See Mary Condren, *The Serpent and the Goddess*, page 82.
[5] See Michael Dames, op cit, page 56.
[6] By Leslie Grinsell in *Folklore of Prehistoric Sites in Britain*, pages 43–4.
[7] By Paul Broadhurst in *Tintagel and the Arthurian Mythos*, pages 132–7, and Charles Thomas in *Tintagel*, pages 96–8.

The Goddess and the Saint: The Bridget/Bride Trail

Moch maduinn Bhride
Thig an nimhir as as toll
Cha bhoin mise ris an nimhir
Cha bhoin an nimhir rium.

Early on Bride's morn
The Serpent shall come from the hollow
I will not molest the serpent
Nor will the serpent molest me.

THIS MYSTERIOUS OLD SCOTS GAELIC INVOCATION leads us from the Cailleach, the Old Hag of winter, to the Goddess of spring. Winter becomes spring in the eternal round of the seasons, and both are aspects of the same Earth Goddess.

Who, then, was this ancient Goddess of spring? We do not know from any early written sources, but her name is remembered in the oral tradition as one of the most important saints of the early Celtic church: St Bridget/Bride (pronounced Breed), meaning literally 'the exalted one'. Disentangling the point where the Goddess ends and the saint begins is virtually impossible. There are many alternative spellings of her name – Brighid, Bridgit, Brid and more – which seem to have been used in different sources, although clearly they all refer to the same 'being'. Whether that being was perceived as saint or pagan deity, a combination of both, or shape-shifting between the two, depends largely on context. For example, in the tenth-century *Cormac's Glossary*, which draws on an earlier oral tradition, Brighid is described as a patroness of poetry and also as a deity of inspiration and prophecy – a daughter of Daghda, a pagan Irish god.

In the *Life of St Brighid*, written by Cogitosus in 650 CE, she is of course a Christian saint, but one with many pagan attributes. Her feast day is 1 February, the Celtic festival of Imbolc, which probably means 'in the belly', referring to the pregnancy of the ewes or to Mother Earth. The iconography associated with her includes cows, which are elsewhere linked with Mother Goddesses, serpents, sheep, vultures, baths, milk, and the sun and the moon, all symbols linked with several other Celtic Goddesses.

Three of her most common symbols – the vulture, serpent and cow – were also symbols of the Romano-Egyptian Goddess Isis, and the rites practised at her shrine at Kildare in Leinster, in Ireland, were said to resemble those of the Romano-British Goddess Minerva, being concerned with crafts and healing.[1]

At this shrine, which the saint is supposed to have founded, there was a sacred fire, similar perhaps to that dedicated to Sulis Minerva at Bath in Somerset, which was tended by either nine or nineteen nuns, both numbers being significant in pre-Christian times. Nine occurs in many Celtic stories and in folkloric rituals associated with healing practices, and nineteen perhaps goes back to the worship of the moon on her 18.6 year cycle through the skies. There can be little doubt that Kildare was once a pagan sanctuary: indeed, some distinctly non-Christian elements came through into the hagiography of the saint and the 'history' of the early abbey there. For one thing, according to Gerald of Wales, the sacred enclosure was surrounded by a hedge and no male was allowed to enter, the nuns taking it in turns to tend the sacred flame to Bridget each night for nineteen successive nights[2]. For another, there is a little-known reference[3] that the abbess of the foundation, also called Bridget (after the Goddess/saint), had a lesbian relationship with a member of her community called Darlughdacha, with whom she shared her bed, and who succeeded her as abbess of Kildare. As Darlughdacha means 'daughter of the sun God Lugh', the pagan anti-patriarchal significance of this incident can hardly be avoided. It is an interesting thought that the worship of Bridget throughout the Catholic world may be based on a pagan Goddess and a lesbian abbess!

Other attributes of the saint hint at her pagan origins: she was born at sunrise, her mother standing at the threshold between the worlds of night and day; she was nourished on the milk of a white cow with red ears who undoubtedly came from the other world; she was brought up in the household of a Druid, who may have been her father; she had power over the element of fire, which was unable to burn the house where she lay sleeping; she was the provider of plenty and protector of cattle (her cows, milked three times a day, could fill a lake with their milk); she was the patroness of the ale-harvest and her larder was a source of limitless food that never dwindled; and, although a virgin, she could cure frigidity and was invoked by pregnant women. She is described in *Cormac's Glossary* also as a triple being: she is the patroness of poetry and the muses, her two sisters being patronesses of healing and craftwork. In other texts she is also described as an aspect of the Goddess Danu[4].

As a saint, Bridget stands at the interface of Christianity and paganism, and a thin veneer of sainthood has been grafted on to what is undoubtedly an ancient Goddess tradition. There was no place for the Goddess in the emerging monotheistic Christian religion, but she was so powerful that she could not be eliminated and was therefore turned into a saint, who effortlessly continued to take on the attributes of her pre-Christian being. We can see this process at work in the continuing significance of Bridget/Bride in the lives of the ordinary people, and her central role in the legend and folklore of her festival day, 1 February, an area we can now examine in more detail.

Much of the material that can shed light on the place Bridget had in the hearts and minds of the people can be found in the manuscript collections of the Department of Irish Folklore (IFC)[5] and in the *Carmina Gadelica* (CG), a six-volume collection of folklore from Scotland[6]. Although much of this folklore was not written down until the earlier years of the twentieth century, nevertheless it is difficult sometimes to know whether the people are thinking of Bridget as a saint or a Goddess: the two aspects are probably conflated in their minds and she was simply a 'holy being':

> According to tradition, the old people had a great belief in Brid in this district (Donegal) and any time they would be in danger or in difficulty they would place themselves under her protection and patronage. This was also the case with regard to their children as can be heard in some of their lullabies to the present day.
>
> *Huis-a-bá, a lil ghil, ó huis-a-bá hi,*
> *Beannacht* Naomh Brid *ar leanbh mo chroi*
>
> Oh, the blessing of Brid on the child of my heart
>
> IFC 904:131

Even to the present day, Bridget continued to be associated with all the earth-nurturing aspects of her Goddess incarnation. A piece of cloth was hung on a bush on the day before 1 February – Bride's Day. It was thought that she would touch it in the night, and the next day it was divided up and a piece given to every female in the house as a protective talisman. This Brat Bride, or Bride Cloth, was supposed to be an infallible cure for cows after calving, and was laid upon the back of the cow to bring good luck for the expelling of the afterbirth and the milk-giving to the calves:

> Usually milk is very scarce in January but the old people used to say during the month when they heard of anyone complaining of the scarcity of milk – 'it won't be scarce very long now as Brid and her white cow will be coming round soon.' I heard that some of the older women of the Parish take a blessed candle to the cow's stall on Bridget's Eve and singe the long hair on the upper part of the cow's udder so as to bring a blessing on her milk.
>
> IFC 899:258–9 AND 900:120

Bridget was believed to have every interest in farming life at heart, especially the *milch* cow. There was a special prayer or charm to her in cases where the cow was unable to give milk, or when it was bad-tempered during milking. A *buarach* (effigy) was made from rushes cut from the riverbank and tied around the cow's legs, and the invocation to Brid recited.

The production of food, the fertility of the land and the fecundity of Mother Nature were all key functions of Bridget, and they underlie the traditions associated with her day. The country people always regarded the advent of Feile Bride (Bride's Feast Day) as marking the end of nature's sleep during winter and her reawakening to a fresh activity of life. In Scotland on the island of Uist the flocks were dedicated to Bride on her sacred day:

> On the Feast Day of beautiful Bride,
> The flocks are counted on the moor,
> The raven goes to prepare the nest,
> And again goes the rook.[7]

In Ireland it was said that jackdaws and crows, and other birds, mated on Bridget's Day. Eggs were put down to hatch if there was a broody hen available, as tradition had it that anything that started its growth on that day would prove to be 100 per cent fertile: 'There is nothing in the water or in the ground that is not thinking of propagating by the Feast of Brid' (IFC 902:57, 902:242, 903:46 AND 903:78).

This role of the Goddess who heralds spring is part of Bridget's symbolism, and is integral to her place in the agricultural wheel of the year. As we have seen, the Cailleach was sometimes thought of as being in the last sheaf of corn harvested on or after the Lughnasad festival, which was then brought into the farmhouse, fashioned into a corn dolly and hung up over the hearth for the winter, before being taken out and re-sown into the land the following spring. We should therefore expect Bridget to be connected with this in some way, and indeed much of her mythic role is associated with straw and rushes. On the Isle of Man, on Bridget's Eve she was invited into homes and rushes were strewn on the floor to make her a bed, the ritual being known as Laa'l Breeshey. In Ireland and Scotland this was also widely observed. This is an account from County Mayo, Connacht:

> Before nightfall [on Bridget's Eve] usually the man of the house procures a garment for the Brat Bride. The man takes out this article of clothing into the haggard, draws a good long sheaf of straw out of the stack, and wraps the garment around the sheaf in a manner giving it as far as possible the rough outline in appearance of a human body. He then reverentially carries the

> object between his arms in the manner one carries a child and deposits it outside the back door. Then when supper is laid on the table, and the inmates are ready to sit, he announces that he is now going out to bring in Bridgit, as she too must be present at the festive board.
>
> IFC 903:51–3

A ritual invocation of set words between the man outside and the people within followed, and then the Brat was brought in and laid carefully beside the table. A version of this amazing survival of Goddess lore was practised widely in Ireland and Scotland: in some places Bridget presided over the whole feast in the form of a straw maiden, while there was feasting and music, and dedications were made to her. She was the Goddess of the coming spring and was felt to be both physically present and invoked in prayer and supplication.

In Scotland, on Bride's Eve the girls of the town would visit every house, carrying the figure of Bride fashioned from corn and adorned with shining shells, sparkling crystals, primroses, snowdrops and any greenery they could obtain. Every person visited was expected to give a gift to Bride and to honour her. The gift could be a shell, a spar, a crystal, a flower or a bit of greenery to decorate the person of Bride. Mothers, however, gave a Bride bannock, cheese or roll of butter:

> The older women are also busy on the Eve of Bride, and great preparations are made to celebrate her Day, which is the first day of Spring. They make an oblong basket in the shape of a cradle, which they call 'leaba Bride' – the bed of Bride. It is embellished with much care. Then they take a choice sheaf of corn and fashion it in the form of a woman. They deck this ikon with gay ribbons from the loom, sparkling shells from the sea, and bright stones from the hill. All the sunny sheltered valleys are searched for primroses, daisies and other flowers that open their eyes in the morning of the year. This lay figure is called 'dealbh Bride' – the ikon of Bride.
>
> When it is dressed and decorated with all the tenderness and loving care the women can lavish upon it, one woman goes to the door of the house, and, standing on the step with her hands on the jambs, calls softly into the darkness '*Tha leaba Bride deiseal*'– Bride's bed is ready. To this a ready woman behind her replies '*Thigeadh Bride steach, is e beatha Bride*' – Let Bride come in, Bride is welcome. The woman at the door again addresses Bride – '*A Bhride. Bhride thig a steach, tha do leaba deanta. Gleidh an teach dh'an Triana*' – Bride, Bride, come thou in, thy bed is made. Preserve the house for the Trinity. The women then place the ikon of Bride with great ceremony in the bed they have so care-

> fully prepared for it. They place a straight white wand (the bark being peeled off) beside the figure. This wand is called 'slatay Bride' – the little rod of Bride. The wand is generally of birch, broom, bramble, white willow.
>
> CG 1:167–8

This fascinating account shows that Bridget as an Earth Goddess and harbinger of spring was still celebrated in her almost completely pagan incarnation. She was fashioned from corn and decorated with the gifts of the earth and sea; her spirit was in the figure and she was addressed and invoked as a real presence; and even her tripleness was remembered in the gloss of 'trinity'. A ritual wand made from the trees of the land was given to her and she entered the house, bringing spring, good luck and fertility with her. It is a moving account that must be a long-held folk memory of a pre-Christian ritualistic ceremony.

Similarly, in Ireland, on the morning of Bridget's Day groups of young children, often restricted to girls only, would travel from house to house to visit Bridget and take part in more ceremonies. The thin veneer of Christianity that overlay these pagan customs is well illustrated in the following example:

> The woman of the house would address the image of Brigit thus: 'A very good morning to you, and, young Christian, this year is spent and you have come to us once again.' She would then take the 'bride' in her arms and kiss it.
>
> IFC 899:154

As an alternative to the straw maiden, the figure would sometimes be made from clothes arranged on a butter dish and padded out with stuffing. The symbolism of the butter, made from the milk of the cow, is also directly pertinent to the role of Bridget as nurturer of the land and provider of food, and there was nearly always some butter on the table at these Bride's feasts. A traditional Hebridean poem collected by Fiona Macleod and entitled *Invocation to Bride* includes the following verse that makes absolutely explicit the Earth Mother/nurturer aspect of Bridget:

> Yellow may my butter be, firm and round;
> Thy breasts are sweet, firm, round and sweet,
> So may my butter be, Bridget sweet.

Sometimes the *brideog* (effigy) would be made in the form of a four-armed straw cross, or *crois Bride*, and smaller versions of these Bride's crosses were widely fashioned and can still be seen in Ireland today. They seem to be a folk memory of the four Celtic agricultural festivals: Imbolc (1 February), Beltane (1 May), Lughnasad (1 August) and Samhain (1

November), the first two being the province of Bride, and the second two of the Cailleach, both aspects of the Earth Goddess wheel of the year. Sometimes a sheaf of straw (the Leaba Bhride), from which the crosses would subsequently be made, was placed under a great pot of potatoes which were boiled to make the *brúitín* (broth) and eaten with butter, while thanks were given 'to Brigid for what she sends us'.

The weaving of the straw crosses was an important part of the ceremony, and on Bridget's Day they were placed in the dwelling house and various outhouses. These crosses were used throughout the year whenever anything needed to be blessed or made fertile, for example in a basket of seed potatoes or when planting new crops. The unused portion of straw or rushes was never thrown away: it might be used to make up a bed for the cattle, or even for Bridget herself. Thus the country people realized intuitively that the spirit of the Goddess remained in the corn, even if they did not articulate it in this way.

As well as the fertility of the land and animals, Bridget would also be invoked for human fertility. In County Mayo, Connacht, when a couple were married the mother or mother-in-law would make a Brigit cross and place it under the bed to ensure a good family, while in the Scottish Highlands it was common practice to hang rowan crosses over infants' cradles while reciting a charm or prayer to Bridget to invoke her protection.

The weaving of the Brigit crosses was linked to another function of the Goddess/saint. There was a specific prohibition on Bride's Day against any turning of wheels, in particular carting, grinding or spinning[8], and yet Bridget's iconography is replete with spinning and weaving references. How can these be reconciled? We can perhaps seek a clue in some of the many 'spinning Goddess' legends from other parts of the world. The Scandinavian Goddess Freya brought the gift of spinning to the people of the earth, as did the Egyptian Goddess Isis, who taught women to spin flax and weave cloth. If Bridget was another such Goddess, then the gift of spinning would have been a sacred one, and honour would need to be paid to her on her day by recognizing this. If she was the Great Spinner, then the people should not 'compete' with her or attempt to emulate her on 'her' day. Bridget's day was thus reserved for weaving Brigit crosses only.

Given all the mythical associations of Bridget in customs and folklore, we should expect to find some evidence for her at special places in the land, and indeed we do in all the countries of Ireland, Scotland, the Isle of Man, Wales, Cornwall and England, although in most places her presence has been Christianized. In Ireland, her birthplace was reckoned to be Faughart in Leinster. A legend tells of a cow called St Brigid's Cow which was milked here by a poor woman and then ran away with her calf out to sea – again linked to Bridget's role as Goddess of fertility. Another legend tells how she plucked out her eyes beside a stream; pilgrims still visit the place and do the 'rounds'. However, as important as Faughart is, the largest and best-known shrine to Bridget in Ireland is at Kildare in Leinster, where her shrine was originally tended by priestesses or nuns. There are also many wells dedicated to her in Ireland, including Brideswell in Connacht, and Liscannor in Munster, which were formerly visited at the time of Lughnasad, and at Castlemagner in Munster, where there is a naked figure on a slab with raised arms that could be a representation of the Goddess herself. Another most interesting well was Tobar Bride in Ulster, the older name for which was Tobar Aibheog, the name of a Celtic fire Goddess. The well was renowned for the cure of toothache, providing a white stone was left as an offering, and legend also tells of a supernatural cow, Glas Gaibhleann, who appeared here and gave milk.

From Ireland, migrant Celtic peoples took the knowledge and worship of Bridget/Bride to Scotland, the Isle of Man and Wales. In Scotland, the Western Isles and the Hebrides are particularly replete with her associations: indeed, the Hebrides themselves are named after her. On the island of Arran, a convent and parish were named after her, through which flows Allt na Bride, the stream of Bride, a memory perhaps of the legend at Faughart. Off the south east of the island of Islay are three small islets which include the Isle of Bride, and a similar isle can be found off the island of Jura. On the island of Mull there is another Bride's stream, Teanga Brideig – the stream of Bride's tongue; on Skye, there is a holy well and standing stone dedicated to her at Kilbride; and on Lewis there is a St Bridget's Well at Melbost.

The Isle of Man is also notable for its Bridget associations, with a parish, a church and some hills in the north of the island all named Bride, and St Bridget's Chapel and nunnery in the south. The route into South Wales is marked by the great sweep of St Bride's Bay in Pembrokeshire, with the village and Church of St Brides built on the site of a sixth-century monastery. There were also a number of holy wells dedicated to Bridget: the key to finding the locations of these is through the Welsh spelling of St Ffraid. These include one in Denbighshire, 0.4km (¼ mile) from Llansanffraid Church, two in Monmouthshire (St Freid's Well near Skenfrith and St Bridewell in Llanuaches parish), one in Cardiganshire (St Frides Well, south west of Ystradmevrig near Treffynnon), and one in Pembrokeshire (Pistyll san ffred, near Henllys in Nevern parish). Brides visited the Bridewell in Monmouthshire on their wedding day, and St Bride appears as the matron of Monmouthshire churches.

By the early Christian period (fifth to seventh centuries) the Goddess Bridget had become the saint. Nevertheless, it is interesting to trace her passage into England, since the people who brought her had only very recently become Christianized and the old Goddess figure elided very easily into the new saint. Several of these 'Bride trails' can be traced into England and Cornwall from Ireland and Wales. One trail came into the north of England, for there are a cluster of Bride's churches in Cumbria,

including Kirkbride, Bridekirk, Brigham, Beckermet and Bride's Well at Stapleton. The Celtic tribes of the north of England must have adopted Bridget eagerly as their tutelary Goddess, and in fact they were already known to the Romans as the Brigantes, literally 'the people of Brigit or Brigantia'. It is hard to tell at this distance in time whether the figure of Bridget, having recently been sanctified, was brought there by early Christian missionaries, or whether the Celtic peoples already knew her as a Goddess and therefore easily accepted her metamorphasis into a saint. Either way, the concentration of places named after her in particular areas indicates her continuing importance at this time of the interface between paganism and Christianity.

Across the Pennines there is another cluster of Bride names on the North York Moors, this time associated with more ancient standing stones and stone rows. We can surmise that these places, as far removed in time from the Celtic tribes of the first century as they are from us, were known to be sacred places of the ancestors in the land where the old goddesses and gods had been worshipped. Therefore, at some point in time, either then or much later in the folklore, the name of the Celtic Goddess Bride was attached to them. As we know from archaeological research, there was continuity of belief in the power of ancient places in the landscape, and the Earth Goddess linked to them could easily be given a new name.

Further south, another trail moved across Wales from St Bride's Bay to the shores of the Bristol Channel, where there is a cluster of churches dedicated to St Bridget, including St Bride's Major, St Brides-super-Ely, St Brides Wentlooge, St Brides Netherwert, and a well dedicated to St Bride at St Briavels in Gloucestershire, near the River Severn. While some early settlement took place in this area, others must have crossed the Bristol Channel to found three churches on the English side, one on the coast at Brean and others further inland at Chelvey and Beckery near Glastonbury, in Somerset. The Beckery one is especially interesting, as there was known to be a site including a chapel and well in an area named Little Ireland. This was obviously a major shrine site to Bridget in the south west of England.

Further west, in the Celtic kingdom of Dumnonia (the present-day Devon and Cornwall) there was another possible branch of the Bride trail. Potters from South Wales (originally from Ireland) travelled into the Camel estuary in north Cornwall, doubtless bringing their Goddess/saint with them. The evidence for this is in certain early-Christian inscribed stones, some with ogham script (inscribed writing), that have their counterparts in South Wales and Ireland. These immigrants moved across north Cornwall and on the way founded St Bridget's Chapel and well at Landue, which still remains.[9] Apposite to this, other holy wells in the area are known colloquially as 'St Bridget wells' even when their dedication is to other saints, indicating a folk memory of the original importance of Bridget in this area. The trail may then have gone on to Bridestow in Devon, where there was another original religious foundation.

Finally, at the very south-western tip of Britain there is another possible Bride's trail, once again from immigrants, this time arriving in Cornwall from the north of Ireland. Here there is some linguistic evidence and similarities in grassware pottery. There is a church at Morvah in West Penwith that is dedicated to St Bridget of Sweden, but which probably had an earlier dedication to the Irish Bridget[10], and a chapel (now lost) at Lanyon that was popularly known to be dedicated to her. Taken all together, it is interesting to note that, with the exception of Bride's Church in London, all the Bridget/Bride church sites are on the western seaboard of Britain. In the east it is only on the Yorkshire Moors that she appears, and here her name is associated not with churches but with megalithic sites, indicating an older, less overtly Christian significance.

We have travelled many miles on our own 'Bride trails', from her earliest incarnation as Goddess of fertility and the spring to her continuing significance under Christianity. She is indeed the 'serpent' who continued to come out of the hollow: the pre-Christian Earth Goddess with her protection over the functions of femaleness in humans, animals and crops. She was honoured, revered and celebrated widely throughout all the lands of the Celtic and early Christian worlds, and an Irish invocation to her on Bridget's Day neatly sums up the esteem in which she was held:

Gabhaigi ar bhur nglúine
Fosclaigi bhur súile
Agus ligigi isteach brid
Is é beatha – Is é beatha
Is é beatha mná vaisle!

Go on your knees
Open your eyes
And admit Brigit!
Welcome! Welcome!
Welcome to the holy woman!

Notes

[1] See Mary Condren, *The Serpent and the Goddess*, page 57.
[2] Quoted by Giraldus Cambrensis in *The History and Topography of Ireland* (twelfth century).
[3] See Peter Berresford Ellis, *Celtic Women*, page 149, and Mary Condren, *The Serpent and the Goddess*, page 71.
[4] See Peter Berresford Ellis, *Celtic Women*, page 27.
[5] The examples given all come from Séamas Ó Catháin, *The Festival of Brigit*.
[6] A. Carmichael, *Carmina Gadelica* (1928–71).
[7] Quoted in Anne Ross, *The Folklore of the Scottish Highlands*, page 130.
[8] See Séamas Ó Catáin, op cit, pages 1 and 23.
[9] See 'St Bridget and her Chapels', *Meyn Mamvro* No 28, pages 6–8.
[10] See 'In Search of Bride',*Meyn Mamvro* No 21, pages 20–3.

The Goddess in the Church: The Pagan Christian Interface

THE COLLAPSE OF ROMAN BRITAIN from about the fifth century onwards happened very rapidly. The Romans withdrew from 409 CE onwards, leaving a vacuum that was filled initially by the petty kingdoms of Romano-British rulers. Then, incomers arrived into eastern and southern England from lands north of the Rhine – the Angles, Saxons and Jutes – while the Celtic west, the Western Isles of Scotland, Wales and Cornwall continued to be visited by peoples originating from Ireland and the continent. Thus, Celtic Goddess traditions remained longer in these western 'fringe' areas, even if they were subsequently assimilated into the new Christian faith, while the Anglo-Saxons, who were still pagan, brought in a different pantheon of deities.

Some of these Saxon Goddess names are known from the writings of the Roman historian Tacitus, who encountered them in northern Gaul; others are more shadowy, for example the Earth Goddess Nerthus. Although no inscriptions or statues are known to be dedicated to her from Britain, nevertheless the account of her worship by the seven tribes of the Inguaeones on an island (probably modern Seeland) is most revealing for the light it sheds on the religious observances of the Germanic peoples, and the important part the Earth Mother played in their lives.

> They worship in common Nerthus, that is Terra Mater [Earth Mother] and believe she intervenes in human affairs and goes on progress through the tribes. There is a sacred grove on the island, and in the grove is a consecrated waggon covered with a cloth. Only one priest is allowed to touch it. He understands when the goddess is present in her shrine and follows with profound reverence when she is drawn away by cows. Then there are days of rejoicing: the places, which she considers worthy to entertain her, keep these days as a holiday. They do not go to war, do not use weapons, and all iron is shut away. Peace and quiet are so much esteemed and loved at that time, until the priest returns the goddess to her sanctuary when she has had enough of human company. Directly, the waggon, the covering cloth and the goddess herself are washed in a secluded lake.

Slaves perform the function, and are drowned as soon as they finish their task.

Tacitus, *Germani*, Chapter 40

The other Goddess known to us from Anglo-Saxon times is Eostre or Ostara, who has given her name to the Christian festival of Easter. She was honoured among Germanic peoples with painted eggs, a tradition that survives to this day in the Greek Orthodox church. Eostre is also associated with the hare, the epiphany of the spring Goddess, and interestingly the Celtic warrior-leader Boudica released a hare before invoking a native Goddess, Andraste, and going into battle, so there may have been a parallel between these two goddesses, one Celtic and the other Anglo-Saxon. The symbols of Eostre are all connected with birth and fecundity, appropriate for a spring Goddess. Bede (673–735CE), writing in *De Temporum Ratione*, refers to a pagan calendar in which the month of April is called 'Eosturmonath', named after Eostre, and the month of March 'Rhedmonath', named after the Goddess Rheda or Hretha.

While southern England was being invaded and settled under its Saxon leaders and kings, the north of England, the Isle of Man, Scotland and Ireland were experiencing a new wave of attacks and invasions from the Norse people of Scandinavia. Scotland, which had retained its ancient Celtic kingdoms of Gododden, Strathclyde and Rheged, had begun to be Christianized from the sixth century onwards, but in the ninth and tenth centuries found itself under sustained and ferocious attack by the Viking people, who still followed pagan beliefs. Shetland, Orkney, Caithness, the Hebrides, the Isle of Man and Ireland were all invaded extensively and then settled by the Norse.

Shetland, Orkney and Caithness came under the direct rule of Norway, and in fact were not handed over to Scotland until 1472. Even today, 99 per cent of the placenames in the Northern Isles are of Scandinavian origin. Many Icelandic peoples settled in the Hebrides, and the Western Isles and Man became the Norderies and the Suderies, ruled by the Norwegian king and bishop, the Isle of Man staying under Norse control until 1266. In the north of England in the late eighth century, the Vikings attacked the Christian monasteries of Lindisfarne, Jarrow and Monkwearmouth in the late eighth century, and from 900 onwards they invaded the Celtic area of Cumbria, from where they moved into Ireland. Lancashire and Cheshire were settled extensively in the tenth century, but Wales suffered only intermittent attacks. In Ireland, the Norwegians and Danes fought each other for possession, and for a while were replaced by the native Irish, but Ireland also succumbed eventually to the Norse occupation, until they were ousted by the English in the twelfth century.

The Viking, Norse, Danish and Icelandic peoples who settled in these lands remained pagan until the tenth to eleventh centuries, and in fact their beliefs were not dissimilar to the Anglo-Saxons who had come originally from Denmark and northern Gaul. We should therefore expect to find evidence of the same or similar goddesses and gods worshipped by both peoples, although once again, as with the Anglo-Saxon material, the traces of Goddess in the Norse territories are few and far between.

This is partly because by the time the Norse people came to Britain their pagan pantheon consisted almost entirely of male gods. The only Goddesses to have come through were Freya and Frigg , the wife of Odin and the mother of Balder. Both Goddesses may be alternative versions of the same one: Freya from the Vanir tradition and Frigg from the Aesir tradition. They gave their names to the English colloquialism for frotterism – frigging – and to the day of the week Friday. One might wonder at the connection between these two meanings, and the answer seems to be that Freya/Frigg was a fertility Goddess, and Friday was also known as Venus' day in the ancient world. She was invoked by women in labour, and it has been suggested[1] that there was some connection between Frigg and her influence over the begetting of children, and the Norns or Parcae, a group of supernatural women remembered for their power to determine the destiny of a newborn child. In Germany, Holland and Britain they are known as 'the mothers', occasionally accompanied on inscriptions by figures in cloaks and hoods called the Genii Cucullati or 'hooded ones'. It is just possible that these Genii Cucullati were themselves meant to represent the Norns and were female deities in disguise.

In the Old Norse, Frig was daughter of Mother Earth and an Earth Goddess herself. Her mother, who may originally have been the Nerthus we have already met, was later turned into her father Niord in a reversal of sex roles. The concept of Mother Earth could not be eliminated, however, so it became attached to the daughter, Freya, whose name literally means 'lady'. She was given many other names, including Gefn (related to giving), Mardoll (suggesting a link with the sea), Horn (connected with flax) and Syr (meaning 'sow'), all of which portray her as a fertility, earth, sea and vegetation Goddess[2]. There are many parallels between her mythology and that of Celtic Goddesses, such as Medb and the Cailleach Bearea, and it is possible that both sets of Goddesses may be traced back to an original pan-European Earth Goddess, who was subsequently given different names by different races of people.

In Britain and Ireland there is little trace left of her, save in one legend and a few placenames in significant locations. These include Freefolk (Frig's people), Frobury (Frig's earthwork) and Froyle (Frig's hill), all in Hampshire, Friden (Frig's valley) in Derbyshire, Fretherne (Frig's thorn bush) in Gloucestershire, Freeborough (Frig's town) Hill in Yorkshire, and an oddity in the Western Isles of Scotland, Clach Bharnach Bharaodag on North Uist, meaning 'the limpet-stone of Freya'. The most significant of these is Freeborough Hill, where the mound, shaped like a breast or the pregnant belly of the Earth-Mother, is directly visible from a megalithic site on Ainthorpe Rigg. In this case, the place was obviously recognized as a sacred site by the later Norse invaders, and either they or their successors gave it the name of their Earth Mother Goddess. The well known as Friday Well in Yorkshire may also have gained its name because of the association of a holy place with a Scandinavian Goddess.

The legend that remains about Freya is a most interesting one. It is found in the Pentland Firth area of Scotland, and in the story Freya was sitting at her golden spinning wheel making the clouds and watching over the women on earth so that she could reward them. She led a poor but hardworking man, whose wife was industrious and content, to a beautiful room where Freya was spinning. She invited him to take his pick of all the riches in the room but, being bewildered by the array of finery, he chose some bright blue, starry flowers. These flowers were in fact flax, and later Freya explained how to tend the flowers, spin the flax and weave it into cloth. In this way, the gift of spinning was brought to the people of the earth[3]. This links Freya to many other spinning and weaving goddesses from all over the world, including Bridget in Ireland.

Eventually both the Norse peoples who settled in northern and eastern Britain, and their Saxon counterparts in the south and west, as well as the still-Celtic Wales, Ireland and Cornwall, began slowly to become Christianized. Augustine had come to England in 597, bringing his mission of Christianity, but it did not gain an immediate hold: indeed, it had to compete with an active and long-established pagan tradition, and many Saxon kings would convert one way and back again, depending on which god appeared to be most efficacious. Pope Gregory's exhortation to his missionaries in Northern Europe in 601CE is an example of how adaptable the early church had to be:

> I have come to the conclusion that the temples of the idols in England should not on any account be destroyed. Augustine must smash the idols, but the temples themselves should be sprinkled with holy water and altars set up in them in which relics are to be enclosed.

It was also faced with the difficulty of incorporating the Goddess, who had existed for so many thousands of years in so many different forms, into a monotheistic, patrifocal religion. This it did, more or less successfully, by turning her into a saint, a virgin, a witch or a spirit. However, the ordinary people's love for their Earth Goddess must have been profound, and it took many years to eliminate her from Christian dogma entirely, as is evidenced by tenth- and eleventh-century 'charms', which show a fascinating blend of Christianity and a much earlier nature religion. One in particular, called *Aecerbot*, contains a pagan hymn to the sun, and one to the earth that was said at the making of the first furrow:

> Erce, Erce, Erce, Mother of Earth...

> Hail to thee, Earth, Mother of men,
> Be fruitful in God's embrace,
> Filled with food for the use of men.[4]

The meaning of Erce is unknown, but it has been suggested[5] that it is either an unknown Goddess, or that it may mean 'high one' or 'exalted one'. In addition, there is a twelfth-century herbal invocation that calls upon Mother Earth in very pagan terms:

> Earth, divine goddess, Mother Nature who generatest all things and bringest forth anew the sun which thou hast given to the nations; Guardian of sky and sea and of all gods and powers... through thy power all nature falls silent and then sinks in sleep. And again thou bringest back the light and chasest away night and yet again thou coverest us most securely with thy shades. Thou dost contain chaos infinite, yea and winds and showers and storms; thou sendest them out when thou wilt and causest the seas to roar; thou chasest away the sun and arousest the storm. Again when thou wilt thou sendest forth the joyous day and givest the nourishment of life with thy eternal surety; and when the soul departs to thee we return. Thou indeed art duly called great Mother of the Gods; thou conquerest by thy divine name. Thou art the source of the strength of nations and of gods, without thee nothing can be brought to perfection or be born; thou art great queen of the gods. Goddess! I adore thee as divine; I call upon thy name; be pleased to grant that which I ask thee, so shall I give thanks to thee, Goddess, with due faith.[6]

This invocation shows how the nominally Christian Anglo-Saxons continued to assimilate traditions of pagan belief, especially those associated with Mother Earth and the agricultural cycle.

Another way of dealing with this nurturing Goddess was to turn her into the Mother of God – the Virgin Mary. An interesting carving at Edenham in Lincolnshire may depict a Mother Goddess figure that has crept through into the church. Housed here is a tenth-century cross-shaft showing a naked female figure breastfeeding a child. It is possible to speculate that this may have been a depiction of the Virgin Mary, shown in an unusually graphic pose, but even if this is so, it is an indication of what the early Christian church had to do to accommodate the Goddess. The Virgin Mary became the Christianized Goddess, although her fertility aspect was denied and sublimated on to the baby boy Jesus. In one sense she was but a later version of Mabon and Modron, the mother and son found in the Welsh mythic literature, or of Tailtu and Lugh, harvest Goddess and sun God of light, from Ireland – but under the new patriarchal religion she became subservient to the power of God. Her role as nurturer and protectress remained, however, as shown by an example from Inishmore, an island in Lough Gill in Connacht, where a cavity in the rock was known as Our Lady's Bed. Here pregnant women would go and turn around three times, in a ritual to give them a safe childbirth.[7]

The way in which the new Goddess of Christianity continued to be related to the old Goddess of the Earth in the minds of the people can be seen from this invocation spoken (originally in Gaelic) at La Feill Moire, the feast day of Mary, which took place in Scotland on 15 August, close to the old pagan Lughnasad festival (before the Gregorian calendar change in 1752):

On the feast day of Mary the fragrant
Mother of the shepherd of the flocks
I cut me a handful of the new corn.
I dried it gently in the sun,
I rubbed it sharply from the husk
With mine own palms.

I ground it in a quern of Friday
I baked it on a fan of sheep-skin
I toasted it to a fire of rowan
And I shared it round my people.

I went sunways round my dwelling
In the name of Mary Mother
Who promised to preserve me
Who did preserve me
And who will preserve me.[8]

CG: 1:95–7

Mary was probably named after the sea Goddess Mare, and the epithet Stella Maris – star of the sea – previously attributed to the Goddesses Isis, Ishtar, Aphrodite and Venus, was given to her by St Jerome[9]. She took over many of the attributes of the pagan Earth Goddess: she was even described in the same kind of terms, as being pre-eminent throughout the universe: 'queen of heaven, empress of hell, lady of all the world'. According to the Office of the Virgin, she was the primordial being 'created from the beginning and before the centuries'. Naturally, this Mariolatry incurred the wrath of the early Christian fathers, who sought to belittle and denigrate her, but to the people she was the Great Female Principle that their grandparents, and their grandparents before them, had celebrated and worshipped. Indeed, it is legitimate to speculate that Christianity in its formative centuries may never have survived had it not allowed some form of Marian worship among the peoples it was trying to convert. 'The Christian figure of Mary was gradually created during the first centuries of the Christian era, out of bits and pieces of the Great Goddess'[10].

Many of the early churches, and later cathedrals, were built on pagan places of the Goddess and re-dedicated to Mary. One in Italy was even called *Santa Maria sopra Minerva*, meaning 'The Church of Holy Mary over [the shrine of] Minerva'! The church, however, had a very ambivalent attitude towards her: terrified that she might be the channel through which Goddess-worship would re-establish itself, they sought to play down her divinity and her role in the Christian theology, while being forced to admit the need for her by the people. That need has lasted down the centuries, as a visit to any Catholic country will attest today. Ireland is a fascinating example: among all the ancient holy hilltops dedicated to Celtic Goddesses, what strikes the visitor most forcibly is the presence of Marian shrines everywhere: beside the roads, in the homes, at the grottoes. On the Catholic island of South Uist in the Western Isles of Scotland, a 38.5m (125ft) statue, being a representation of Mary as the Lady of the Isles, adorns the slopes of the hill of Revval, as indeed it does also on Barra, where a marble Madonna as The Lady Star of the Sea stands on the shoulder of Heavel mountain. In all these places, Mary is still intuitively recognized as the nurturing, caring, protective Goddess of the land and sea.

However, Mary alone could not carry the full weight of all the multifarious goddesses of the pagan era, and many other Goddess archetypes were turned into saints. One of the most interesting of these is St Milburga, celebrated particularly in Shropshire, where there is a well dedicated to her. It has been shown[11] that Milburga took on the attributes of a pagan grain Goddess, the information about this being encoded in her legend. While fleeing on her white horse from her enemies, she fell where some men were sowing barley in a field. The horse struck his hoof on a rock and from it flowed clear running water, a liminal place that became her holy well. Milburga passed by the sown field, where she commanded the barley to grow. It sprang up instantly, allowing her to pass safely, so that when her pursuers arrived, it was being harvested by the farmers. The men asked for information about her and the farmers were able to say that she had been there at the time of sowing, ensuring that the men went away, their pursuit a failure. This most interesting story contains elements of Milburga as an Epona figure on her horse, and an Earth Mother figure who endows the earth with great fertility and the seed with miraculous growth energy. The land protects her, and she in turn fertilizes the land.

There may have been other localized versions of the grain Goddess as well. It has been suggested[12] that Iseult in the medieval Cornish tale of *Tristan and Iseult* was one such. In the story, the land shelters, protects and nourishes her, and at the same time it is only through her that the lands of Cornwall and Ireland can be joined, so the grain Goddess is also the Goddess of sovereignty.

Other localized versions of the Earth Mother may also have existed. There are a plethora of holy wells in Yorkshire dedicated to St Helen, such as that at Eshton, and it has been suggested[13] that Helen may have been a Christianization of an earlier Goddess Ellen, who appears in the Welsh *Mabinogi* as Sara Ellen. In Herefordshire, St Catherine was something of a local goddess[14], especially in Ledbury, where the church bells rang of their own accord to welcome her, and at Stretton Grandison, where there was a well dedicated to her. She was also remembered at St Catherine's Chapel near Guildford in Surrey, and at Temple Church on Bodmin Moor in Cornwall. Catherine was originally a Gnostic Goddess, who was an aspect of Kali, the Hindu Goddess of death and transformation. She was dancer of the fiery wheel at the hub of the universe, and was martyred as a Christian saint on a wheel of fire. She was brought to England by the Cathari or medieval Gnostics, who revered her almost as a female counterpart of God.[15]

St Ann/Anne is another saint with possible pagan antecedents: her name may be derived either from Anu, the eponymous Goddess of Ireland, or from *tain*, a Celtic word meaning 'fire', and often associated with holy hilltops lit by beacons. There are many wells dedicated to her, for example at Aconbury in Herefordshire, near Chertsey in Surrey, at Hempstead in Gloucestershire, at Trelleck in South Wales, and at Whitstone in Cornwall, which contains a stone head that may be a depiction of her. The most amazing one of all is at Llanmihangel in the vale of Glamorgan, South Wales, where a bust of the saint issued forth healing water from her nipples and vagina.

Some saints are peculiar to the Celtic lands, and many hint at a pagan origin. St Madron's Well in Cornwall may derive its name from St Madrun, a Welsh saint who was probably a Christianization of Modron, the Mother

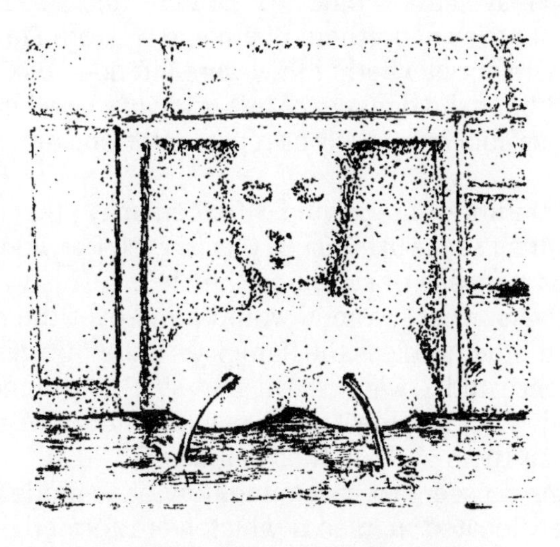

ST ANNE'S WELL, LLANMIHANGEL.

Goddess in the *Mabinogi*. Madron's Well has many traditions of healing – effecting cures – and of divination – dropping pins into the water to forsee the future. St Senera at Zennor, also in Cornwall, may be a version of a pagan Goddess of the sea. Her legend includes her survival on the sea in a barrel, and her transportation from Brittany to Ireland and back to Cornwall. A mermaid legend associated with the church also reinforces this interpretation. St Warna's Well on the Isles of Scilly may be another latter-day Goddess of the sea, who became in historical times the patron saint of shipwrecks – and therefore of bounty from the sea! Finally, from North Wales come St Winifred and St Melangell. St Winifred's Well had healing properties and nurturing Mother Goddess associations: cures were effected here and the well gave forth milk. She was supposedly beheaded on 22 June, the time of the summer solstice. St Melangell may be a local variation of the Earth Goddess and the Goddess of hares, Oestre: her legend has her shielding a hare from harm, and her church was built in the shadow of a beautiful breast-shaped hill.

There are many other saints whose names, feast days and legends hint at the Christianization of earlier Earth and Mother Goddesses. Taken all together, we have a rich tapestry of vibrant Goddess colours, woven by the church out of the pagan threads from the past. Often hidden and remote, and far off the beaten track, the churches and wells show that the Goddess never really died under the Christian faith: she just metamorphosed into the saints, who continue to keep her spirit alive in the sacred places of the land today.

Finally, the Goddess of the land may have gone into the churches themselves. Sheela-na-gigs are a form of female exhibitionist carving found on the walls of some churches in England and on churches and castles in Ireland. Most are medieval in origin (from the twelfth century onwards) and may have come to Britain and Ireland from the Romanesque countries of northern Spain and western France. There has been much debate about whether they were intended as Christian warnings to people about the dangers of lust and vice, or whether they were carved by masons subconsciously as representations of the old Goddess of the land.

Some of the traditions associated with them may give clues as to their meaning. Early Irish sagas like *Táin Bó Cúailnge* refer to women displaying their genitals as a means of subduing the enemy. This was carried over into Celtic festivals, where women would jump over the fires, exposing their genitals, in order to bless the flames with their power, to receive its beneficial influence and to ward off evil spirits[16]. Some of the sheelas have similar traditions, and at some it was considered lucky, or a good presage of fertility, to visit them and rub their vaginas.

Some sheelas do seem to have a memory of a Goddess association, or to have been located at places which were formerly sacred to the Goddess. At Killiniboy in Munster, the sheela was known locally as Baoith,

SHEELA-NA-GIG FROM BALLYPARTY CASTLE, IRELAND
(CRAIG CHAPMAN)

named after the cow-Goddess Boand. At Ballyvourney in County Cork, Munster, there is a shrine dedicated to St Gobnat that incorporates a sheela. St Gobnat is the patron saint of bees, and this may be a Christianized version of the old Earth Mother bee goddess[17]. At Copgrove in Yorkshire, a sheela is carved with the letter T, which may mean *terra*, making her an Earth Mother figure. And at Rodel on South Harris in the Western Isles is a sheela depicted with an animal or child that may have been carved in the same tradition as the nurturing Mother Goddesses. Some – including Copgrove in Yorkshire and Kiltinan Castle in Munster – have symbols that could make them a form of sun or moon Goddess, but that could be said to be in the eye of the beholder.

The locations of the sheelas also varied widely. Some are in churches and are clearly meant to be seen, such as that at Killinaboy in Munster, where she sits over the doorway, so that entering the church is akin to entering her womb. Others, however, are much more hidden, adding to the puzzle. We know that other votive figures were sometimes brought into churches for safe-keeping – such as the one of Fortuna at Marlborough in Wiltshire, Verbia in Ilkley Church in Yorkshire, and the Mother Goddess in Lund Church in Lancashire – so it is not inconceivable that some sheelas may have been considered to be pagan. Two are carved on megalithic stones: St Adamnan's Pillar at Tara and the cross at Stepaside, Jamestown, both in Leinster. These are either a paganization of a Christian monument or a Christianization of a pagan megalith.

Some sheelas may have been conceived of as protective spirits of the buildings, inheriting a tradition of Goddesses at important places in the land such as river crossings and pagan temples. One is on a bridge, two are at holy wells (the one at Kiltinan Castle being known as The Guardian of the Well) and several are on the walls of buildings at quoins or corner joints. One was known as The Hag and two as The Witch, hinting at their pre-Christian significance as depictions of the 'divine hag' of Celtic mythology transmuted into iconographic image.[18]

Whatever their precise meaning, whether they were symbols of lust personified or apotropaic talismans to ward off evil spirits, whether they were a deliberate Christian attempt to show the wickedness of the daughters of Eve or an unconscious recividism to their pagan roots by the masons, they are a fascinating example of a very basic and physical image of femaleness, the counterpoint of the female saints. The sheelas may or may not have been conceived of as Goddesses, but they clearly share some of the same traditions, and they must have touched a deep chord in the people, as indeed they still do today.

NOTES

[1] By H.R. Ellis Davidson in *Gods and Myths in Northern Europe*.
[2] See H.R. Ellis Davidson, *The Lost Beliefs of Northern Europe*, pages 108–113.
[3] Taken from Bette Hochberg, *Spin Span Spun*.
[4] Translation from A.K. Gordon, *Anglo-Saxon Poetry*, pages 89–90.
[5] By Pamela Berger in *The Goddess Obscured*, pages 65–6, and Kathleen Herbert in *Looking for the Lost Gods of England*, page 23.
[6] Translation by Dr Charles Singer in *Early Magic and Medicine*, and reproduced in Paul Hudson, *Mastering Herbalism*, pages 232–4.
[7] See Patrick Logan, *The Holy Wells of Ireland*, page 83.
[8] From Lorraine McDonald, 'The Feast of Tailtu', *Dalriada*, vol 7/3, page 27.
[9] See Barbara Walker, *The Women's Encyclopedia of Myths and Secrets*, page 958.
[10] Ibid, pages 602–3.
[11] See Pamela Berger, *The Goddess Obscured*, pages 67–70.
[12] By Caeia March in 'In Search of Iseult', *Meyn Mamvro*, no 23, pages 16–19.
[13] By Rob Wilson in *Holy Wells and Spas of South Yorkshire*, page 6, and by Chesca Potter in 'Helen, Goddess of Leys', *Northern Earth*, no 29, pages 4–6.
[14] See Jonathan Sant, *The Healing Wells of Herefordshire*, page 60.
[15] See Robin Ellis and Cheryl Straffon, 'Cornwall's Mysterious Places', *Meyn Mamvro*, no 23, pages 4–5.
[16] See P. Rawson, *Primitive Erotic Art*, page 76.
[17] See Jack Roberts, *The Sheela-na-Gigs of Britain and Ireland*, page 22.
[18] See Anne Ross, 'The Divine Hag of the Pagan Celts' from *The Witch Figure* (ed Venetia Newall), pages 139–164.

The Goddess Today: The Pagan Legacy

WE HAVE COME A LONG WAY IN following the story of the Earth Goddess, from the earliest settlements and megalithic sites of our Neolithic and Bronze Age ancestors around 7,000 years ago, through the Romano-British period with its plethora of Goddess reliefs and names, looking at the Celtic stories and traditions of the Goddess in many forms and places, tracing the Anglo-Saxon and Norse invasion with their particular Goddesses, and arriving at the Christianization of Goddess into saint and legend. However, we cannot leave the story without asking what, if anything, remains today? There are a number of answers to that question.

The first can be found in the area of folklore and storytelling. Tales and legends remain in the folklore and oral tradition sometimes for a very long time, but they have to be treated with caution. They can change a lot over a long period of time, or have additional parts added to them from other oral and literary sources. They are almost impossible to date: the date when they are first recorded is simply that, and it gives no indication as to how long or short a time they were current before then. However, even with these reservations in mind, it is interesting to look at some particularly prevalent themes that might be an indication of the continuity of Goddess belief, as she was turned into a *genus loci* or 'spirit of place'.

One such figure may have been Figgy Dowdy/Madge Figgy in Cornwall. She gave her name to a well on Carn Marth, and has a rhyme attached to her about her selling her bed and lying on straw. It has been suggested[1] that her name may be a corruption of the Cornish for 'the reaper Goddess' or 'good Goddess of the scythe'. The custom of baptizing dolls in her holy well water may link her to a Cornish fertility Goddess, closely related to Bridget/Bride. Other figures are recorded elsewhere. Queen Mab, the queen of the fairies, who was written about by Shakespeare, was probably a version of the great Irish queen Goddess Maeve. She has given her name to Mab's Well in Yorkshire. Other wells, rivers, pools and lakes have their own female spirits who haunt the place and often claim victims from the unwary – perhaps a folk memory of sacrifice to a Goddess. These include Peggy's Well in Lancashire, where Peg O'Nell claims a victim every seven years; The Strid in Yorkshire, where the spirit of the River Wharfe appears as a white horse on May Day morning to warn of death in the river; and Doxey's Pool in Staffordshire, where the mermaid threatened to drown the town of Leek if she were disturbed.

Elsewhere, the spirits of the rivers and wells did not threaten doom and death, but were nevertheless treated with some awe and respect. In Ireland, pilgrims went to a well called Tobar na mBan Naomh (Well of the Holy Women) near Teelin in County Donegal on midsummer night to keep a vigil in honour of the three women: Ciall (sense), Tuigse (understanding) and Naire (modesty). Although the women were envisaged as nuns, this is in all probability a Christian continuation of the worship of the Three Mothers. The presence of the women at this well was known to be so powerful that when sailing out of Teelin Bay fishermen would lower their sails in salute and take off their caps as they passed the well[2].

Further themes and motifs associated with the Goddess appear into other legends. Many ancient sites have legends of petrifaction, particularly young maidens turned into stone for dancing on the Sabbath (for example, Merry Maidens in Cornwall and Nine Ladies in Derbyshire), or witches greedily overmilking other-worldly cows (for example, Mitchell's Fold in Shropshire), or themselves being turned to stone for practising witchcraft (for example, Long Meg in Cumbria). What we seem to have in all these cases are late (seventeenth- to nineteenth-century) glosses on the original meaning of the sites: that they were pagan places (and therefore, in Christian eyes, evil) where the goddesses and gods of old were remembered (as hags, giantesses and devils) and celebrated by women who were originally the priestesses of the Old Religion (maidens and witches). By now the Goddess has become but a faded memory, a trace of some strange old belief from long ago, but nevertheless faintly recalled in half-remembered songs and stories handed down by mothers and grandmothers.

Sometimes the old goddesses and gods became part of the fairy belief that lingered until very late, especially in the Celtic lands of Ireland, Wales, the Isle of Man, Scotland and Cornwall. When Evans Wenz went to collect this material at the beginning of the twentieth century[3] he found that these fairy-folk or Sidhe (pronounced 'shee'), or 'little people' as they were often called, were thought to be either spirits of the dead or the spirits of mounds, rivers, wells and hills – precisely the places where the Goddess was formerly thought to dwell. He himself suggested that the Sidhe were the original people of the Goddess Danu of the Tuatha De Danaan. It has also been suggested recently[4] that the 'bean side', or the banshees – the women of the other world who are supernatural death-messengers in Irish legend and folklore – are a memory of an earlier Earth Goddess. Evans Wenz also found traces in the material he collected of memories of old Goddesses transmuted into fairy beings. In Scotland he came across a guardian Goddess called Gruagach, who watched over the cows (cf Bridget) and to whom libations were still made by pouring milk into special hollowed stones called Leac na Gruagach. And in Wales he discovered that the Goddess of heaven or Mother of All was known as Brenhines-y-Nef.

If it is surprising to find that a living tradition of this kind continued to exist into the twentieth century, it is even more surprising to discover that it may also have lingered in remote places right up until very recent times. In the Longdendale valley in Derbyshire an anonymous woman has claimed[5] that a community of farming folk living in scattered farmsteads has retained a belief in the Earth Goddess, and that she is represented in significant stones in the landscape in which there is a V shape denoting her vulva. This Earth Goddess was known as the Mother or the One. Another writer[6] has claimed that as a young girl living in the south west she was brought up in a living pagan tradition that still celebrated the Goddess as part of its seasonal round. Among the things she remembers was the tradition that mothers of newborn children would place the placenta at the foot of a standing stone to thank the Goddess for their successful delivery. If these are genuine remains, they are indeed an amazingly long-lasting oral tradition.

The second main area where fragments of the old tradition have come down to us is through the folk customs that take place every year in different parts of the country. Although some of these are modern revivals, many contain ancient elements in their observance. One of the most powerful is the Padstow Obby Oss in Cornwall, which involves the whole community of this small harbour town and attracts thousands of visitors every May Day. There are now two Osses, or hobbyhorses, involved – the Red and the Blue – each consisting of a fearsome-looking 'beast' that dances through the streets from morning to evening, accompanied by a 'teaser' who leads it on, and a band that plays the ritual song to which the Oss dances. The current programme of the Red Oss that is given out on the day makes explicit the link between the festival and the old Goddess religion. It points out that at one time the Oss would have been a version of the Celtic horse goddess, known as Epona, Rhiannon and Magog, and the teaser who danced it through the streets a man. Nowadays the position is reversed, and the Oss is usually a man covered by a heavy metal hoop draped with the black costume, and the teaser a woman. Until 1850 the Oss was accompanied by an old woman in a scarlet cloak and cape, who 'could have been an earlier link with the crone of Celtic mythology'[7]. Reference to the Oss goes back as far as 1346–7, and it is undoubtedly much older than that.

A similar type of Obby Oss called the Mari Lwyd was once seen extensively in South Wales between Christmas Day and the old New Year (6 January). This horse's head was carried from house to house, where it tried to gain admittance, accompanied by a ritual exchange of verses in Welsh between the people outside and those inside. Eventually the horse was let in, and there was much feasting and merrymaking. Remnants of this festival still take place in Llangynwyn and Pencoed, and may form a direct link back to the old story of Rhiannon.

In other places, spring is welcomed in with egg-rolling – in Preston in Lancashire and Edinburgh in Scotland, for example – and ball games, such as bottle-kicking on Easter Monday at Hallaton in Leicestershire, where the victors win a hare pie, and hurling the silver ball on Shrove Tuesday at St Columb Major in Cornwall. All these were doubtless associated originally with the pagan Goddess Oestre. In Derbyshire, well-dressing takes place at various holy wells between May and August; it is now a Christian festival, but originally was almost certainly a pagan thanksgiving to the water-goddess.

Harvest time brings the last great remnant of the agricultural ritual cycle. In Cornwall, the ceremony of 'crying the neck' takes place, revived during the early years of the twentieth century and continued ever since. The last sheaf of corn, called the 'neck', or in some places the 'neck of the mare', is ritually cut and held aloft with a special formula of words incanted between harvester and onlooker. This was formerly a widespread custom, symbolizing the ritual sacrifice of the grain Goddess. In the Highlands of Scotland, the last sheaf was called the Maiden before the Celtic festival of Samhain (31 October) and the Cailleach afterwards. This was thought to contain the spirit of the grain Goddess, so the 'maid' from the farm ran to the farmhouse with it, where it was fashioned into a corn dolly and hung up over the hearth for the winter. The Cailleach presided over the home, and was taken out and scattered on the fields prior to sowing time in spring. Thus was the cycle of the Earth Goddess complete.

In many places, these customs died out only in the early years of the twentieth century, with the changes to traditional agriculture and the total disruption caused by two World Wars. In many places they were revived soon afterwards, although few of them still carry the traditional power and deep sense of continuity provided by Padstow's Obby Oss. There was, however, only a short time between the last remnants of these festivals and the extraordinary revival, reinvention or reinterpretation (depending on your point of view) of traditional 'witchcraft' that took place in the mid 1950s and has grown stronger ever since, as a whole neo-pagan movement has gathered pace.

There are many strands and versions of this wiccan and/or pagan movement, but the significance of it perhaps is that the Goddess, in many different forms and guises, is central to this eclectic and polytheisic movement. Old Goddesses have been rediscovered, and long-lost Goddess meanings and symbols reinstated. Some of these build on the anthropological studies of Sir James Frazer in *The Golden Bough* (1890–1915), together with the theories of archaeologist Margaret Murray, although many of their ideas have since been questioned. Some have been inspired by the research of archaeologist Marija Gimbutas into the Goddess-celebrating civilizations of the past, and the visionary application of contemporary Goddess studies by the feminist artist and writer Monica Sjöö. Others have been influenced by the revivalist Gerald Gardner (1884–1964), whose brand of Gardnerism has spawned a whole neo-wiccan movement. And still others have come to Goddess through the Women's Spirituality movement and the work of organizations like the Matriarchy Research and Reclaim Network. The central focus on Goddess by all these groups and others can perhaps best be summed up by the invocation written by modern witch Doreen Valiente, that begins:

> Listen to the words of the Great Mother, who of old was called Artemis Astarte, Diana, Melusine, Aphrodite, Cerridwen, Diana, Arianrhod, Brigit and by many other names... For you who seek to know her, know that your seeking and learning will avail you not, unless you know the Mystery; for if that which you seek, you find not within yourself, you will never find it without. For behold, she has been with you from the beginning, and she is that which is attained at the end of desire.[8]

And that perhaps is the message of this whole Goddess story. Although we have travelled many miles throughout Britain and Ireland, covered vast aeons of time from 5000 BCE to the present day, and encountered multifarious Goddesses along the way, yet all of them in all their different contexts and from their different cultures are only the outward form of an inner spiritual direction. There are many paths to the centre of this being, the spiritual force of the universe that has been called the Goddess, but in all cases those who celebrated or worshipped or placated or loved their Goddesses were seeking only to find the truth of humankind's existence within themselves. The Earth Goddess was out there in the land, but she was also within the inner landscape: she was the focus of the individual's relationship between themselves and the forces of the universe that gave them life, nurtured and sustained them, and finally brought this incarnation to an end.

The Goddess has never really died, never disappeared from this and other worlds: she has shape-shifted, metamorphosed, gone underground and re-emerged in a different form. But we are the daughters and sons of that elder of the tribe who entered the megalithic tomb to commune with her 7,000 years ago, and as long as there are people who have need of her in their lives, then the Goddess of the Earth will never go away. If she ever does, if we ever decimate our precious planet so that it is incapable of bearing life any more, then we are all doomed. Our Neolithic ancestors knew this all those thousands of years ago; let us hope we never forget.

Notes

[1] By Andy Norfolk in 'Bride's Bed Revisited', *Meyn Mamvro*, no 27, pages 18–19.
[2] See Patrick Logan, *The Holy Wells of Ireland*, page 42.
[3] Evans Wenz, *The Fairy Faith in Celtic Countries*.
[4] By Patricia Lysaght in 'Aspects of the Earth Goddess in the Traditions of the Banshee in Ireland' in *The Concept of the Goddess*, pages 152 – 165.
[5] See David Clarke with Andy Roberts, *Twilight of the Celtic Gods*, pages 20–3 and 58–9.
[6] Rhiannon Ryall, *West Country Wicca*, page 54.
[7] David J. Eddy, *A Brief History of the Obby Oss*.
[8] Quoted in Starhawk, *The Spiral Dance*, pages 90–1.

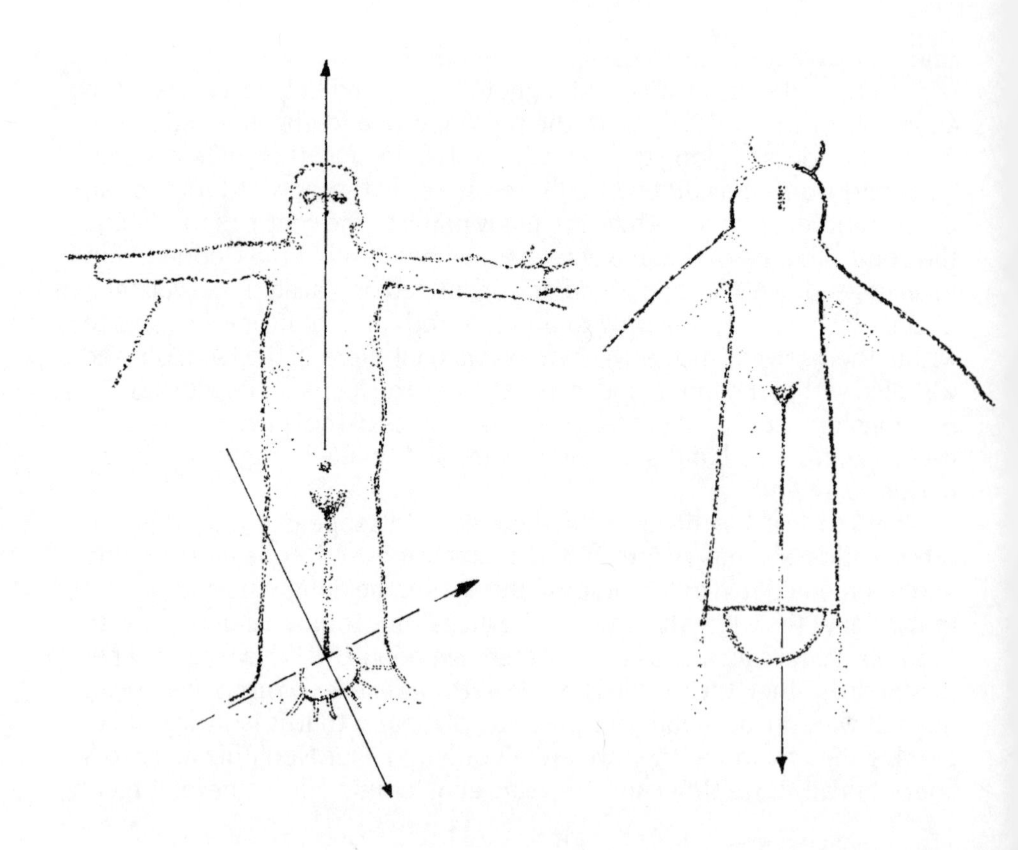

BIDSTON HILL FIGURES, MERSEYSIDE (CRAIG CHAPMAN).
(SEE PAGE 140)

Part 2:

The Gazetteer

England

ENGLAND IS DIVIDED HERE INTO FIVE AREAS and then into counties. The county boundaries are those established under the most recent (1996) local government reorganization. It also includes the Isle of Man, 64km (40 miles) off the English coast in the Irish Sea, and the Channel Isles, 160km (100 miles) off the south coast, near France.

South West

Cornwall and the Isles of Scilly

Isles of Scilly

The Isles of Scilly are a group of about 200 isles, islets and rocks lying some 43km (27miles) off the SW coast of Cornwall. Five of the larger islands – St Mary's, St Martin's, Tresco, Bryher, and St Agnes/Gugh – are inhabited, and the islands as a whole contain a wealth of ancient sites.

In prehistoric times the Isles of Scilly were one land mass, but by 3000 BCE, when the first settlers began to arrive, the waters had started to rise and the islands began to separate out. To these first Bronze Age inhabitants it is likely that the original island was still seen as the body of the Mother Goddess, and cairns and entrance graves were placed strategically to mark various solar alignments. In the Eastern Isles, for example, the three distinctive peaks of Great Arthur (SV 942 135), Middle Arthur (SV 939 138) and Little Ganilly (SV 939 141) may well have represented three aspects of the Earth Mother. Two entrance graves on Middle Arthur are placed to face the winter solstice sunrise and sunset, perhaps working together on the shortest day of the year. The latter cairn was excavated in 1953 and some pottery and a bone of a female were found – perhaps she was the attendant priestess of the sacred burial sites?

By the Romano-British period (500 CE), the Scillies in general and the Eastern Isles in particular had become a major Goddess shrine. On Nornour (SV 944 148), now an uninhabited island, a shrine settlement was established. Eleven circular stone huts were in use and were modified over a period from the second millennium BCE to about the fourth century CE. In two of the huts, which formed the shrine, a large number of votive offerings were found including about 300 brooches, 35 bronze rings,

11 bronze bracelets, 84 Roman coins, 44 glass beads and several clay figurines, including Mother Goddess and Venus depictions (see page 23). This was clearly a significant Goddess cult centre, and one that was probably dedicated to a specific marine Goddess, perhaps called *Sillina, which may have meant something like 'she who looks out, the watcher Goddess'. Interestingly, the root of this word – *sul/sil*, meaning 'eye', 'light' or 'vision' – is the same as that of the Celtic Goddess Sulis, who was the presiding deity at Bath, some 280km (175 miles) away (see page 94). It has been suggested[1] that the two Goddess centres may have been linked by a chain of holy hilltop beacons, running from St Martin's next to Nornour up through Cornwall to Bath. There was formerly a chapel beacon fire on Chapel Downs on St Martin's, and the tradition of lighting midsummer bonfires on the holy hilltops in Cornwall has been kept up until the present day.

Following the Christianization of the islands, the old Goddess of the sea may have been turned into a saint, Warna. She became the patron saint of shipwrecks, and in the past offerings were laid at her well on St Agnes (SV 880 079) to encourage the sea to give up its storm bounty to the islands. Nearby is the famous Troy Town Maze (SV 877 078), a walkable stone maze that overlooks the western Atlantic ocean. It dates from at least 1729, although it may have been built on an earlier site. Such mazes have been used in Scandinavia as a means of giving protection and luck to fishermen, so it too may relate to the propitiation of a Goddess of the sea. Indeed, there was a custom in Finland and Sweden for a maiden representing the Goddess to stand at the centre of such stone mazes, waiting to be set free[2]. The power of the sea Goddess in the Isles of Scilly is ever present and still very strong.

The Scillies are reached from Penzance *in* Cornwall *by boat or helicopter, or from* Land's End *airport by* Skybus. (*There is a railway station at* Penzance.) *Contact the* Tourist Information Centre *on* St Mary's (*tel*: 01720–422536) *for more details. Boats run regularly from* St Mary's *to all the off-islands, including* St Agnes, *and there are sometimes trips to the* Eastern Isles, *including* Nornour.

Merry Maidens stone circle (SW 433 245)

The West Penwith peninsula – that part of Cornwall W of the River Hayle as far as Land's End – has in its 130sq km (50sq miles) or so about 500 extant archaeological sites: perhaps the densest concentration in Britain. Much has been lost, but enough remains for us to be able to piece together a picture of an ancient ritual landscape. The stone circles are at the heart of that landscape, and their Cornish names and legends give us a hint as to their ancient origins. Known in Cornish as Dans Maen, meaning 'the dancing stones', many of the circles have legends of petrifaction attached to them.

At the Merry Maidens near Lamorna, the 19 stones are supposed to be a group of women turned to stone for dancing on the Sabbath, a legend that applies to some other stone circles in Britain. This may be a folk memory of the original use of the site for ritual dancing activity. Some sites are called the Nine Maidens, which may be another aspect of the same legend, nine (triple three) being a sacred number to ancient peoples. In the case of the Merry Maidens, the legend is given a double confirmation by another legend applying to the nearby Boleigh fogou (underground chamber), where a coven of witches held sabbats. One of the witches assumed the form of a hare, an animal traditionally sacred to the moon goddess, so we may be looking here at a distant memory of a cult of priestesses connected with the Goddess of the moon, a connection reinforced by the number of stones in the circle – 19 reflecting the moon's 18.6 year cycle around the earth.

From the circle, as from other significant places in the Penwith landscape, the twin hills of Chapel Carn Brea and Bartinney are clearly visible. Both hills were famed 'holy hill' sites: Chapel Carn Brea has a Bronze Age entrance grave near its summit, and formerly a chapel to St Michael was built there to Christianize a pagan spot; while Bartinney is the 'hill of fire' where midsummer bonfires were lit, an act of sympathetic magic. The twin hills – seen perhaps by our ancestors as the breasts of the Mother Goddess – were part of the same ritual landscape as the stone circles that were deliberately constructed to reflect the creative power of the cosmic deity, who was seen to be alive in the land and in the stones[3].

The Merry Maidens stone circle lies beside the B3315 *Penzance–Land's* End *road (there is a railway station at* Penzance*). The hills of* Chapel Carn Brea *and* Bartinney *are accessible from a minor road leading from the* A30 *at* Crows-an-Wra *signposted to* St Just.

Fogous

Fogous are Cornish *souterrains* – underground passages – confined in distribution to the West Cornwall area and dating from the Iron Age/Celtic period (500 BCE–500 CE). They usually consist of a curved underground passageway, sometimes with another passageway leading off it, and a narrow side entrance known as a 'creep' sloping towards the surface, and are most often associated with courtyard house settlements.

Theories as to their purpose include storage, refuge or ritual. These have all been examined in turn[4], and the first two at least found severely wanting.[5] The third explanation – ritual – has been questioned[6], but criticism has been soundly rebutted by researcher Ian Cooke[7]. He argues that the orientation of the fogous indicates a ritual function and, by analogy with other prehistoric sites, he believes that they were built both to appease the Earth Mother for the extraction of tin by mining (the tin lodes run in the same direction as the fogous), and to celebrate the rebirth of the sun Goddess or God each year at the winter and summer solstices.

In eight of the eleven extant fogous, the main passage curves from NE to SW, marking the midsummer solstice sunrise, and in two others it faces NW, marking the midsummer solstice sunset. In at least one site (Carn Euny fogou) this orientation is superimposed on an earlier one that marked the midwinter solstice sunrise.

The legends associated with the fogous are also interesting. The one at Boleigh fogou is recounted elsewhere (see Merry Maidens stone circle, page 84); another, at Pendeen fogou, warns that a woman in white with a red rose in her mouth travels from Ireland to appear at the fogou entrance on Christmas morning and portends death to anyone who sees her. This could well be a folk memory of the Earth Goddess worshipped at the site, her whiteness linking her to the rites of the moon (similar stories of white ladies are known from elsewhere – see, for example, Parc-y-Meirw on the Preseli Hills, page 163). Her red rose represents her menstruating or fertility aspect. Her journey from Ireland recalls the link between Celtic peoples who worshipped the same goddesses, and her appearance on Christmas morning is perhaps a memory of the time of the winter solstice and the rebirth of the sun Goddess. Whatever the precise nature of the rituals performed at them, it seems likely that fogous were powerful places of communion with the Earth Mother.

The best-preserved fogous are at Carn Euny (SW 402 288), *reached by a minor road* N *of the* A30 *at* Tregonebris; Pendeen (SW 384 355), *reached from a turning from the village to the coast on the* B3306 St Just–St Ives *road*; Boleigh (SW 437 252), *on private property at* CAER *near* Lamorna (*tel:* 01736–810530 *for permission to visit*); *and* Halligye *on the* Trelowarren *estate* (SW 713 239), *reached via a turning off the* B3293. *This last site is closed during the winter because of the resident bat population. Good footwear and a torch will be required at all the sites.*

The Mermaid of Zennor (SW 454 385)

There are many legends around the Cornish coast of mermaids, who seem to be a folk memory of an ancient Goddess-worship together with much later Greek myths of sea-sirens, who were themselves derived from earlier Greek worship of the Goddess Aphrodite[8]. The word 'mermaid' derives from the ancient 'merrymaid' or 'meremaid', which is identified in folklore with the moon and Aphrodite, Goddess of love, who shape-shifted into a fish tail to escape the attentions of the pursuing sun God. Her common possessions of a mirror and a comb may originally have represented the full moon and phases of the waxing and waning moon.

One of her most potent manifestations is as the Mermaid of Zennor, the latter a tiny hamlet nestling among ancient Celtic fields on the remote N coast of Penwith. In the legend, she appears in the church and seduces the best choir singer, Mathew Trewella, to share her watery home with her. She may be based in part on St Senara, whose parish church this is and who herself had legendary origins. Originally a pagan princess – Asenora

of Brittany – she was cast adrift on the sea in a barrel when pregnant and was eventually washed up on the coast of Ireland. From here she returned to Brittany via Cornwall, where she founded the small granite church at Zennor. Mermaid, saint and sea-creature seem inextricably intertwined and may all be aspects of an other-world, sea Goddess shape-shifter from prehistoric times. In the church at Zennor there is a carving of the mermaid in black wood on the side of an ancient chair. The carving may be over 600 years old, and a notice above the chair makes the pagan/Goddess origins of the Mermaid quite explicit.
Zennor lies to the N *of the* B3306 St Ives–St Just *road (there is a railway station at* St Ives*). There is access to the church at most times.*

Saints and wells

Cornwall boasts about 100 holy wells, many of them dedicated to particular Celtic saints found elsewhere only in Wales, Ireland and Brittany – areas with which Cornwall had particular contact in the early Christian period. These wells were doubtless already in existence when Christianity came to Cornwall, so behind the legends of the saints we can sometimes glimpse a more ancient Goddess-celebrating past.

At Sancreed Well in West Penwith (SW 418 293), which has a powerful liminal entrance into the womb of Mother Earth, there is a legend of St Credan, who became a swineherd. In Celtic mythology, pigs were totem animals of the other world and swineherds often represent an initiation into the mysteries of the dark Goddess[9]. At Madron Well, also in West Penwith (SW 446 328), the saint's name may be a metamorphic rendering of Modron, the Mother Goddess from the Welsh *Triads*. Modron became Christianized into the Welsh saint, Madrun, who is etymologically identical with the Cornish Madron. The well is a place with many legends of healing and divination. Morvah Church, once again in West Penwith (SW 402 355), is dedicated to St Bridget of Sweden, but there may have been an earlier link with the Celtic Goddess/saint Bride[10]. Her feast day at Morvah is 1 August, the old Celtic Lughnasad festival. Another Bridget link is at Landue near Launceston, where St Bridget's Well stands in a wooded grove on a private estate (SX 350 796). It was perhaps established there by Irish immigrants, who came up the Camel estuary and moved on into Devon (see Bridestow, page 90).

Finally, at Whitstone in North Cornwall there is St Anne's Well (SW 263 985), which has a strange carving over the well entrance of a head, supposedly that of St Anne but looking much more like a pre-Christian effigy – perhaps the original spirit of the well itself, the Celtic Goddess Anu.
Sancreed Well is signposted from Sancreed Church near St Just-in-Penwith. *Madron Well lies down a beautiful lane* N *of Madron village, near* Penzance. *Morvah Church is on the* B3306 St Just–St Ives *road. Landue estate is beside the* A388 *Launceston–Callington road, about 8km (5 miles)* S *of Launceston. The estate is pri-*

vate and permission must be sought to visit St Bridget's Well. St Anne's Well *is behind the church at* Whitstone, *to the* W *of the* B3254, *halfway between* Launceston *and* Kilkhampton.

Tintagel (SX 050 390)

Tintagel Castle is famous the world over as the dwelling place of the legendary King Arthur. While there is no historical basis for this identification, nevertheless we know that in the fifth century CE it was an important citadel, probably occupied seasonally, with strong trading links with the Mediterranean. What is less well known is that on the headland to the S of the twelfth-century castle is a curious footprint-shaped cavity in the natural rock, known as King Arthur's Footprint. It has been suggested[11] that this could be a very early feature of the site, associated with an inauguration ceremony: the ritual crowning of a king or chieftain who could only gain his authority to rule by a sacred joining with the Goddess of the land, or sovereignty. Such a custom is known from elsewhere, particularly in Scotland and Ireland, and it would help to explain why this particular site retained its notion of power and authority for so many years.

Tintagel lies on the N *coast of* Cornwall *to the* W *of the* A39 *at* Camelford. *The castle is on the headland (a steep climb!), and the footprint is on a rock above the castle. There is an admission charge. For details of opening hours, tel:* 01840–770328.

River Tamar

Most of the boundary between Cornwall and Devon is marked by the River Tamar, which rises at Woolley Barrows near Youlstone (SX 265 162) and meanders its way along the border until it reaches the sea at Plymouth (SX 460 550). Such a significant feature in the land, which renders Cornwall a peninsula (almost an island, except for some 8km /5 miles in the N), would always have been important to prehistoric peoples: the name Tamar is recorded as long ago as 120 CE by Ptolemy as one of the three principal rivers in the ancient kingdom of Dumnonia.

There is also a legend[12], first recorded in the seventeenth century, about the river nymph Tamara, who was the lovely daughter of an earth gnome. She wandered freely over the land exploring where she pleased, until one day two giants, Torridge and Tavy, fell in love with her. She would have none of either, but when her father found out he turned his daughter into the river that to this day carries her name. Torridge and Tavy were similarly turned into the rivers that flow from Dartmoor, but only Tavy joined the Tamar. Although it has been suggested[13] that this is a relatively late legend, possibly deriving from literary influence, it nevertheless contains the kernel of an identification of the river as Goddess, so may have been adapted from much earlier sources.

The River Tamar *is crossed at* Greystone Bridge *on the* A384 *between* Launceston *and*

Tavistock; at Horsebridge on a minor road from Stoke Climsland to Sydenham Dameral; and at Newbridge on the A390 between Callington and Tavistock.

DEVON

DARTMOOR

Dartmoor contains a wealth of prehistoric remains: stone circles, burial cists, stone rows and standing stones. Many of the sites are quite remote and require good walking and a decent map, but very much repay the effort. Like other prehistoric sites, they seem aligned to significant sun and moon risings and settings, and it has been suggested that stone rows in particular could have been 'avenues for the dead', for shamans and shamankas of the prehistoric tribes to travel over in spirit paths of altered consciousness. Recently it has been suggested[1] that some of the sites contain stones which have significant bosses – breast-like protuberances – on them, often in pairs. These are known from sites in Brittany, where the raised relief carvings are sometimes associated with fertility rites: women would rub themselves on the 'breasts' to avoid barrenness.

The breast-like carvings are most noticeable at Scorhill stone circle (SX 655 875), which interestingly lies just above the River Teign with its Tolmen holed stone – a large natural boulder with a perforated hole that is renowned for healing. According to Dartmoor archaeologist Deborah Griffiths and stone circle expert Aubrey Burl, these breast-marks are probably natural geological inclusions, or xenoliths. However, it remains a possibility that, because of the parallel with the Breton sites, such distinctive features were recognized by the prehistoric builders and incorporated into the stone circles as Goddess features: both Griffiths and Burl concede this possibility, although they say it must remain a speculation worthy of observation but impossible to prove.

According to tradition, a female skeleton lies under each of the seven fallen stones of the Scorhill circle, and this may relate to other legends of women dancing at the circles. At the Nine Stones stone circle at Belstone (SX 612 928), maidens were once again turned into stone for dancing on the Sabbath. Ruth St Ledger Gordon has suggested[2] that this notion is a corruption of the old word 'sabbat' – the witches' gathering-time at the old festivals taking place at the stone circles.

Scorhill stone circle is best approached from Teigncombe, near Chagford. There is limited car parking on the edge of the moor; from here, walk NW towards the river and cross it via stepping stones. The circle is on a rise of ground above. Belstone stone circle can be reached from a track leading S from a road in the village and is signposted.

SPINSTERS ROCK (SX 700 908)

This is a dolmen (the remains of a Neolithic burial chamber once covered by an earth mound), now consisting of three upright stones supporting a capstone measuring 14.5x3m (47x10ft) and weighing about 16 tonnes. It collapsed in 1862 and was subsequently re-erected. It may originally have been orientated to face NE, the direction of the midsummer solstice sunrise, the sun being viewed coming up over a hill when sighted along the under-edge of the capstone (or entrance to the mound)[3].

The name Spinsters Rock refers to the legend that it was put up by three spinsters or spinning women one morning before breakfast – Legends of spinning women as supernatural Fates are common to many ancient peoples, and one of these may subsequently have become attached to this site. The Greeks had spinning Goddesses, the Moerae or Fates; these were supernatural women who decided the fate of mortals: Clotho spun the thread of life, Lackesis measured the lifespan and Atropos cut the thread. The Scandinavian trinity of Norns or Three Fates sometimes wove the golden threads of fate, and the Valkyries spun a loom of human body parts while singing a song of death and battle. The Celts, too, may have had a similar concept of spinning Goddesses: an altar from the Rhineland depicts the Three Matres, the central one of which carries a distaff. These ancestral motifs may be relevant to this site, combining as they do an ancient place of burial and ritual with a legend of the spinners of the web of life and death.

Spinsters Rock is in a field beside a minor road that runs from the A382 *Okehampton–Moretonhampstead road to Drewsteignton.*

Frithelstock Priory (SS 464 195)

In the village of Frithelstock near Great Torrington lie the ruins of an old priory. As late as the fourteenth century the monks of the priory used to worship a statue 'like the unchaste Diana' at a temple altar in the woods – much to the shock of the Bishop of Exeter, who made them destroy it. This is a remarkable survival of Goddess-worship so late into the Christian era. There is a record[4] of the location of the sacred grove as being near a wood called Wadeclyve, close to the priory. An isolated cottage on Pencleave Farm nearby was still known as Waddacleave in the early twentieth century, and between there and the priory, only about 0.4km (¼ mile) away, is the wooded valley of a tributary to the River Torridge. The pagan temple is likely to have been here; once it was demolished, the stones were brought to the priory for use there. The statue and temple are gone, but the ruins of the priory and the wooded grove by the river remain.

The priory ruins are behind the church in Frithelstock village, which lies on a minor road between the A386 N *of Great Torrington and the* A388 S *of Monkleigh. There is a small admission charge to the ruins, but they are visible from the back of the church. The* B3227 *from Great Torrington runs* SW *for 3km (2 miles) or so to Watergate Bridge, from where there is a path (The Tarka Trail) running* N *through the woods beside the tributary stream.*

Bridestow (SX 513 895)

A village on the N fringes of Dartmoor, Bridestow lies at the junction of the rivers Lew and Cranbrook. Its significance lies in its name, which means the village of the Goddess/saint Bride. The present fifteenth-century parish church dedicated to St Bridget is the third one, replacing two much earlier foundations, and there was a former convent known as Sanctuary Moor, a place of refuge perhaps not dissimilar to St Bridget's sanctuary in Kildare, Ireland (see page 195)[5].

Bridestow lies just S *of the* A30 *Launceston–Okehampton road, about 8km* (5 *miles*) W *of Okehampton.*

River Erme (SX 615 470)

This river rises on Dartmoor and flows S through Ivybridge and Ermington to the coast near Kingston. In the mouth of the river, divers searching wrecked ships have come across the remains of a Bronze Age vessel, one of the oldest shipwreck sites in Britain[6]. This wreck contained tin ingots, possibly from Dartmoor, and a small bronze figurine of a goddess, who may have been the protectress of the tin streamers or the sailors, or may possibly have been traded from the Mediterranean for the precious tin. At any rate, here is a fascinating association of a goddess with both the earth from whence came the tin and the sea where she was found.

The Erme estuary marks the start of a beautiful stretch of coastline and is approached by minor roads off the A379 *Plymouth–Kingsbridge road. The course of the river on Dartmoor may be followed* S *from Green Hill.*

Sheela-na-gig
In the church at South Tawton, to the E of Okehampton, there is a headless sheela among the medieval roof bosses.

Somerset

Glastonbury (ST 510 390)

Long believed to be the 'mystical heart' of England, Glastonbury attracts a wide variety of pilgrims, from Arthurian questors to New Age Christians. The place resonates with myth of various kinds, including the abbey as the legendary resting place of Arthur and Guinevere, and the Tor as the mythic entrance to the Celtic underworld of Annwn and the home of Gwynn Ap Nudd, king of Faery. There is also an active Goddess-celebrating community, who see the shape of the hill of Glastonbury Tor as being a deliberate representation of the body of an ancient Earth Mother figure, and Annwn as the womb of the Great Mother and/or cauldron of

Cerridwen. This is all very imaginative, and doubtless inspirational to some seekers, but is there any foundation for a Goddess link with Glastonbury?

Interestingly, the answer lies not in Glastonbury itself, but about 2km (1¼ miles) to the SW at a place called Beckery (ST 492 383), which stands beside the River Brue. Here a daughter-house to Glastonbury Abbey was established in the Anglo-Saxon period (pre-1100 CE), which legend ascribes to Irish connections and in particular to St Bridget. A charter of 971 implies that there was a chapel here and the site is named as Little Ireland. A thirteenth-century document mentions repair to 'the chapel in honour of St Bridget', and says that the chapel had a hole or opening in the S side for penitents to pass through in order to obtain forgiveness for their sins, which is reminiscent of the legends attached to holes in some prehistoric megaliths. The site of the chapel was rediscovered in 1887 and excavated in 1967, when flints and Roman pottery were found. Nearby there was also a well associated with a spring called St Bride's Well, which up until the 1920s consisted of a shallow basin among brambles marked by an inscribed stone, and a thorn tree on which women would tie rags. The fields around the site are still called The Brides.

There is also a small mound near the foot of nearby Wearyall Hill called Bride's Mound (ST 484 383)which legend says was the gateway to Avalon, where pilgrims would spend the night in vigil before proceeding along a processional way to Glastonbury. John of Glastonbury, writing in around 1400 CE, speaks of a visit there by King Arthur, who had a vision of Mary – described as 'Mistress of the Earth and Queen of Heaven' – and he also recounts the existence of a 'monastery of holy virgins' on Wearyall Hill. This probably relates to a legend[1] of a community of women who lived on Bride's Mound after a visit by St Bridget, and kept a perpetual fire burning there: a tradition that parallels that of Bridget's shrine at Kildare in Ireland (see page 195).

The importance of the Goddess/saint Bridget was also remembered on the Tor itself, where St Michael's Tower has a carving on the entrance arch of the doorway showing St Bridget milking her cow. She can be found similarly depicted in the twelfth-century ornament over the entrance to St Mary's Chapel in the abbey. Nicholas Mann comments that 'She signifies the strong connection Glastonbury enjoyed with Ireland. The Irish identified Bridget with Mary and both saints were identified with the earlier tradition of the Great Goddess'[2]. Later legends (recounted by Geoffrey of Monmouth) suggest that Glastonbury, the 'fortunate isle', was ruled by nine sisters, led by the enchantress Morgan-le-Fay. The name Morgan can be traced back through Irish mythology to the Morrigan, the fearful and deadly aspect of the Goddess, who became secularized into the Arthurian figure of Morgan of the fairies.

Behind the early Christian foundation at Glastonbury lie probable pagan origins: archaeological evidence shows traces of an Iron Age settlement on the Tor. With its red-staining chalybeate (iron) waters, the beautiful and peaceful Chalice Well at the foot of the Tor (ST 507 385) would also have been a notable feature. It is sometimes known as the Blood Spring, and a second spring – the White Spring – rises nearby. An excavation in 1961 showed that the spring had been frequented in earlier times, and would probably have been the principal water supply for the Romano-British and Anglo-Saxon settlements on the Tor above. The stump of a yew tree was found and dated to around 300 CE: it may have been part of a sacred pathway to the well. All this points to a probable early spiritual site at Glastonbury, focused around the wells at Chalice Hill and Beckery, which later became Christianized into a Bridget site by Irish immigrants. The presence of the Goddess in Glastonbury is subtle, but she is there.

Glastonbury is on the A39/A361 *road. There is access to the Tor at all times; Chalice Well is open every day (tel:* 01458–831154). *There is an admission charge. Beckery lies to the* W *of the* A39 *Glastonbury–Street road, and the site of* St Bridget's Chapel *is on low-lying land between* Mill Lane *and the* River Brue. *Although none of the original remains are now visible, a local group is hoping to restore* Bride's Mound, *part of which is now on the site of a sewage works. The stone that marked* Bridget's Well *has been moved and is now* 100*m* (325*ft*) *away from the original site.*

The Bell Tracks – The Somerset Levels (ST 428 423)

To the W of Glastonbury lie the Somerset Levels, a wetland area first settled in the Neolithic period, when people occupied the higher ground and islands of dry land. The Neolithic coppicers cleared the forests and used the wood to make wooden trackways across the wetlands, in order to link the settlement areas together. These have become known by names such as the Sweet Track, the Meare Heath Track and the Bell Tracks. The Sweet Track has been dated precisely by dendochronology (tree-ring dating) to 3807–3806 BCE, and the Bell Tracks to around 2890 BCE.

It was close to the second Bell Track that a remarkable discovery was made: a roughly carved block of ashwood 16cm (6½ in) high, that appears to be the depiction of a goddess with two breasts, although an ambiguous 'stump' at the bottom has caused it to be interpreted[3] as an hermaphrodite god-dolly. However, the stump is on the left-hand side of the body, so it may have carried an entirely different symbolic meaning altogether. In any case, it is probable that the figurine was an offering made to the Goddess in token for the cutting down of the trees, or as a protective talisman against any malevolent forces in the swamp. Along with the Grimes Graves chalk Goddess from Norfolk (see page 122), it is one of the few ritual offerings from this early period still extant.

About 11*km* (7 *miles*) NW *of Glastonbury on the* B3151 *is the village of* Westhay. *A further* 1.5*km* (1 *mile*) SW *of* Westhay *on a minor road to Shapwick is the* Peat Moors Visitor Centre *(tel:* 01458–860697), *which contains a small but informative display* *on the Somerset Levels and reconstructions of the wooden trackways.* A *reproduction of the figurine can be found in the* Somerset County Museum *in* Taunton Castle (*tel:* 01823–255504), *while the original is in the* Cambridge University Museum of Archaeology and Anthropology, *Downing Street, Cambridge* (*tel:* 01223–333516). At *the time of writing it is not on display, but arrangements can be made to view it.*

Wimble Toot (ST 560 280)

One of the famous visionary discoveries of Glastonbury is that of the Glastonbury Zodiac, a pattern of zodiacal shapes outlined by topographical features on the land, discovered by Katherine Maltwood in the 1930s[4]. This is the ultimate ink-blob test – you either see it or you don't – but it does have one particularly curious aspect worthy of note. The figure of Virgo, the fertile Earth Mother, in the Zodiac is outlined by Wheathill at her feet, and her breast is formed by a tumulus called Wimble Toot, the name of which comes from the same root as 'teat'. The toot is a very pretty green mound, unmistakably breast shaped, with very old trees forming a protective canopy. It all seems rather more than just coincidence.

Wimble Toot lies in a field near the village of Babcary, *to the* E *of the* A37 *Yeovil–Shepton Mallet road. Take the lane running* S *by the village pub and after about* 0.75*km* (½ *mile*) *you will find the Toot in a field on the right.*

Wookey Hole (ST 557 460)

Wookey Hole cave was formed over millions of years by the erosion of limestone from the River Axe, and was inhabited during the Neolithic period. Stalactites and stalagmites formed here, one of the most famous being the Witch of Wookey Hole, so-called from the legend of a witch who lived in the cave and was turned into stone in a confrontation with a monk, who sprinkled holy water on her. This Christian legend alerts us to the possibility that originally some kind of pagan presence or deity was known to be associated with the place, and this was confirmed in 1912, when excavations uncovered the skeleton of a Romano-British woman, together with a dagger, a white alabaster ball (a witch ball) and the remains of a goat and kid. Also uncovered between 1946 and 1949, in an underground pool between the first and third chambers of the cave, were 14 human skulls, together with Romano-British pottery of the first or second century CE. The skulls were probably placed there for some ritual purpose, and the whole site, with its association of water, pools and underground cave, plus its witch legend, seems likely to have been an ancient underground Goddess place.

Wookey Hole caves are to the E *of the* A371 *Wells–Cheddar road. They are open daily, with guided tours.* (*tel:* 01749–672243).

St Bridget's Church, Brean (ST 297 562)

There has been a settlement on Brean Down from a very early date[5]. It was originally an island, and by 3000 BCE was being farmed by people who grazed stock and perhaps even cultivated land. In 300 BCE a large hill fort was built, and some barrows can still be seen there. Between 340 and 367 CE the Romans erected a temple at the E end of the Down near the sacred site where barrows had once been, but within 30 years it had fallen into disuse.

To the S of the Down was sea marsh, rich in fish and birds, but too wet and easily flooded for settlement. The earliest settlement therefore took place inland on the dune line, where the ground was highest. Here there was an early sacred site that later became the Church of St Bridget, probably founded by immigrants from Ireland or Wales who came across the Bristol Channel, and who may have gone on to found St Bridget's Chapel at Glastonbury, as well as St Bridget's Church at Chelvey (ST 474 689) some 24km (15 miles) to the NE.

Today, St Bridget's Church at Brean remains over the back of the sand dunes, with a beautiful contemporary stained-glass window depicting the saint with a sheaf of corn, suggesting an earlier role as a vegetation Goddess, and a map on the wall showing all the Bridget sites in Britain. To get a sense of how and where this Goddess/saint was brought into the country – one of the branches of the Bride Trail – St Bridget's Church is certainly worth a visit.

St Bridget's Church lies on the coast to the S *of* Weston-super-Mare. *It is best reached by a turning to the* W *of the* A38 (*Junction* 22 *of the* M5) *on to the* B3140 *Burnham-on-Sea road, and then by a minor road heading* N *to* Brean. *The church is normally open during the day. Continue on to* Brean Down *which juts out over the* Bristol *Channel. It is owned by the* National Trust, *and a steep flight of steps climbs 98m (320ft) up on to the headland.*

Sheela-na-gigs

At St Martin's Church in Fiddington village, near the coast at Bridgwater Bay, a weathered sheela is carved on an outside cornerstone. At St Mary's Church at Redcliffe in Bristol there is a sheela over a wall-plate.

Bath and North-east Somerset (formerly Avon)

Bath (ST 751 647)

The hot mineral waters of Bath rise from a deep natural spring at a rate of ¼ million gallons a day and at a temperature of 49°C (120°F). The site was probably venerated in Neolithic times, and may have been dedicated to a sun Goddess, the memory of whom is contained in the name Sul or Sulis[1]. By the Celtic period it was called Aquae Sulis – the waters of the Goddess Sul(is), whose name may have come from a root word meaning 'eye'. Certainly by the time the Romans came, it was such an important sacred place that they grafted their own Classical Goddess Minerva on to the native Goddess, and built a shrine to the now renamed Sulis Minerva.

From the first century CE the site became a huge temple complex, consisting of a Roman temple, sophisticated bath buildings, a great altar and a reservoir for the sacred spring water. This steaming water was viewed as the living body of the Goddess and became the focal point of the complex. The temple (now buried under Stall Street) was dedicated to Sulis Minerva and a gilded bronze head of the Goddess, found under the street in 1723, would have been part of a cult figure of the temple. Other finds from the site have included model bronze and ivory breasts, indicating either that Sulis was a nurturing goddess, or that the supplicant may have been a nursing mother. Also found were many inscribed stone, lead and pewter tablets that had been cast into the waters: these ask the Goddess for her help in finding lost items or in cursing those who had stolen personal possessions. Some 16,000 Celtic and Roman coins were also discovered, which provide interesting evidence that the habit of throwing coins into wells and fountains for good luck goes back to Goddess-invoking times.

As the site was such a large and complex one, its nature was probably multifarious. Minerva was a Roman warrior-Goddess, and the gilded bronze head described above would originally have been a Corinthian helmet. A gorgon's head with serpent-like hair found here, which now adorns the entrance to the Baths, may be connected to this. But she was also a Goddess of wisdom, music and crafts, and may have been invoked as the Goddess of medicine and healing. The temple shrine was probably a healing sanctuary, and supplicants would have come to bathe in the waters and perhaps undergo sleeping and dreaming therapy in the hope of a curative vision. There may be an explanation here of the name Sulis meaning 'eye' and, by extension, 'vision' – a Goddess of visionary trances.

There would have been appropriate rituals and festivals at this most important of shrines. The original spring, the source of the Goddess site, was later enclosed, making access available only through a dim passageway – perhaps an attempt to reflect initiation ceremonies into the Goddess caves and tombs of the prehistoric ancestors. There was also an ornamental pool (now situated beneath the main bath) which was surrounded by several smaller baths with water at different temperatures, the whole forming a great water and healing complex.

Minerva is clearly the principal Goddess celebrated at the site: another relief shows her in association with an owl and a gorgon's-head buckle. But other goddesses were also invoked there. One, Nemetona – whose name means 'Goddess of the sacred grove' – is depicted with her consort Leucetius in a relief probably imported from Gaul (see also Buxton, page 138). She was a Goddess of the Nemetes tribe in Germany, and seems to be especially associated with thermal waters and fertility cults, so her presence here is doubtless connected with the reputation of the site as an aquatic healing shrine. Another pediment found beneath the Pump Room in 1790 depicts a moon Goddess, Luna or Selene. Although rather worn, it shows her holding a thong or whip in her left hand, with her head surrounded by a double-crescent moon, appearing as a kind of horned crown. She too may be connected with moon rituals performed at the site, the moon governing the ebb and flow of the waters of the earth. The Earth Goddess and her waters are powerfully represented at this foremost shrine.

Bath (which has a railway station), lies 16km (10 miles) to the SE of Bristol. The site of the Roman Baths was subsequently abandoned and lost to the marsh, so the layout that can be seen today is a Victorian reconstruction. For details of opening hours, tel: 01225–477791. There is an admission charge. An on-site museum houses the Minerva head and the other Goddess reliefs mentioned above.

Stoney Littleton (ST 735 577)

This is a prehistoric Cotswold–Severn chambered mound, one of the best preserved of a number of similar Neolithic long barrows in the area, such as Hetty Pegler's Tump (SO 789 000), Nympsfield (SO 794 013), Notgrove (SP 096 212) and Belas Knap (SP 021 254). They each have slightly different structures, but share a number of features in common, including an entrance passage with side passages leading off. The whole structure is covered by a mound (still present at Stoney Littleton, Hetty Pegler and Belas Knap).

It has been suggested[2] that the tombs were constructed deliberately to imitate the body of the Earth Mother, the Neolithic Goddess who was the provider of all life. The chamber represented the womb, and the entrance passage and door the vagina and vulva. The stone-lined forecourt curved gently into the shape of a pair of horns, which were symbols of the Goddess. The entrance passages were often aligned to significant times of the year, in the case of Stoney Littleton to the midwinter solstice sunrise. Every year the sun rises over the hill on 21/22 December, and for just a few minutes shines to the end of the long passage, where it illuminates a stone on the right-hand side that bears a deep, broad, natural cup-mark. Although the midwinter solstice sun rises in the SE at an angle of 128 degrees, the steep incline of the hill delays its appearance here until it has reached 138 degrees – the precise angle at which the entrance is aligned.

There is also a possible moon alignment. The maximum midsummer full moon, which occurs only once every 18.6 years, rises in its most S position at an angle of 149 degrees and illuminates a prominent ammonite fossil contained in the stone of one of the side chambers. There are two other ammonite fossils (well known for their spiral-centred

shells) in rocks in the tomb, the presence of which must have been noticed by the Neolithic tomb builders. There is here a holistic joining of the world of the dead with the world of the living, the sun, moon and earth all interlinked in a complex web of Goddess energy.
Stoney Littleton tomb lies above the Wellowbrook river between the A367 Radstock–Bath road and the A366 Radstock–Trowbridge road. The nearest village is Wellow. Obtain the key at Stoney Littleton Farm, then walk the 0.75km (½ mile) uphill to the tomb. A torch is advisable.

Dorset

Eggardon camp hill fort (SY 541 948)

This is a large and impressive Iron Age hill fort with spectacular views across the surrounding hillside. It has three banks, two ditches and about 500 depressions in the ground, inside which were probably huts and storage pits. Legends associated with the site are of the Goddess Diana and her hounds hunting the souls of the dead. These also occur elsewhere, often connected to the devil or Odin with the wild hunt, and are probably a memory of the pagan significance of the site. Diana was a Roman Goddess known at Ephesus as the Mother of animals and Lady of the wild creatures – the many-breasted nurturing deity. She remained the Goddess of wild woodlands and hunting late into Christian times (see also Frithelstock Priory, page 89).
Eggardon hill fort is about 4km (2½ miles) SE of Powerstock, and is reached by lanes N of the A35 Bridport–Dorchester road, or S of the A356 Crewkerne–Dorchester road.

Maiden Castle hill fort (SY 669 884)

This is one of the largest and most impressive sites in the country, covering an area of about 24 hectares (40 acres), with massive ramparts and ditches. Building commenced in the Neolithic period (3000–2000 BCE) and the fort was extended and developed in the Iron Age, when it became an important centre of trade, commerce, dwelling and probably ritual. The Romans attacked it and the fort was abandoned, but was reoccupied in the fourth century CE, when a small Romano-British temple was built, the foundations of which can still be seen.

A fragment of a statue of the Goddess Diana found at the site probably dates from this period. Also found was a three-horned bronze bull with the remains of three goddesses on its back, which may be connected with Dianic worship or a native version. The presence of three horns and three goddesses is significant, being an example of the triplicity of the Goddess, which is found elsewhere in the Three Matres reliefs. Not far from Maiden Castle are some prehistoric megalithic sites, including Nine Stones at Winterborne Abbas (SY 610 904), which preserves in its name the magical number of triple three and the legend of children turned to stone for playing on the Sabbath.

Maiden Castle is about 1.5km (1 mile) to the SW *of* Dorchester *(which has a railway station) and is reached by a road leading off the* A354 Dorchester– Weymouth *road. The bull and goddesses may be seen in* Dorset County Museum, High Street, Dorchester *(tel:* 01305–262735).

Notes

Cornwall and the Isles of Scilly

[1] By Charles Thomas in *Explorations of a Drowned Landscape*, pages 154–9.
[2] See John Kraft, *The Goddess in the Labyrinth*.
[3] See Cheryl Straffon, *Pagan Cornwall: Land of the Goddess*, pages 22–33.
[4] See Rachel MacLean, 'The Fogou: An Investigation of Function, *Cornish Archaeology*, no 32, page 41ff.
[5] See Ian Cooke, *Mother and Sun: the Cornish Fogou*, pages 267–291.
[6] By Ronald Hutton in *The Pagan Religions of the Ancient British Isles*, pages 168–70.
[7] In Ian Cooke, op cit, pages 275–6.
[8] See Ian Cooke, 'Merry Maiden of the Sea' in *Journey to the Stones*, pages 37–8.
[9] See Cheryl Straffon, op cit, page 75.
[10] See Cheryl Straffon and Caeia March, 'St Bridget and her Chapels', *Meyn Mamvro*, no 29, pages 6–8.
[11] In Paul Broadhurst, *Tintagel and the Arthurian Mythos*, pages 132–7, and Charles Thomas, *Tintagel*, pages 96–8.
[12] See Robert Hunt, *Popular Romances of the West of England* – second series, pages 440–1, and John Coxhead *Devon Traditions and Fairy Tales*, pages 69–71.
[13] By Jeremy Harte, in a letter in *Wisht Maen*, no 3, pages 15–16.

Devon

[1] By Calum McIntosh, see *Wisht Maen*, no 1, pages 16–17; no 2, page 10; and no 4, pages 20–1.
[2] *In The Witchcraft and Folklore of Dartmoor*, page 54.
[3] See Hugh Franklin, 'Spinsters Rocks', *Wisht Maen*, no 3, pages 20–3.
[4] See R. Pearse Chope, 'Frithelstock Priory', *Transactions of the Devonshire Association*, 1929, vol 61, pages 167–191.
[5] See Christine Kitt, 'In Search of Bride in Devon', *Wisht Maen*, no 2, pages 12–15.
[6] See Kendall McDonald, 'Devon's Bronze Age Tin', *Diver*, October 1993, pages 26–8.

Somerset

[1] See Serena Roney-Dougal, 'Bride's Mound', *Avalon*, summer 1996, pages 10–11.

[2] From Nicholas Mann, *Glastonbury Tor*, page 21.
[3] By Bryony and John Coles, *Sweet Track to Glastonbury*, page 81, and John Coles, 'A Neolithic God-dolly from Somerset', *Antiquity*, XLII 1968, pages 275–7.
[4] Katherine Maltwood, *A Guide to Glastonbury's Temple of the Stars*.
[5] See Rev William St John Kemm, *The Story of Berrow and Brean*.

Bath and North-east Somerset
[1] See Miranda Green, *The Sun-Gods of Ancient Europe*, page 126.
[2] By Terence Meaden in *The Stonehenge Solution*, pages 46–9.

South East and Wessex

Wiltshire

Stonehenge (SN 123 422)

Stonehenge has been all things to all people: from John Aubrey in the seventeenth century to Aubrey Burl in the twentieth, antiquarians and archaeologists have probed, prodded and picked away at its secrets. There have been as many interpretations of its form and function as there are stars in the sky (to which some think it may have been dedicated). What we do know is that the remains we see today are the end-product of about 1,500 years of development from about 3000 BCE[1], a period of prehistory in which it is probable that the peoples were still celebrating and worshipping the Goddess and, possibly by this time, the sky God as well.

The original site of Phase 1 (c2950–2900 BCE) consisted of a circular ditch and an internal bank. Fifty-six pits were dug in the chalk (the Aubrey holes), and in Phase 2 (2900–2400 BCE) were refilled with cremated remains as possible foundation offerings, perhaps to the Goddess of the site or the underworld. One hole (hole 55) had antlers placed in it, which may have been an offering to a lunar Goddess[2]. At this time there may have been a timbered building inside the circle. In Phase 3 (2550–1600 BCE) the stones were put in place. Tall, thin blocks of volcanic rock – the Bluestones – were probably brought from the Preseli Hills in South Wales (see page 163), a sacred holy hilltop landscape, to be followed by 30 huge, upright sarsen megaliths of about 20 tonnes apiece, with lintels at the top, to form a circle of trilithons. Carvings have been found on some of the sarsen stones: on stone 53, daggers and axe-heads, and on stone 57, a possible carving of a Mother Goddess figure[3]. The Bluestones were then dismantled and re-erected as a circle and oval among the sarsens. Also at this time an avenue of parallel banks was constructed, running from the sarsen Heel Stone down a slope to the Avon river – a linking of the site with the tutelary Goddess of the river. Finally, some of the

Bluestones were again removed, leaving a womb-shaped horseshoe setting of stones, and a series of other holes were dug around the perimeter (Y and Z holes), which may originally have been intended to hold the other Bluestones or to have had a ceremonial function.

The purpose of Stonehenge is still a matter for interpretation. In its earlier period, it may have been constructed to view the most northerly rising point of the moon's 18.6 year cycle, and/or the maximum moonset at right angles to the midsummer solstice sunrise[4]. Later it became a sun-oriented site. The midsummer sun would have risen to the W of the Heel Stone, perhaps between that and another stone, now missing, and then would immediately have been eclipsed by the Heel Stone in a dramatic earth-and-sky symbology[5]. There was also a possible reverse alignment through the trilithons at the midwinter solstice sunset – a linking together of both halves of the wheel of the year. Recently it has been suggested that the whole of Salisbury Plain, with its wealth of barrows and cursuses, was a sacred landscape dedicated to the Goddess, and the discovery (in 1620) of many skulls of bulls and oxen in the central area of the site may be evidence of a bull cult that was part of this. The precise meaning of Stonehenge can only ever be a matter of speculation, but for a Goddess-celebrating people the functions of moon, sun and stones must have been part of the mystery of birth, death and renewal at this site.

Stonehenge is one of Britain's most visited sites, but at the time of writing its future management is a matter of some controversy, involving a possible re-routing of roads and the creation of a special approach to the site. At present it is reached from the A303–A344 junction, about 5km (3 miles) to the W of Amesbury. There is an admission charge. For opening hours, tel: 01980–623108. There is a fence around the stones, allowing them to be viewed but not touched.

AVEBURY (SU 103 699)

'The Avebury sanctuary doth surpass the much renowned Stonehenge as a Cathedral does a parish church'. So said John Aubrey in 1648, and today the complex is still an impressive site, despite part of the modern village being inside the stone circle. The site originally consisted of a Neolithic burial mound and a great circular earthwork of 11.5 hectares (28 acres), enclosed by a ditch and bank nearly 1.5km (1 mile) round. Today, this earthwork contains a total of 27 massive standing stones (each weighing about 40 tonnes) from an original 100 or more. Within this great circle are the remains of two smaller circles, each originally containing about 30 stones, but many are now missing – numerous stones were deliberately destroyed in the seventeenth century. There are four entrances in the outer bank, and from the S one an avenue of paired stones – the West Kennet Avenue – runs for about 2.5km (1½ miles) beside the road. This originally terminated at a small double stone circle on the top of Overton Hill known as the Sanctuary, which is now marked by concrete posts. In the eighteenth century, the antiquarian William Stukeley noted a second avenue leading from the w entrance to the longstones w of Beckhampton, of which two – the Adam and Eve stones – now survive.

Like Stonehenge, Avebury is closely connected with a nearby river, the Kennet, and this may be a clue to its significance. As long ago as 1977 Michael Dames suggested[6] that the whole landscape of Avebury and the surrounding sites was a physical representation on the land of the Goddess. In his interpretation, the Sanctuary (called by Stukeley the Temple of Ertha) was the womb-eye of the complex, where the Lughnasad full moon rose; the West Kennet and Beckhampton avenues were the snake Goddess; the West Kennet avenue, with its break in the paired stones at 29 ½ pairs, was a reflection of the lunar Goddess; and the Henge was the living image of the Goddess as bride with her male consort, in a Beltane festival wedding. This aspect of the theory has recently been echoed by Terence Meaden[7], who sees the whole Avebury complex functioning as an earthly embodiment of the divine marriage between sky God and Earth Goddess, with certain stones deliberately shaped to represent the vulva of the great cosmic Goddess.

On the other hand, Aubrey Burl[8] believes it to be a place of ritual and ceremony for the dead ancestors. He suggests that the N circle cove of stones facing the moon's most northerly rising, and the cove at the end of the Beckhampton Row facing the midwinter solstice sunrise, point to winter rituals for the dead, while the s circle, with its huge central obelisk (destroyed in the eighteenth century), became the focus of springtime rituals of fertility and renewal of the earth. Recently, Alastair Service[9] has elaborated on this by suggesting that the Avebury monuments form a great landscape calendar through the whole wheel of the year. It is all a matter of interpretation. What can definitely be said is that we have here all the elements of a sacred landscape: the huge stone circle, the two rows leading off to sacred enclosures, tombs for the dead, and the magnificent Earth Goddess shape of Silbury Hill – with all of it in relationship to the liminal River Kennet.

Avebury lies about 9.5*km* (6 *miles*) *to the* W *of* Marlborough, *to the* N *of the* A4. *The* A361 *Swindon–Devizes road cuts through the middle of the village. There is a carpark and refreshment facilities.*

Silbury Hill (SU 100 685)

About 1.5km (1 mile) to the s of Avebury lies Silbury Hill, the largest artificial mound of prehistoric Europe. It covers an area of 2.2 hectares (5 acres), and is 60m (320ft) in diameter and 40m (136ft) high. It comprises 354,000 cu m (455,000cu yd) of chalk and would have taken 18 million people-hours to construct, perhaps over a period of some ten years at around 2500 BCE, the same time as Avebury was begun. It is surrounded by a ditch of varying width. Despite digs in 1776 (by tin miners from

Cornwall), 1849 and 1968–70, no burials have ever been found.

It is now widely accepted that Silbury was a representation on the land of the Goddess, specifically to celebrate the festival of harvest time in August. It was Michael Dames who first pointed out that the shape of the hill, together with the surrounding ditch or moat, resembled a squatting pregnant female (see page 15). In his interpretation, she was the Goddess, her womb Silbury Hill itself, and her head, neck, breast and back the water in the surrounding ditch, which was the source of all life: 'Mother Earth gave rise to Silbury Hill, and in the process revealed her whole body'[10]. The water table has since lowered in this part of Wessex and part of the ditch has silted up, so that it is now wet only in winter, but at the time it was built the site would have been surrounded by water all year round. Reflected in the water (the blood of the Mother), the hill would have become the primordial mound of the Goddess – the sacred mountain, the holy hill.

From this hill, various solar and lunar alignments could have been seen. The midwinter solstice sunrise aligns with the moat (thigh/vulva) in the SE, while the midwinter sunset seen from the SW edge of the summit aligns with the tip of the breast (areola), turning it pink in the reflection of the water. The taking of the midwinter sun into the Goddess' body has parallels with other sites, such as Newgrange in Ireland (see page 189). The midsummer solstice sunrise, seen from the NE, would have created a fiery reflection in the water along the base of the Goddess' spine, and the midsummer solstice sunset would have illuminated the base of her neck and top of her spine. At the Lammas/Lughnasad full moon in August, the Goddess would have been observed giving birth, as the reflection of the passage of the moon across her body provided a lumière performance of harvest birth and lactation.

We know from the preservation of grass and insects at the centre of the mound that the construction of Silbury Hill was begun at precisely the end of July/beginning of August, and it has been suggested[11] that the mound has a summit terrace constructed specifically for viewing a double sunrise at this time. From the summit of the hill, the Lughnasad sun would have been seen to rise over the crest of Waden Hill, about 0.75km (½ mile) to the ENE. Descending to the lower terrace just below the crest of the mound, the sun disappears, but then rises again 71 seconds later in a viewing 'window' where the top of Waden Hill coincides with the skyline. If this was deliberate – and given the precise construction of the hill and its relationship to the surrounding landscape features, it seems likely – we have an extremely impressive artificial mound, built deliberately to reflect and celebrate the bounty of the Earth Mother and the ripening power of the sun Goddess at harvest time is a living landscape temple.

Silbury Hill lies beside the A4, 8km (5 miles) W of Marlborough. There is a carpark to the W of the site, from where it can be viewed. The hill is fenced off, with no official access, but that does not seem to prevent people climbing it!

River Kennet

The river that runs to the S of Avebury and Silbury Hill has its source at the Swallowhead Spring, about 1.5km (1 mile) S of Silbury (SU 101 681). Here there is a horseshoe-shaped enclosure, where waters rise from within the chalky earth and issue forth, to flow E towards West and East Kennet. The positions of Silbury and Avebury may be intimately related to this stream, the old name for which was Cunnit, deriving from the Middle English *cunte* and Latin *cunnus*, before finally becoming the modern Kennet. Here we have the strongest indication of the significance of the river as the source of all life – the very sexual orifice of the Goddess herself. It has been suggested[12] that the original word for the great Earth Mother Goddess may have been Cunti. Goddess names in other parts of the world have similar meanings: for example, the name of the Greek Earth Goddess Hera literally means 'womb'. The word 'cunning' comes from the same root, meaning originally 'knowing' or 'skilful', so she is not only the the source of life and fertility, but also of wisdom and knowledge, the place where understanding of the Goddess begins. In the past, villagers used to go to Swallowhead Spring and also climb Silbury Hill to have fig feasts on Palm Sunday; figs are universal symbols of fecundity, and a basket of figs traditionally represents woman as Goddess and Mother[13].

The river flows to the N of West Kennet Long Barrow (SU 104 677), an impressive chambered tomb over 100m (325ft) long, and East Kennet Long Barrow (SU 116 668), which so far remains unexcavated, before looping around the site of the Sanctuary (SU 119 679), which leads to the Avebury site. The whole prehistoric landscape is thus built in relationship to the river, which would have been seen as a living embodiment of the Great Earth Mother.

A lane leads S *from the* A4 (*where there is a layby*) *for about* 0.75*km* (½ *mile*) E *of Silbury Hill to West Kennet Long Barrow. About 90m (100yd) along the lane, a public footpath heads* W *towards the Swallowhead Spring. However, due to water extraction and dry summers, the source of the water is sometimes dry.*

Winterbourne Monkton (SU 097 720)

Lying below the huge Neolithic camp of Windmill Hill (SU 087 714), from where chalk figurines, balls and phalli have been excavated, is the village of Winterbourne Monkton. Its church has a most interesting twelfth-century font, showing a female figure with vegetation springing from her vulva: a blending of sheela-na-gig and Goddess of nature.

Winterbourne Monkton lies 2.5km (1½ miles) to the N *of Avebury, on the* A361 *to Swindon.*

St Mary's Church, Marlborough (SU 189 692)

A votive figure, probably the Goddess Fortuna, dating from Romano-British times is now built into the inside of the W wall of the church, on the N side of the arch linking the nave with the tower. The upper part of the figure has been mutilated, but it is still possible to see in her left hand what appears to be a cornucopia (horn of plenty), behind which is a spoked wheel, and in her right hand what appears to be the tiller of a rudder, whose broad blade is resting on what is probably a globe[14]. She is certainly much older than the church itself, but how she came to be here is not known.

Marlborough is on the A4, 9.5*km* (6 *miles*) E *of* Avebury. St Mary's Church *is at the* E *end of the* High Street, *immediately behind the* Town Hall.

Westbury White Horse (ST 900 516)

On the edge of the downs above Westbury lies Bratton Castle hill fort, an Iron Age site containing a Neolithic long barrow. This was also the site of an original White Horse carving, which may have been a landscape depiction of the Goddess Epona. (A bronze carving of Epona with her ponies which came from Wiltshire is unprovenanced, but could be evidence of an Epona cult in this area.) The original horse was a strange creature, with a crescent moon on the end of its long, thin tail. In 1778 it was completely remodelled with the horse that can be seen today, which faces in the opposite direction. Nevertheless, this is a spectacular location for a site with a long continuity.

The site lies to the S *of the* B3098 *between* Westbury *and* Bratton, *from where it is signposted, and about* 8*km* (5 *miles*) S *of* Trowbridge. *The carving of* Epona *is now in the* British *Museum*.

Sheela-na-gig

On the outside N wall of the church at Oaksey to the SW of Cirencester, is a sheela with pendulous breasts, enormous genitalia, and a well-defined clitoris.

Hampshire and the Isle Of Wight

Froyle (SU 757 422)

The name of this village is one of the rare ones in Britain derived from the Scandinavian Goddess Freya. It comes from 'Freohyll', meaning Freya's Hill. There are no other obvious Norse or pagan links with this area, although a Roman road runs a short distance to the W and crosses the River Wey at a place called Holybourne 'sacred river'.

Froyle is to the N *of the* A31 *Farnham–Winchester road.*

Sheela-na-gigs
The abbey at Romsey (on the A31) has a sheela on the outside W wall that has been interpreted as St Cecilia, or perhaps the original abbess herself. At Binstead on the Isle of Wight, there is a very weathered sheela at the Holy Cross Parish Church, positioned over a gate leading to the churchyard. She is known locally as The Idol.

Sussex

St Uncumber's Church, Burton (SU 968 176)

Burton Parish Church is an early Saxon foundation, dating originally from about 1075 and restored in the nineteenth and twentieth centuries. Although there is no 'official' dedication of the church, there is an amazing unofficial one: on the E splay of the N window of the nave is a remarkable early sixteenth-century wall painting of St Uncumber, crucified upside down[1]. Although the painting is deteriorating badly, she presents a startling appearance, with her mass of deep red hair cascading downwards.

St Uncumber, also known as St Liberata or St Livrade, was a 'renegade' saint, specially invoked by wives who had grown tired of their husbands. She was an Anglicized version of Wilgefortis, a daughter of a pagan king of southern France, who, when her father wanted to give her in marriage, prayed she might become unattractive to men, and subsequently grew a beard. For this she was put to death by her father, who was furious at her for refusing to get married.

This extraordinary apocryphal tale, together with the wall painting of a (clean-faced) St Uncumber in an upside-down crucifixion, is almost a parody of patriarchal Christianity. St Uncumber/Wilgefortis seems to be of the same order as Lilith, the first wife of Adam, who would not submit to his authority and was subsequently 'written out' of Christian theology. It has also been suggested that she may be a variation of the Goddess Amathus of Cyprus, who wore the dress of a woman with the beard of a man, although this has been dismissed as unlikely because of a 1,000 year gap between Mediterranean paganism and mediaeval Christianity[2]. But we know that other saints were probably modelled on earlier Goddess archetypes (see St Milburga's Well, page 132), and perhaps a more apt antecedent for St Uncumber is Artemis/Diana, who was certainly known in Roman Britain as the virgin moon Goddess roaming the forest with her band of nymphs, avoiding men and killing any male who looked upon her. Perhaps not altogether coincidentally, the old Roman road of Stane Street runs nearby, and there are Roman remains and mosaics at Bignor Villa. Wherever she comes from, St Uncumber's presence here raises many more questions than it gives answers, and she is by no means just a historical curiosity, having as she still does a strong following among

lesbians in the surrounding area.
Burton Parish Church lies to the E *of the* A285 *Petworth–Chichester road, near the village of* Duncton. *From here, a path leads* E *across some fields to the* Burton Park *estate, and the church is at the junction of three minor roads, close to a school.*

Kent

Lullingstone Villa (TQ 529 651)

This is one of the most important villa sites in the country, begun in the first century CE, rebuilt over subsequent centuries, and not abandoned until the fifth century. There are fine fourth-century floor mosaics, including one of Europa, Goddess of the moon, and the bull, and a former shrine dedicated to a local water nymph, perhaps the Goddess of the River Derwent.
Lullingstone Villa lies to the W *of the* A225 *and* E *of the* M25 (Junction 3/4), *about* 5*km* (3 *miles*) S *of* Swanley. *It is signposted from* Eynsford (*which has a railway station*). *For opening hours, tel:* 01322–863467. *There is an on-site museum.*

Minster Abbey (TQ 956 730)

Minster Abbey is a sixth to seventh-century early Christian site, founded by the legendary Saxon saint, St Sexburga, who subsequently became abbess at Ely in Cambridgeshire. St Sexburga and her holy sisters were traditionally said to have had a vast knowledge of healing waters, herbs and medicines, and they used the waters from certain magical springs and wells for drinking and for bathing the wounds of injured people and animals. It has been suggested[1] that Sexburga may have replaced an earlier Goddess figure such as Bridget/Bride, and pottery found on the site dating from earlier than the sixth-century foundation suggests that the abbey was built on an earlier pagan site. Sections of the original Sexburga Chapel survive today as part of the Parish Church of Minster, and a pagan image of the Green Man adorns the priest's door. There is also a tradition that a pre-Christian temple at Minster, dedicated to the Goddess Diana, stood on the site on which Minster Abbey was later built[2].

There are two wells on the site: the Abbess' Well, part of the garden at Abbot's Gate, and the Abbey Gatehouse Well, a 12m (40ft) deep shaft, which was excavated by a team led by local archaeologist Brian Slade in 1991[3]. Finds from both wells have included late Bronze Age pottery, ten varieties of Roman ware, and Anglo-Saxon bronze dress pins, some with decorated heads. However, the most startling find came from the Abbey Gatehouse Well, where the team found figurines of iron and wax in the shape of a triple-headed goddess marked with a cross, at the bottom of the well. Anne Ross has suggested[4] that this cross may have been a Bronze Age solar symbol rather than a Christianized icon. The three-headed goddess is in a squatting position, and Ralph Merrifield believes[5] that she may be a pregnant goddess figurine. Whoever she is and from whatever period she dates, she is certainly a fascinating find – the pre-Christian goddess of the well subsequently Christianized by Sexburga.

Minster Abbey is on the B2008 *at* Minster *on the* Isle *of* Sheppey, *5km (3 miles)* W *of* Sheerness *(which has a railway station). For further information about the wells, the excavations and the triple* Goddess, *contact* Brian Slade *on* 01759–875036. *The* Abbess' Well *is in a private garden at* 5 Falcon Gardens, *but it is open to the public by request (tel:* 01759–872882). *The* Abbey Gatehouse Well *is situated against the* N *wall of the gatehouse, and has recently been restored.*

Richborough (TR 325 602)

The Roman fortress of Rutupiae (Richborough) grew up at the bridgehead where Claudius first landed his troops in 43 CE, but because of silting it is now 5km (3 miles) inland. Here the Saxon shore defences were also built, and the walls still stand up to a height of 8m (25ft). From here, too, came a Venus figurine and a fragment of pottery of local ware, showing the bust of a horned Goddess – an unusual find that may be a portrayal of Diana the huntress.

Richborough stands on the W *side of a loop in the* River Stour, W *of the* A236 *and 2.5km (1½ miles)* NW *of* Sandwich *(which has a railway station). There is a small museum by the fortress entrance (tel:* 01304–612013).

Dover (TR 326 418)

Dover was the base of the Roman fleet and there was a Roman settlement (Dubris) here. Some years ago, a three-quarter life-size statue was found here[6] which may have depicted the tutelary Goddess of the Dour, the small stream that flows through Dover into the sea. Its present whereabouts are unknown.

In 1994, an excavation of a fifth- to seventh-century CE pagan burial-ground site on a hilltop at Buckland, overlooking Dover, yielded an extraordinary treasure trove of jewellery. Individual items included richly decorated gold pendants, garnet-inlaid silver brooches, an amethyst and silver necklace, and three mysterious crystal balls, probably used for magical purposes. Much of the finery comes from the grave of a woman aged about 30, who was buried with a miniature crystal ball. The indications are that this was the grave of a high-ranking pagan priestess, and some of the zoomorphic iconography on the jewellery may be Goddess imagery, including a bronze brooch in the form of a horse, perhaps depicting the Goddess Epona.

Dover is on the S *coast at the terminus of the* A2 (Watling Street). *The treasures are due to be displayed at the* British Museum.

Springhead (TQ 618 725)

Here, at the confluence of three springs, a temple complex called Vagniacae was established in the first century CE and later developed. Groups of shrines were surrounded by shops and other buildings to form small settlements, which attracted pilgrims who came to give votive offerings to the Goddess of the waters[7]. Finds included a clay horse, a pair of purple shoes (perhaps to assist the dead in walking to the other world) and two fragments of pipe-clay Venus figurines[8]. It is likely that the temple was dedicated to a local Goddess deity, who presided over the sacred waters that flowed into the creek, which fed the Thames Estuary.

Springhead was about 1.5km (1 mile) NW *of Southfleet and 3km (2 miles)* E *of Swanscombe, beside the* A2 (Watling Street). *The site was located in a field called* One Tree Field, *but it is now backfilled. A public footpath runs through the field.*

Canterbury (TR 145 575)

The pre-Roman Celtic tribe of the Cantiaci had a settlement at this crossing-place of the River Stour, which was subsequently built on by the Romans in the third century CE. A stretch of wall has been uncovered, and the remains of a town house with mosaic floors and a possible temple site have been revealed. From various locations in the city – St Dunstan's Roman Cemetery, St Margaret's Street, St John's Lane and more – have come fragments of Venus figurines[9] and five Dea Nutrix, at least two of which are complete and in a beautiful condition[10]. All the Dea Nutrix figurines – except one that is shown holding a small dog – are depicted holding infants in their arms: manifestations of the cult of the nurturing Goddess. It has been suggested[11] that this could be a representation of the Goddess Nehalennia, who in numerous monuments at her temple at Domburg in Holland is shown with a dog at her side. Nehalennia was a vegetation Goddess, concerned with fertility and the abundance of crops, and was depicted with the same attributes as the Dea Nutrix figurines. These votive offerings may have been carried by mariners as protective talismans on their journey to and from Gaul.

Canterbury lies on the A2 *road, and has a railway station. The figurines are in the* Royal Museum *in the* High Street *(tel:* 01227–452747).

Chart Sutton (TQ 804 495)

A Roman villa here yielded a very fine Venus figurine, probably from a sacred shrine in the villa (see page 30).

Chart Sutton lies to the W *of the* A274 *Maidstone–Headcorn road. The old Roman road runs to the* W *of the village. The site of the* Roman villa *was behind* Chart Sutton Church. *The figurine is in* Maidstone Museum *(tel:* 01622–756405), St Faith's Street, Maidstone *(which has a railway station).*

Surrey

Pilgrim's Way, Guildford

The ancient track known as The Pilgrim's Way runs S of Guildford on its way into Kent. At this point there are two holy hilltop sites that have been Christianized with a chapel and a church. On one hill, St Catherine's Chapel (SU 944 482) was built in the fourteenth century on what was probably already a pagan site: a shrine to the Goddess of the River Wey that flows nearby[1]. A traditional fair took place here every 2 October, which was known for its general lawlessness. On the other hill, St Martha's Church (TQ 028 483) was also built on a sacred site, with magnificent views across the Surrey countryside. There was formerly a stone circle here, and beacon fires were lit.

St Catherine was a fictional saint, possibly derived from the eastern Goddess Kali, whose symbol was the sacred wheel. She is often found as a dedication on high places, and was also known as a dragon slayer. St Martha is an unusual dedication, the only one in England. She was the biblical sister of Mary, and became the symbol of hospitality and the home. Interestingly, she too is often represented with a dragon whom she is supposed to have tamed, so the two 'dragon' saints may be a reference to the powerful 'earth energies' at these sites. These two saints, Catherine and Martha, were also thought in local folklore to be sisters, and seem to be two aspects of the same deity. We have here the probable remnants of a prehistoric Goddess in the landscape.

The ruins of St Catherine's *Chapel lie* 0.75*km* (½ *mile*) S *of Guildford (where there is a railway station), off the* A3100 *Godalming road. There is a carpark at the foot of the hill. The Pilgrim's Way can be walked from here across the River Wey to St Martha's Church, which lies* 0.75*km* (½*mile*) *to the* E *of Guildford off the* A246. *There is parking at the base of the hill.*

St Anne's Hill and Well (TQ 027 675)

At the junction of two of Britain's busiest motorways, the M3 and M25, lies a reminder from a much more ancient past. At a height of 73m (237ft), St Anne's Hill commands wide views over the Thames basin and was occupied from Mesolithic times (12000–3000 BCE) to the Bronze and Iron Ages. A hill fort was constructed here in the Bronze Age, and halfway down the hill is a holy well, St Anne's or Nun's Well. The River Bourne, a tributary of the Thames, flows nearby, and all the elements of a holy hilltop and sacred shrine are present: the hill, the river and the holy well, dedicated to a female saint. The well is a shallow spring, now covered with a brick canopy, but was doubtless a venerated spot sacred to the Goddess in prehistoric times. Into recent times, it was still renowned for the curing of eye disorders.

St Anne's Hill is to the NW *of Chertsey, at junction* 12 *of the* M25 *and junction* 2 *of the* M3. *The well is accessible from a small carpark off* Saint Anne's Hill *road and lies about a quarter of the way down the side of the hill, facing the motorway.*

LONDON

LONDON'S RITUAL LANDSCAPE (TQ 320 810)

In the E central area of London, now overlaid by the streets and buildings of the modern city, lies a hidden landscape. There are now only tantalizing glimpses of what might have been, but enough perhaps to put together a paradigm of an ancient ritual area. The area is centred on two hillocks around Blackfriars. Between these two hillocks once ran the sacred river now called the Walbrook stream. From here, we move eastwards on a trail that leads from St Paul's Cathedral to Cannon Street, a distance of about 1.5km (1 mile).

On the westerly hillock there was an original Bronze Age settlement and perhaps also a stone circle, which later, when the Romans founded Londinium, became Diana's Temple; the site is now occupied by St Paul's Cathedral. In 1830, a stone altar to Diana, 58cm (23in) high, was found 4.5m (15ft) below the surface, built into the foundations of Goldsmith's Hall in Fosters Lane, to the NE of St Paul's. The Goddess, accompanied by a hound, is shown as a slim young huntress wearing a short, belted tunic, with a bow in one hand and a quiver of arrows on her shoulder. In addition, a 64mm (2½in) tall bronze statuette of the horned huntress, holding a *patera* (ritual libation dish) in her right hand and cornucopia (horn of plenty) in her left, was found supposedly between the Deanery of St Paul's and Blackfriars, to the SW of the cathedral. And in Leadenhall Street nearby, a pipe-clay figurine was found, representing Diana as Luna with the crescent moon behind her head, a similar motif to that found in the child's grave in Arrington, Cambridgeshire (see page 121).

There was also a most interesting custom that lingered into the late medieval period[1], in which a deer, symbol of the Goddess, was ritually sacrificed, actually in the cathedral. Two animals were led to the high altar in procession, attended by keepers who wore garments with the animals embroidered on the breast. The beasts were received by the dean and chapter, and were blessed before being ritually slaughtered. The buck's head and antlers were retained and fixed on a pole, which (taking precedence over the cross!) was then led by a procession of clerics to the W door, where a horn was loudly blown, to be echoed by other blasts all over the city. The contemporary historian Camden commented: 'Certain it is that this ceremony savours more the worship of Diana than the Christian religion'. This ceremony was still being performed up until the sixteenth century, and if it was a memory of the original Dianic temple on the site, it represents a remarkably long continuity of tradition.

A short distance to the S of St Paul's Cathedral, a Mithraic temple was discovered in 1954. Among its reliefs and statuettes, it contained a rare marble roundel of Atargatis, the Syrian Mother Goddess, and a superb head of the Goddess Minerva. This has interesting parallels with the Mithraeum at Carrawburgh on Hadrian's Wall (see page 150), which also contained a statue of the Mother Goddess in the ante-room. A short distance to the W, at Blackfriars, a relief was found in excellent condition portraying (uniquely) four Matres, having been reused as foundation material in the late Roman riverside wall.

Also found here was a limestone altar that records the restoration of a Temple of Isis in London by a third-century governor of Upper Britain, Marcus Martiannius Pulcher. A third-century wine flagon found in Tooley Street, Southwark, was also inscribed to Isis, and may have come from the same Iseum, the location of which was probably in Southwark.

About 1.5km (1 mile) to the E of the Mithraic temple flowed the Walbrook stream, from whence have come some interesting finds. Numerous human skulls have been discovered, which may date from the time of Queen Boudica, who made her stand against the Romans here, or they may have been ritual offerings to the stream from the Bronze Age. Other finds include a leaf-shaped plaque made from tin showing the Three Matres, and many fragments of white pipe-clay figurines of 'Venus', probably representing a local Celtic divinity. The whole area may have been a special religious complex dedicated to the Goddess of the waters.

To the E of the Walbrook lay the second hillock, which may originally have housed a standing stone, perhaps an outlier to the stone circle on the W hillock[2]. This stone could then have become the sacred central stone of London – the omphalos – a fragment of which remains today and is called the London Stone. Tradition says that it was set up by Brutus, founder of the city, as an altar to Diana. It was mentioned as far back as the *Anglo-Saxon Chronicle*, and was still in good shape up until the end of the sixteenth century, when proclamations were made from it.

Finally, to return to St Paul's Cathedral: a short distance to the W lies St Bride's Church, which stands beside the old Roman road from Ludgate. It has been suggested[3] that the church, dedicated to the Goddess/saint Bride, has pagan foundations: a large pit (3.7m/11ft deep) found in the apse of the church could be evidence of its possible earlier ritual significance. Nearby is Bride's Well Place, indicating the former presence of a holy well.

So, within a relatively compact area there is a Bronze Age settlement, twin hills (perhaps seen as the breasts of the Mother Goddess), a sacred river with offerings, temples to Diana, Isis and possibly Bride, a holy well, a tradition of deer sacrifice, and Mother Goddesses, altars and statuettes. It seems that we are looking at the remnants of an ancient continuous ritual landscape.

St Paul's Cathedral area is at Ludgate, EC4 (*nearest railway station* Blackfriars; *near-*

est underground station St Paul's). *The* Mithraic *temple has been rebuilt about* 45m (146*ft*) *to the* W *of its original site in Temple Court,* 11 Queen Victoria Street, EC4 (*nearest underground station* Mansion House *or Bank*). *Walbrook lies between* Queen Victoria *Street and* Cannon *Street. The stream now runs underground, although a street still bears its name. The fragment of the* London *Stone can be seen behind railings in the wall of the* Bank *of* China*, opposite* Cannon *Street railway and underground stations.* St Bride's *Church is in* Fleet *Street, where it meets* Ludgate *Circus. The site of* St Bride's Well *is marked by a pump in a niche in the* E *wall of the churchyard adjoining* Bride's Lane (*nearest underground station* St Paul's).

Finds that include the altar to Diana, *the* Minerva's *head, the* Matres *reliefs and the* Isis *wine-flagon from the* Mithraeum/Iseum, *and the pipe-clay figurines from the* Walbrook *are in the* Museum *of* London, Aldersgate Street, EC1 (*tel:* 0171–600–3699; *nearest underground station* St Paul's *or* Barbican). *The horned Goddess is in the* British Museum, (*nearest underground station* Russell *Square*). *Tel:* 0171–636–1555.

Channel Islands

Guernsey

This island has two extraordinary Goddess statue-menhirs, quite unlike anything else to be found in Britain[1], although there are similar pieces in France and Spain. They are known locally as *grandmeres* (grandmothers) and are often referred to as 'Earth Mothers'. They both stand in churchyards, and were revered and honoured right up to the present day.

The older of the two is La Grandmere du Castel at Castel Church (WV 311 788), who stands at the top of a slight rise on the left-hand side of the W porch. She has been dated to 2500–1800 BCE, which makes her late Neolithic in origin. She is a standing stone 2m (6ft 6in) tall, carved in local granite in a female form with two breasts, although one has been defaced. There is slight carving, possibly representing a headband, a U-shaped necklace around the neck, and a girdle midway up the back. She was discovered in 1878 buried under the floor of the N chancel of the church, so the assumption is that the church was built on a site previously sacred to her. It is noticeable that offerings of fruit and flowers are still made to her today.

The other Goddess megalith is La Grandmere du Chimquiere at St Martin's Church (WV 324 765), who stands at the entrance to the circular churchyard. She is 1.5m (5ft 6in) tall and probably dated originally from the late Neolithic period, but was reworked in Gallo-Roman times (200 BCE–200 CE), when the face and cloak were added. She has a striking face, a neck ruff and two round breasts. There is a crack running across her lower half, which is where she was broken in two by a churchwarden in the nineteenth century in order to discourage the veneration of her that still persisted. However, this was quite counter-productive, as the locals put her back together again and placed her by the church gate, where she continued to be honoured. It was considered propitious to offer her fruit or flowers, and even today garlands of flowers can sometimes be seen around her neck. It is believed that if certain rites are performed correctly and at the proper time, she not only confers favours on those who seek her, but can be seen to move and 'come to life'[2]. Both stones represent an amazingly long continuity of active and respectful Goddess celebration here.

The Channel Islands lie 96km (60 miles) to the S *of mainland Britain, and can be reached by aeroplane and boat. A ferry service runs from* Weymouth (Dorset) *to* Guernsey. *Castel Church lies at the junction of* Rectory Hill *and* Rohais de Haut, *about 3km (2 miles)* W *of* St Peter Port. *St Martin's Church is situated in the* SE *of the island beside* La Grande Rue, *about 3km (2 miles)* SW *of* St Peter Port.

Notes

Wiltshire

[1] See Cleal, Walker and Montague, *Stonehenge in its Landscape*.
[2] See George Terence Meaden, *The Stonehenge Solution*, page 170.
[3] See R.J.C. Atkinson, *Stonehenge*, pages 45 and 179.
[4] See Aubrey Burl, *The Stonehenge People*.
[5] See George Terence Meaden, op cit, pages 146–164.
[6] In *The Avebury Cycle*.
[7] In *The Stonehenge Solution* and personal communication.
[8] See Aubrey Burl, *Prehistoric Avebury*, pages 216–18.
[9] With Jean Bradbery in *The Standing Stones of Europe*, pages 241–2, and *Guide to Secret Avebury and Silbury* (forthcoming).
[10] Michael Dames, *The Silbury Treasure*, page 55.
[11] By Paul Devereux in *Symbolic Landscapes*, pages 137–164.
[12] By Michael Dames, recounted by Terence Meaden, in personal communication.
[13] See Janet and Colin Bord, *Earth Rites*, page 200.
[14] See S.R. Tufi, *Corpus Signorum Imperii Romani*, vol 1, fasc 3, pl 102.

Sussex

[1] See Francis W. Steer, *Guide to Burton Church*, page 8.
[2] See Tristan Gray Hulse, 'Masks and the Androgyne', *Wood and Water*, vol 2, no 51, pages 12–13.

Kent

[1] By Marija Gimbutas, quoted in Brian Slade, *The Well of the Triple Goddess*, page 28.
[2] See Augustus Daly, *History of Sheppey* (1904).
[3] See Brian Slade, op cit and personal communication.
[4] In Brian Slade, *The Well of the Triple Goddess*: What the Experts Say, page 19.

[5] Ibid, page 26.
[6] See Frank Jenkins, 'The Cult of the Pseudo-Venus in Kent', *Archaeologia Cantiana*, 1958, page 66.
[7] See W.S. Pean, 'The Romano-British Settlement at Springhead', *Archaeologia Cantiana*, 1957, pages 53–106; and 1958, pages 77–110.
[8] See Frank Jenkins, 'Clay Figures of Venus', *Archaeologia Cantiana*, 1958, pages 107–8.
[9] See Frank Jenkins 'The Cult of the Pseudo-Venus in Kent', *Archaeologia Cantiana*, 1958, pages 60–76.
[10] See Frank Jenkins, 'The Cult of the Dea Nutrix in Kent', *Archaeologia Cantiana*, 1957, pages 38–46.
[11] By Frank Jenkins in 'Nameless or Nehalennia', *Archaeologia Cantiana*, 1956 pages 192–200.

Surrey
[1] See John Michell, *Sacred England*, pages 78–80.

London
[1] See Dave Hunt, 'Pagans in St Paul's', ASH, no 18, pages 22–3.
[2] See Rob Stephenson, 'London Stone', *London Earth Mysteries Newsletter*, no 1.
[3] By Ralph Merrifield in *The Archaeology of Ritual and Magic*, page 95.

Guernsey
[1] See Asphodel Long, 'The Goddess is Alive in Guernsey', *Matriachy Research and Reclaim Network Newsletter*, no 99, pages 6–8, and Ian Dawson, 'Sacred Sites of the Channel Islands 2', ASH, no 21, pages 12–13.
[2] See Anne Ross, 'Celtic and Northern Art', in *Primitive Erotic Art*, page 79.

Central and East

Essex

Dianic church sites

A couple of churches in the Brentwood area of Essex have interesting Dianic associations in the form of carvings, dedications and legends. Hornchurch (TQ 544 870) is named after the 'horned church' of St Andrew, where on the E end of the chancel there is a stone figure of a bull's head. The earliest reference to a 'horned church or monastery' here was in 1222, but there may have been a church on the site before the twelfth century. In 1604 the village was known as Herne Church, after the pagan figure of Herne the Hunter, but a legend[1] attributes it to a pagan priestess who dedicated a temple site here to the Roman Diana, Goddess of the hunt and the moon, and who subsequently converted to Christianity and built the church to atone for her former ways. The bull's head in the church may well be a memory of its former pagan origins.

Near the mouth of the River Thames at Mucking (TQ 685 812) there is another Dianic connection[2]. In the former church, which is now converted and privately owned, was a chancel dating from the thirteenth century. In its central pillar was a carving of a Green Man and a moon Goddess, with a horned lunar crescent resting in a horseshoe. This is a startling thing to find in a church, and is evidence that the area must have had some strong Dianic traditions, perhaps not unconnected with those in London nearby (see page 110).

Hornchurch *(which has a railway station) is on the* A124 *road near* Upminster, E *of* London. Mucking *is* 14.5*km (9 miles) further* E, *and lies just* S *of the* A13 *at* Stanford le Hope *(which also has a railway station). The former church is in the centre of the village.*

Sheela-na-gig

In Colchester Museum in the castle keep is a sheela which came originally from Easthorpe Church. She was known locally as The Clunch Stone and has a large vulva and clearly defined clitoris.

Hertfordshire

Royston cave (tl 355 415)

Royston stands at the crossing of two Roman roads – the Icknield Way and Ermine Street. Exactly under the crossroads is an artificial cave cut into the chalk – bell shaped, nearly 10m (33ft) high and 7m (23ft) in diameter. Its date is unknown, but it may originally have been a Neolithic flint mine that was taken over in the fourteenth century by the Knights Templar, an esoteric order who had a church 6.5km (4 miles) away at Wendy. Almost every part of the walls is covered with religious and quasi-pagan imagery, including a crowned woman holding aloft an eight-spoked wheel, which is possibly an image of either St Catherine or the Romano-British Goddess Fortuna[1]. There is also a sheela-na-gig, standing between images of a horse and a sword with nine circular rings. This is indeed an enigmatic and powerfully liminal place.

Royston *(which has a railway station) is at the junction of the* A10 Cambridge–Hertford *road, the* A14 Huntingdon *road and the* A505 Letchworth *road. The cave is open to the public on Saturday and Sunday afternoons from* Easter *to the end of* September.

St Albans (tl 136 073)

This town was a major Roman centre known as Verulamium, with well-furnished houses, beautiful mosaics, piped water and a theatre (which can still be visited). One house had an underground shrine, and excavations yielded a beautiful and unusual bronze Venus figurine, with a crown of fruits in her hair and an apple or pomegranate in her left hand. She seems to be an Earth Mother figure, perhaps guarding the fertility of the land and the well-being of the house.

St Albans (which has a railway station) is on the A5 (Watling Street) and A6, 13km (8 miles) S of Luton. The Roman city lies close to the River Ver, to the W of the modern city. The Verulamium Museum (tel: 01727–819339) at St Michael's in St Albans houses the bronze figurine, as well as two or three other Venus pipe-clay figurines and other Roman remains.

Buckinghamshire

Thornborough (SP 732 333)

At a loop of the Padbury Brook, a tributary of the River Ouse, there is a prehistoric river crossing, now the A421. Here stand two large Roman barrows about 4m (13ft) high, which were opened last century and yielded a rich collection of grave goods, including two bronze jugs, a lamp and a *patera* (ritual libation dish). There was also a gold ornament (now lost) with the figure of Cupid on it. Just across the river is the site of a Romano-British temple[1], standing on a slight natural rise with its entrance facing the river. It consisted of a central square or *cella* 5m (16ft) square, with a small inner sanctum which probably housed a statue of the Goddess of the river. The site is similar in many ways to Little Dean in Gloucestershire (see page 128), although it is closer to the river. To the NW of the temple, traces were found of a second sacred building, with a foundation sacrifice of a horse's skull ringed with oyster shells and crowned with a large, smooth pebble. This building may have been one of several overlooking a courtyard facing the temple.

In 1981 a small bronze Goddess figurine was found on the footpath near the temple (see page 24). She appears to be an unusual statuette of the Goddess Isis, crowned with a distinctive high ostrich-feather diadem. Isis was a Goddess of the waters of the Nile, so her transplantation to this riverside site by the Romans would make sense. She may also have been grafted on to an existing native goddess (there is some evidence for a possible pre-Roman temple site) in the same way as Sulis Minerva in Bath (see page 94). Other finds have included around 2,000 coins, again typical of other Goddess water shrines, and several small representations of deities in bronze, including a head of Minerva, as well as other miniature votive offerings. The temple was burned down in the fifth century, perhaps by Christians.

Thornborough lies about 5km (3 miles) to the E of Buckingham. The temple site is just S of the A421, W of the river; the barrows are N of the A421, E of the river. The Isis figurine is in Buckinghamshire County Museum, Church Street, Aylesbury (tel: 01296–331441).

Sheela-na-gig
At the Parish Church of All Saints in Buckland, to the W of Aylesbury, there is a sheela on the outside wall of the nave. It is quite worn, perhaps by frequent rubbing.

Oxfordshire

Rollright stones (SP 296 308)

This well-known stone circle has a number of legends associated with it. The 77 or so stones of the main circle (30m/100ft in diameter), called The King's Men, are supposed to be the petrified remains of a king's army, with the King Stone itself (a 2.5m/8ft outlier to the circle) on the opposite side of the road. About 0.4km (¼ mile) to the ESE of the circle are The Whispering Knights, a collapsed dolmen. The legend[1] tells that the king and his army, who were campaigning across England, came to this spot, where they met a witch who owned the land and who stopped them in their tracks by means of a strategem. She told the king: 'Seven long strides thou shalt take, and if Long Compton [a nearby village] thou can see, king of England thou shalt be'. The king took the steps, expecting to see the village, but a large hillock rose up to obscure his view. So, laughing, the witch said: 'As Long Compton thou canst not see, king of England thou shalt not be. Rise up stick and stand still stone, for king of England thou shalt be none. Thou and thy men hoar stones shalt be, and I myself an elder tree'. All were then transformed as she promised, and the witch herself – in the form of an elder tree – still stands near to the site.

It is worth recounting this legend in some detail, as it contains some very interesting hints of a much earlier meaning to the site. As can be seen from elsewhere, kings and heroes of old could only get their power and authority to rule from the Goddess of the land, or sovereignty. Here the witch, who owned the land, was not prepared to give that power away, and thus prevented the king from becoming ruler. The king or hero had to be worthy of the gift of power, and in this case he showed he was not clever enough for the witch. Her progeniture as Goddess of the land is indicated by her metamorphosis into an elder tree: she is the shape-shifting Goddess of nature, and the elder tree was sacred to the Celts. That it was still viewed as a 'living tree' is evidenced by the fact that it was supposed to bleed when cut into, and this was still performed ritually by gatherings of local people at Midsummer Eve up until the 1700s[2]. At the climax of this bleeding ritual, the King Stone was supposed to move its head. The link between the ancient stones and the power of fertility is also evidenced by the custom of infertile women rubbing the stones with their bare breasts at the full moon. The Rollrights are a site replete with much ancient magic and remnants of a far-distant Goddess aspect that has never quite died out.

The stones are all beside a minor road (formerly a prehistoric trackway) linking the A3400 *with the* A44 N *of Chipping* Norton. *There is access during daylight hours and a small admission charge.*

The White Horse of Uffington (SU 302 866)

This is one of Britain's most dramatic – and most enigmatic – hilltop sites. On the hilltop itself lies Uffington Castle, an Iron Age hill fort, just below which is the White Horse, 110m (358ft) long and 40m (130ft) high, outlined in gleaming white chalk on the green land. This is certainly Britain's oldest extant chalk figure, probably dating to at least 1000 BCE, when it may have been carved as a representation of a pre-Celtic horse Goddess who became known as Epona. The 'horse' is very stylized in a typically Celtic manner, perhaps resembling a dragon more than a horse. Interestingly, the small, flat hillock below the horse is known as Dragon Hill, from a legend that St George slew the dragon here, which may be a folk rendering of the Christianization of a pagan spot, symbolized by the building of a chapel here in the eighteenth century.

Recent research[3] has shown that the whole area was a ritual landscape, dating back over 5,000 years. A Bronze Age burial mound was excavated just above the horse's head dating to about 1900 BCE, and the head also looks towards a 24m (78ft) long, 5,500 year old burial mound, which was still used in the Romano-British period (third to fourth century CE). The reason for the carving of the White Horse here, which would have required regular scouring over thousands of years, becomes apparent: it was an integrated part of this funerary landscape, the horse symbolizing a native Epona, protector of the dead and guardian of souls.

The White Horse *can best be seen from the* B4507 *between* Ashbury *and* Wantage. *A one-way road leads from the* B4507 *up over the hill and down to a carpark, from where you can walk to the figure itself. From a point close to the carpark runs* The Ridgeway, *a prehistoric track across the downs that carries on to* Waylands Smithy *burial chamber.*

Bablock Hythe (SP 435 042)

On the upper reaches of the Thames at an ancient crossing of the river, a relief of what could be a Goddess was found in the river in 1932. Anne Ross suggests[4] that she is a native Goddess, fashioned from local forest marble. A recent catalogue[5] lists the figure as a male 'genius', although as 'he' is wearing a veiled head-dress and holding a cornucopia (horn of plenty) in the right hand and a *patera* (ritual libation dish) in the left, that seems to be a somewhat unjustified piece of gender re-assignment! In the light of the location and nature of the find, it seems more than likely that she was a votive offering to the Goddess of the river crossing.

Bablock Hythe *can be approached on its* W *bank from a minor road to the* E *of* Stanton

Harcourt on the B4449 (*there is a public house by the water's edge*), *or on its* E *bank by a minor road from the* A420, 5*km* (3 *miles*) S *of* Oxford *signposted to* Eaton. *There is a pretty area in which to sit by the river and have a picnic. The relief is on loan to the* Ashmolean Museum, Beaumont Street, Oxford (*tel:* 01865–278000).

St Margaret's well, Binsey (sp 486 081)

On the NW outskirts of the city of Oxford lies Binsey, a small, unspoilt 'typically' English village. To the N of the village beside the Seacourt Stream lies the twelth to thirteenth-century foundation of St Margaret's Church, where two holy wells may be found, one inside and the other just outside the church. Its peaceful remoteness (despite the busy A34 nearby) belies the fact that in medieval times this was a great pilgrimage centre, with its claim to fame deriving from St Frideswide, who also became the patron saint of Oxford itself. St Frideswide was a Saxon princess who spurned all her suitors, much to the chagrin of Alfgar of Mercia, who tried to hunt her down, but he was punished with a blindness that rendered him unfit for kingship. He tracked her down in her refuge at Binsey, where she cured his affliction, and he then left her in peace to found her oratory and well.

Frideswide sounds very much like a Christianized version of the Goddess of sovereignty, representing the power of the land and the giving of authority to kings to rule. It has also been suggested[6] that her name may derive from the Celtic *Sanct Ffraid Delwes yd* which translates as 'the holy one of bride the corn idol'. This would make her a Bridget archetype, and another example of the grain Goddess in the land.

The well outside the church is also known as the Treacle Well, the name deriving from *Tre-Kel-Wynle* – 'the water place of the hidden house' – an apt name for Frideswide/Bridget's secret place.

Binsey lies about 1.5*km* (1 *mile*) N *of the* A420 *on the* E *side of* Oxford, *and* St Margaret's Church *is about* 0.75*km* (½ *mile*) *further on. There is a well situated within the* W *end of the church, and another one outside but close to the church.*

Sheela-na-gig

St Michael's Church in the centre of Oxford formerly had a sheela set into the wall of the tower, where it was the custom for brides to visit her on the way to getting married. She is now on display in the church treasury. There is an admission charge to the tower.

Cambridgeshire

Wandlebury/Gog Magog Hills (tl 493 533)

This range of low hills, named after the legendary giants Gog and Magog, contains Wandlebury hill fort, a circular, tree-covered, Iron Age fort dating from the fifth century BCE to the first century CE. There was formerly a giant figure cut into the turf on the slope of the hill, which was recorded in the eighteenth century but subsequently became overgrown. In 1954 Tom Lethbridge[1], a local antiquarian, attempted to locate the position of the hill figure by means of placing rods through the turf to the chalk layer beneath, and to his amazement found the outline of what appeared to be a Goddess, some 37m (120ft) tall, sitting astride a horse. He felt this may have been a representation of Epona, a tutelary Goddess of the Iceni tribe, whose territory it was in the Iron Age/Romano-British period. Although his work met with stubborn resistance from the then Cambridge archaeological establishment, his findings excited the attention and support of leading academics of the day, including Dr Margaret Murray.

Part of the hill figure was excavated (see page 9), and the possible outline of a chariot and a second giant warrior figure was suggested. Hill figures are known about from other places, and this one has interesting links with the suggested Epona white horses at Uffington in Oxfordshire (see page 118) and Westbury in Wiltshire (see page 104). Interesting legends about a knight riding into the place on a moonlit night on horseback, and a giant horse buried under Little Trees Hill to the W of the site, may be a memory of the existence of this figure. It has also been suggested[2] that the whole site may have been a gigantic solar and lunar observatory in Neolithic times, and that it lies on a line linking together other ancient sites, ending at Hatfield Forest earthwork, and was used as a landscape astronomical calendar. If so, this would perhaps explain why the site was reused in the Iron Age as a sacred place.

The site has been allowed to grow back again, so nothing of the hill figure can now be seen. If Epona does still lie beneath the turf, and her precise location could be discovered by dowsing, then she is a Goddess still awaiting re-excavation.

Wandlebury hill fort is on the E *side of the* A1307/A604 *Cambridge–Haverhill road, and is approached from the* Gog Magog Country *Park,* N *of the* A1307. *There is parking at the entrance to the site.*

Nene Valley (TL 085 985)

There was a settlement called Durobriuae here in the lower Nene Valley in the Romano-British period. In 1844 a number of statue fragments were found, including a headless figure of Minerva, depicting her wearing a long tunic with a gorgon carving on the breast and a vase with a snake slithering up the back of the vessel. Her right hand holds an owl (now detached), symbol of the Goddess of wisdom. Excavations in 1959 indicated that these statues were made on the spot from a quarry of Jurassic limestone that was used to service the extensive potteries which existed in the area.

The site is to the E *of* Water Newton, *a village beside the* A1, *8km* (5 *miles*) W *of* Peterborough. *The route of the* Roman *road* (Ermine Street) *runs nearby, and the site of the Roman town and the old quarry lies between the* A1 *and the* River Nene. *The* Nene Valley *Railway runs to the* N *of the settlement (nearest station* Wansford *near* Sibson). *The statue is now located in* Woburn Abbey *in* Bedfordshire (*tel:* 01525–290666). *There is an admission charge.*

ARRINGTON (TL 325 504)

Arrington lies on the old Roman road of Ermine Street, and it is here that a remarkable burial was recently discovered. The digging of a water pipeline revealed the burial of a child, originally in a wooden coffin with lead lining. Buried with the ten-month-old baby were a number of 'toys', perhaps ritual objects chosen to accompany the child to the afterlife. These included two figurines of children, two rams, a bullock and a Mother Goddess figurine. She has an elaborate head-dress, a cloak fastened at the breast with a brooch (see page 32), and a girdle around her waist. She is seated, and carries a basket of apples or pomegranates, representing life and renewal. Around her neck she wears a necklace from which hangs a moon-crescent, which may represent Diana, Goddess of fertility and childbirth. Miranda Green has commented[3] that: 'The goddess possesses abundant symbolism of death and regeneration, and is a symbol of protection in death and rebirth in the other world'. Her presence in this tomb shows the persuasive power of the Goddess in all aspects of life, death and rebirth in the ancient world.

Arrington is on the A14 Huntingdon–Royston *road. The statuette and toys are in the care of* Cambridgeshire *Archaeology Department, and at the time of writing were not on public display. For up-to-date information, tel:* 01223–317312.

Sheela-na-gig

At Whittlesford Church, to the S of Cambridge, there is a sheela on the S side of the tower, on the arch of a Norman window. She is squatting and is accompanied by a large ithyphallic animal, which may make her a Lady of the beasts. Another sheela was discovered in 1956 on a stone slab from St Ives Priory, to the W of Huntingdon, and this is now in a private collection.

NORFOLK

GRIMES GRAVES (TL 818 898)

Hidden among the pine and fir forests of Beckland in SW Norfolk is an area of heathland known as Grimes Graves. Here there is an extensive area of prehistoric flint mines, dating from 4,000 years ago. It consists of 25 galleries all leading off the main pit shaft, covering about 38 hectares (93 acres) in all. Although only about 14 hectares (34 acres) have been investigated, some 700–800 shallow pits have so far been found. All of this was dug with antlers shed by red deer, and as some of the pits go very deep (15m/49ft) to get at the good-quality flint, this was an amazing achievement. The rewards were great – a single mine might have yielded 50 tonnes of flint material, and it is from the bottom of one of these shafts (Pit 15) that the chalk figure of a Mother Goddess was found (see page 16), along with other ritual deposits, including a heap of flint blocks with seven antlers on top, chalk balls, a carved chalk phallus and a chalk cup lamp. Although it has been claimed[1] that the figure may be a fake, recent research[2] suggests that Grimes Graves was a site of intense ritual activity, making its provenance more, rather than less, likely. Although unique to Britain, this Goddess has much in common with other Neolithic Goddess figurines found in Old Europe, such as the Goddess of Willendorf and Goddesses from Çatal Huyuk in Turkey. Placed ritually in this context, she is clearly a propitiatory offering to Mother Earth herself – the Goddess of the Earth in the earth.

Grimes Graves lies to the W *of the* A134 *Thetford–King's Lynn road, and to the* E *of the* A1065, 5*km* (3 *miles*) NE *of* Brandon (*which has a railway station*). *There is an admission charge. One pit* (Pit 1) *is open to view. For further information, tel*: 01842–810656. *The Goddess is on display in Gallery* 36 *of the* British Museum.

Snettisham (TF 675 349)

Hoards of Iron Age treasure have been found at a site at Ken Hill, Snettisham, discovered during ploughing that unearthed gold, silver and bronze torques. Hoards A–C were first discovered in 1948, to be followed by Hoards D and E in 1950, and a recent find, Hoards F–L, in 1990 with the aid of metal detectors[3]. It is in this most recent discovery (Hoard L) that two torques were found which were intricately decorated with stylized faces that have been interpreted[4] as Goddess representations, possibly a Goddess of the beasts, suggesting that they may well have been sacred objects.

Snettisham is on the A149 *King's Lynn–Hunstanton road. Ken Hill lies to the* W *of the road. The site is on private land and has now been backfilled. The torques and other treasures from the hoard are in the* British Museum.

Lincolnshire

Lincoln (SK 975 714)

The Roman town of Lindum, which was founded on the hilltop site and later spread down to the River Witham, still contains stretches of the Roman wall and gates. Also discovered from excavations in the city are two reliefs of three Mother Goddesses, one showing them in a naturalistic and relaxed setting, holding a basket of fruit, a small animal or child and a sheaf while the other fragment displays a more formal pose.

Lincoln (which has a railway station) is on the old Roman road of Ermine Street *(the* A15). *The first Mother Goddess relief is in the* British Museum, *the second in* Lincoln City and County Museum, Broadgate, Lincoln *(tel:* 01522–530401).

Witches' flight path

A local legend[1] tells of a possible 'witch way' stretching in a straight line across the Lincolnshire countryside. Stones were supposedly stolen by a witch from a 'temple which stood on high ground' not far from Ewerby Waithe Common. As she was flying towards the Fens, she was seen by some shepherds who fired arrows at her, causing her to drop the stones. This seems to be a folk memory of a kind of spirit line or shamanic flight path, and has parallels with other legends of witches and giantesses dropping stones from their aprons on to the land, all of which could relate to a primordial Goddess-shaper of the land.

It has been observed[2] that there is a straight line that runs across the land from Dorrington Church (TF 083 534) to the Drake Stone, a large boulder stone outside Anwick Church (TF 115 507), then running parallel with a path beside the River Slea, before entering Ewerby Waithe Common and continuing on to Ewerby Fen. Dorrington Church was reputed to be a witches' meeting place, and Mrs 'H', a well-known local witch, was frequently seen on Church Hill in the form of a hare, an epiphany of the Goddess Eostre. This obscure legend at the remote edge of the Fens may be a memory of some kind of Goddess lore in the area.

The area is to the S *of* Lincoln *and the* E *of the* A15. *Dorrington is on the* B1188 *Lincoln–Ruskington road. Anwick Church is 5km (3 miles) to the* SE *on the* A153, *and Ewerby Waithe Common is on a minor road 3km (2 miles) to the* S *of Anwick.*

Edenham (TF 063 218)

A most interesting Anglo-Saxon cross-shaft can be found inside the Norman church here, which was built on a Saxon site, and before that doubtless on a place of pre-Christian worship. On one side of the cross-shaft is carved the body and feet of a tall standing figure, and on the other is what appears to be a Mother Goddess figure – a seated naked female breastfeeding a child. It may be an early depiction of the Virgin Mary, and if so, was clearly influenced strongly by ideas of the nurturing Mother Goddess. The whole area is one of strong Anglo-Saxon pagan influence, as witnessed by the preponderance of Grimsthorpe placenames.

Edenham is on the A51 *between Bourne and Colsterworth, 19km (12 miles)* SE *of Grantham.*

Ancaster (SK 983 435)

A small, walled Romano-British town grew up here on an earlier Iron Age site, as part of a native settlement along Ermine Street. Sections of rampart and ditch from a rectangular earthwork can be seen, but most of the first-century CE fort is buried beneath the modern cemetery. The most interesting find from here was a relief of the Très Matres, holding a dish of fruit, a *patera* (ritual libation dish), and a large, round loaf. This was found in the SE corner of Ancaster churchyard, together with an altar forming a shrine.

Ancaster (which has a railway station) is on the B6403 (*Ermine Street*) *and* A153 *Sleaford road. The Très Matres and altar are on display in Grantham Museum (tel:* 01476–58783).

Sheela-na-gig

In the church at Torksey, to the S of Gainsborough, is a very worn sheela, set high up in the S wall.

Rutland

Braunston (SK 833 066)

The church in this prosperous Rutland village is very old, but probably even older is a unique Goddess figurine who stands around the side of the building. She has an ancient-looking, hag-like appearance, with pronounced breasts and a short body. No-one knows for certain from when she dates: Anglo-Saxon, Celtic and medieval experts all say she is unlike anything known elsewhere. It has been noted[1] that the church overlooks the River Gwash, the ancient boundary between Rutland and Leicestershire, so she may have been a later version of an earlier Iron Age tribal boundary landmark, or Goddess of the land. On the other hand, with her ambiguous mouth/vagina, she seems to have certain affinities with the sheela-na-gig carvings. Whenever she dates from, she remains a challenging and powerful totem figurine staring out from the Christian church.

Braunston lies 3km (2 miles) to the SW *of Oakham in Rutland. The church is in the centre of the village, opposite the inn.*

Leicestershire

Dane Hills (SK 565 055)

On the outskirts of Leicester are the Dane Hills, named after the Celtic Goddess Danu. Here there was a legend of Black Annis, a fearsome figure who in turn may derive from Anu, a variation of the Goddess Danu. There was formerly a cave here known as Black Annis Bower, where she was supposed to lie in wait for young children, to suck their blood and hang their skins up to dry! This sounds like some negative stereotyping under Christianity of a former Goddess, who was worshipped in a cave on

the hills. Formerly, a ritual hare hunt took place on the hills at Easter, and in the nearby village of Hallaton there is still a Hare-pie Scramble that takes place every Easter Monday. The linking of the hare with the time of year dedicated to the Goddess Eostre is another indication of the strong pagan links in the area.
The Dane Hills are located on the W *outskirts of Leicester, between the* A47 *and* A50, *but they are now urbanized. Hallaton lies to the* S *of the* A47 *Leicester–Peterborough road.*

Nottinghamshire

East Stoke/Thorpe (SK 755 500)

From this Roman settlement (Ad Pontem) came a relief, fashioned from local stone, of a god and goddess. They are not named, but by comparison with Gaulish depictions, it has been suggested[1] that they are Sucellus and Nantosuelta, the former being a hammer God whose name means 'good striker', and the latter a Goddess of the home whose name means 'meandering stream'. She is depicted with long hair and a large torque about her neck, and holds a bowl of apples in front of her. Perhaps she was dedicated here because of the meandering nature of the River Trent at this point, which would make her a Goddess of the river itself.
East Stoke is on the A46 *Leicester–Newark road, to the* E *of* Nottingham, *and the settlement was at a river crossing of the* Trent. *The relief is now in* Nottingham University Museum, *which lies to the* SW *of* Nottingham, *near* Beeston (*tel:* 0115–9514820). (*There are railway stations at* Nottingham *and* Beeston.)

Notes

Essex

[1] Recounted in David Clarke, A *Guide to Britain's Pagan Heritage*, page 112.
[2] See Ian Dawson, 'Paganism in Essex Churches Part 2, ASH, no 4, page 22.

Hertfordshire

[1] See Nigel Pennick, 'The Royston Cave', *Mercian Mysteries*, no 15, pages 5–10.

Buckinghamshire

[1] See Shelagh Lewis, *Buried Around Buckingham*, pages 10–25.

Oxfordshire

[1] Recounted in Katherine M. Briggs, *Folklore of the Cotswolds*, pages 13–14.
[2] See Mike Howard, 'From Thor to Rollright', *The Cauldron*, no 72, pages 12–15.

[3] See 'White Horse Hill', *Current Archaeology*, no 142, pages 372–8.
[4] *In Pagan Celtic Britain*, page 274.
[5] *Corpus Signorum Imperii Romani* 1/7, no 35.
[6] By Michael Bayley, in personal communication.

Cambridgeshire
[1] T.C. Lethbridge, *Gogmagog – the Buried Gods*.
[2] By Tim O'Brien in 'The Wandlebury Enigma Solved', *Sunday Telegraph Magazine*,
[3] In *Current Archaeology*, vol 130, pages 420–2.

Norfolk
[1] By Gillian Varndell, *Excavations at Grimes Graves* 1972-76
[2] In *British Archaeology*, no 18, October 1996, page 5
[3] See I.M. Stead, 'The Snettisham Treasure', *Antiquity*, 1991, pages 447–64.
[4] By Miranda Green, in personal communication.

Lincolnshire
[1] Recounted in Ethel Rudkin, *Lincolnshire Folklore*, pages 56–7, and 74.
[2] By Bob Dickinson in 'Lincolnshire Spirit Lines', *Markstone*, no 8, pages 8–9.

Rutland
[1] By Bob Trubshaw in 'Goddess or Queen?', *Mercian Mysteries*, no 21, pages 4–5.

Nottinghamshire
[1] By Miranda Green in *Celtic Goddesses*, pages 128–130.

West Midlands & Welsh Borders

Gloucestershire

The River Severn

The River Severn is one of Britain's longest rivers, rising in mid-Wales and flowing in a huge loop through Shropshire, Herefordshire, Worcestershire and Gloucestershire, to discharge into the Bristol Channel at Avonmouth. It was also originally a Goddess, both figuratively and literally, known to the Celts as Sabraan and Romanized to Sabrina. Gloucestershire is an area particularly rich in sites that relate to the Goddess of the river, a liminal deity whose waters would have been the source of all life and fertility in the area.

AUST-ON-SEVERN (ST 564 898)

One could be forgiven for thinking that Aust's main claim to fame is as the E end of the original Severn Bridge: a place to zoom through on the A48 on the way to and from Wales. However, it was here right under the bridge at the base of the cliffs that a little-known Goddess artefact was discovered in 1901[1]: a bronze statuette 14cm (5½in) high, depicting a goddess with eyes inset with glass beads. She wears a crescent-shaped head-dress, her hands are at her sides, her buttocks are well developed and her breasts are firm and pronounced. The style is Cycladic (Mediterranean) and, given the location, she may have been a prized imported or traded artefact. There is evidence of Romano-British occupation here, so could she have been seen as the Goddess Sabraan herself? The deity of the river found at its mouth was perhaps ritually placed there as a thanksgiving and/or a protective talisman.

Aust is at Junction 1 of the M48 *on the original* Severn Bridge. *The figurine is now in the* British Museum, *but is not on display. There is a copy in the* Bristol Museum, Queens Road, Bristol, *which also is not on display at present due to refurbishment, but is due to be reinstated. For up-to-date information, tel:* 0117–9223571 .

FRETHERNE (SO 734 092)

This village, on the E bank of the Severn, bears one of the few names in Britain to have come from the Scandinavian Goddess Frig/Freya. Its original name was Frithorne, meaning 'Frig's Thorn Tree'. There are many hawthorn trees growing hereabouts, and an interesting church with distant views of the river from the churchyard. It is dedicated to St Mary and was lavishly rebuilt in 1847 with windows, buttresses, pinnacles and gables, and a plethora of angel carvings, as well as a nineteenth-century Madonna marble statue and a Madonna picture from a Russian triptych! The church stands on the site of an earlier one, which in turn probably occupied the site of a much earlier sacred shrine.

But what is the Scandinavian Goddess Frig/Freya doing here, far removed from the Anglo-Saxon territory of eastern and southern England, where she would have been most widely known? Perhaps the site was originally dedicated to another Goddess, maybe that of the Severn nearby, and only later became 'Frig's place', as a general epithet used for something so strongly pagan in origin. Or perhaps there really was a pocket of Norse influence here, situated as it is between the sacred river and Barrow Hill above. At any rate, it is tempting to think of all those Victorian additions of angels and Madonnas as an unconscious manifestation of the original Goddess spirit of the place!

Fretherne is reached from the B4071 W *of the* A38 *at* Frampton on Severn, *on to a minor road towards* Arlingham. *The church is normally locked, but the churchwardens can be contacted on tel:* 01452–740959/740275.

Hempsted (SO 815 172)

The well at Hempsted is known as Lady's Well, but the 'lady' referred to is not the Virgin Mary but St Anne. Her restored well (1992) lies on a sloping field overlooking the River Severn to the SW, and water from it issues out into a trough and eventually runs over the fields and into the Severn itself. There is a carving of St Anne and two other figures at the rear of the well, and such a dedication to this female saint near to the Severn is probably a Christianized version of an older sacred spring used for dedicatory rites to the Goddess of the river.

Hempsted is about 2.5km (1½ miles) SE *of Gloucester city, to the* W *of the* A38. A *path at the rear of the churchyard leads across fields to the well.*

Little Dean (SO 672 131)

In January 1984 the remains of a Roman temple were discovered in the grounds of Little Dean Hall, which lies close to the W bank of the River Severn. Excavation was carried out through 1984 and 1985, and the site was shown to have been occupied as far back as the Mesolithic (middle Stone Age) and Neolithic periods. It was in use during the pagan Celtic period and then became Romanized, the remains dating from the first to fifth centuries CE. The on-site archaeologist, Barry Jones, confirmed that it was a water shrine, and co-excavator Anne Ross added that in her opinion it was a Romanized Celtic cult shrine of Sabraan/Sabrina, Goddess of the Severn.

The site consisted of a sacred pool, fed from a spring beyond the N side of the temple, which may have been the sacred springhead, as at Bath (see page 94). There was a cult shrine at the E end (which was robbed and destroyed in the fifth century), a sacred pool for cleansing and bathing, and buildings that may have contained niches in the walls for statues of the Goddess. Later, a church was built on the site and the earlier remains destroyed. Today, a hypothetical reconstruction of the walls at ground level can be viewed.

The location of the shrine is of great importance, overlooking as it did a horseshoe-shaped bend in the River Severn. The horseshoe was a sacred symbol to the Celts, who are credited with inventing it, and the shrine was placed around the spring that stood on the central axis of an imaginary line through the bend of the river at the lowest fordable point (Newnham). Furthermore, this alignment faced the rising equinoxical sun in spring and autumn, the times of the year when the tidal surge of the river, called the Severn Bore, was – and still is – at its most dramatic. Seen from the hill slope above Little Dean Hall, the Goddess would have seemed literally alive as the wave surge raced dramatically up the course of the river.

It has also been suggested[2] that the phenomenon would have been

The Goddess in white appears at Pendeen fogou in Cornwall on Christmas morning. (Cheryl Straffon)

An other-world sea Goddess, the Mermaid of Zennor, is carved in a remote Cornish church. (Cheryl Straffon)

The well at Landue in Cornwall dedicated to St Bridget, on her trail across the West Country. (Cheryl Straffon)

Monks from Frithelstock Priory in Devon worshipped the Goddess Diana in the fourteenth century. (Cheryl Straffon)

THE BLOOD-RED WATERS OF THE CHALICE WELL AT GLASTONBURY IN SOMERSET WERE A PROBABLE SACRED SITE TO THE GODDESS. (CHERYL STRAFFON)

THE TEMPLE SITE OF SULIS MINERVA AND HER SACRED SPRING AT BATH. (JO PACSOO)

This 'vulva' stone at Avebury in Wiltshire stands on a site that may have been dedicated to the Goddess. (Terence Meaden)

The Goddess of the land looks over the Rollright Stones in Oxfordshire in the form of a witch's elder tree. (Cheryl Straffon)

Silbury Hill in Wiltshire: the mound of the Goddess at the harvest festival birth. (Cheryl Straffon).

The Sheela-na-gig from Kilpeck in Herefordshire whose enigmatic smile may be remembering a pagan past (Cheryl Straffon)

Grandmere Du Castel: the standing stone with breasts that is still revered on Guernsey
(Pamela Soden)

A Celtic Goddess was venerated here at Diana's Well on witton fell in Yorkshire.
(Cheryl Straffon)

Grandmere Du Chimquiere: the Guernsey Goddess adorned with flowers and berries. (Pamela Soden)

The Mother Goddess carving in the church at Edenham in Lincolnshire, at harvest time. (Cheryl Straffon)

THE FIERCE GODDESS WHO SITS BEHIND THE CHURCH AT BRAUNSTON IN RUTLAND. (CHERYL STRAFFON)

THE BEAUTIFUL HILL BREASTS OF THE PAPS OF ANU, THE ANCIENT GODDESS OF IRELAND. (DAVID CLARKE)

The headless statue of Peg O' Neill that still stands beside the River Ribble in Lancashire. (Cheryl Straffon)

A Romano-Celtic shrine to the Goddess Sillina was found on Nor-Nour, one of the Isles of Scilly (Cheryl Straffon)

The fantastically shaped natural rocks of the High Bridestones in Yorkshire are named after the Goddess Bride. (Jon Barker)

High on the North York Moors, the Low Bridestones is the stone row named after the Goddess Bride. (Jon Barker)

Ainthorpe Rigg in Yorkshire: this site is aligned to the hill of Freya. (Cheryl Straffon)

The breast-shaped hill of the Goddess Freya – Freeborough Hill in Yorkshire.(Cheryl Straffon)

Branwen's Seat viewed from Moel-ty-Uchaf cairn circle in North Wales. (Cheryl Straffon)

Long Meg in Cumbria: the witch stone with the mystic spiral who bleeds with her daughters. (Cheryl Straffon)

Cerridwen's womb at Pentre Ifan in Pembrokeshire, South Wales, through which the mystical Preseli Hills can be seen. (Cheryl Straffon)

Pennant Melangell in North Wales: the patron saint of hares, the Goddess Oestre and her breast-shaped hill. (Cheryl Straffon)

THE STANDING STONES AT BALLOCHROY ON THE WEST COAST OF SCOTLAND POINT TO THE PAPS OF JURA AT MIDSUMMER SUNSET.
(CHERYL STRAFFON)

THE CAILLICHE'S HOUSE THAT LIES DEEP WITHIN THE HIDDEN GLEN LYON IN THE GRAMPIAN MOUNTAINS.
(DAVID CLARKE)

The magnificent stone circle at Callanish on the Isle of Lewis, which aligns to the sleeping woman mountain. (Cheryl Straffon)

Newgrange in County Meath, Leinster: the home of the Goddess Boann, with her spiral entrance stone. (Cheryl Straffon)

From Cairn L at Loughcrew in County Meath, the breast-shaped cairn of Slieve na Cailleagh is directly visible. (Cheryl Straffon)

Ancient symbols of the Goddess illuminated at Loughcrew by the rising sun at the equinox. (Cheryl Straffon)

best viewed from Little Dean Camp nearby (SO 676 135), a small earthwork about 184m (600ft) high which was excavated in the 1950s. The dating of the camp is not known for certain for, although the excavators suggested it was Norman in date, it is possible that the Normans adopted an existing henge-type earthwork dating from an earlier period. Certainly, the spectacular panoramic view of the Severn from here makes it a strong contender for a ritual viewing site, in conjunction with rites performed at the temple site to the Goddess Sabraan.
Little Dean Hall lies to the S *of the* A4151 *between* Cinderford *and the* A48 Gloucester *road (signposted at* Little Dean*). The house, gardens and grounds are open to the public – there is an admission charge (tel:* 01594–824213*). There is an informative display about the temple site in the entrance barn, and the site lies just inside the grounds. Walk up the slope behind the site to see the river through a gap in the hedge.* Little Dean *Camp is on private land and is not accessible.*

Lydney (SO 616 027)

In Lydney Park lies the remains of another Romano-British temple, a parallel site to Little Dean, which also stands near the W bank of the River Severn. Originally the river would have been even closer to the site, so in earlier times it may have been a similar cult site to the river Goddess, and there is evidence of pre-Roman occupation. However, by the time the site was Romanized it had become dedicated to a healing God, Nodens, who is known only at this site. It was also a dream incubation place, where pilgrims would come to bathe, be sent to sleep with drugs and herbs, and in the morning have their dreams interpreted by the site priest/priestess or therapute.

Finds from the site include over 7,000 coins, brooches, beads and bronze figurines, found in the temple as offerings. Many of these were of female objects, such as a bone pin with the head in the form of breasts, and women's bracelets, causing the excavators to suggest that 'this marked concentration of female offerings indicated that the presiding god or goddess dispensed relief in connection with childbirth and its attendant ills'[3]. Also found was a (headless) stone statue of a Goddess carrying a cornucopia (horn of plenty), strengthening the link between the site, the Goddess of the river and/or land, and the aspects of healing and fertility.
Lydney Hall lies on the A48 *just outside Lydney (which has a railway station), between Gloucester and Chepstow. It is open for a limited period in spring only, and there is an admission charge (tel:* 01594–842844*). There is an on-site museum containing the Goddess statuette.*

St Briavels (SO 559 046)

St Briavels (pronounced 'Brevels') is a small village lying near the Forest of Dean. It has been suggested[4] that it may be named after the Welsh saints St Briamel or St Brioc. St Brioc travelled on to Cornwall and Brittany, and his feast day is 1 May, the old Celtic Beltane festival. However, the holy well at St Briavels is named not after St Briamel or even St Brioc, but St Bride, the Irish Goddess/saint. Could the source for St Briavels be not St Brioc but St Breaca (pronounced Brecha), who was one of the 'nuns' at St Bridget's shrine in Kildare, Ireland (see page 195)? To compound matters even further, the well is known locally as St Anne's Well, and the present church is dedicated to St Mary! We thus have a proper cornucopia of female saints at a site lying between two Goddess rivers, the Severn to the E and the Wye to the W.

St Briavels lies just off the B4288 between Chepstow (which has a railway station) and Coleford. The well is not far from the church, on the Lower Road below the tump with the flagpole. There is a Youth Hostel in the castle in the village.

Crickley Hill (SO 928 161)

This hilltop site began as a Neolithic causewayed camp. A long mound was added in the Bronze Age, and it became a hill fort in the Iron Age. It was abandoned, but was then reoccupied in the Romano-British period, making it one of the most important sites in Britain due to its long continuity of use. It appears always to have had a sacred element to it. The Bronze Age long mound contained a stone cairn and a small stone circle, to which offerings of bronze brooches and bracelets were made, as well as some soil from further up the valley – perhaps gifts from the earth to the Earth Mother.

In the Romano-British period a large enclosure was built, which housed somewhere between 50 and 200 people. A smaller long mound was also constructed, perhaps in imitation of the larger Bronze Age feature. An excavation here in 1992 revealed a striking find of a small pregnant Goddess figurine, less than 25mm (1in) high, in a red fabric. The head and lower legs were missing, but it is not known whether or not these were ritually removed before burial[5]. Altogether, this is a most fascinating sacred site, at which excavation is still continuing.

Crickley Hill lies to the N of the A436 Gloucester–Andoversford road, W of a junction with the B4070 at Air Balloon Inn, about 5km (3 miles) S of Cheltenham. It is owned by the National Trust and there is an admission charge.

Roman villas

Private villas were a feature of Roman occupation, and some have yielded Goddess figurines and shrines. Woodchester villa (SO 838 032) had in its nymphaeum (a shrine to a water goddess) an amazing great mosaic, which is now unfortunately buried underground. There was also a (headless) statuette of the Goddess Diana, depicted with the head of a bull beside her right foot, recalling the statue found at Maiden Castle in Dorset (see page 97), as well as third-century coins showing the Goddess Luna standing in a biga (chariot) drawn by bulls. Here, evidently, is depicted a Goddess of the moon and Lady of the beasts.

Chedworth villa (SP 053 135) also contained a nymphaeum, together with private rooms and baths, and another floor mosaic. The on-site museum houses a Goddess relief, originally from Leamington, of Dea Regina – the queen-Goddess – plus two worn remains of statues, possibly of Diana.

The site of Woodchester villa *is* 1.5*km* (1 *mile*) *to the* S *of* Stroud, *but it now lies beneath a graveyard. The Goddess statuette is in the* British Museum. *Chedworth villa lies on a minor road to the* W *of the* A429 *and* S *of the* A40, *about midway between* Cheltenham *and* Cirencester. *It is owned by the* National Trust *and there is an admission charge* (*tel*: 01242–890256).

Cirencester (SP 025 018)

Cirencester was the local tribal capital of the Celtic Dobunni, which then became Romanized. By the second century CE it was the largest town in Britain and a crossing-place of major routes: the Fosse Way, Akeman Street and Ermine Street. Much of the ancient town has been built over, but an amphitheatre can be viewed. However, it is the Corinium Museum that is worth a visit for any Goddess-lover. Statues and carvings housed here include heads and friezes of Ceres, Fortuna, Diana, Minerva and the Three Matres (see page 27). One (from Daglingworth) shows three *cucullati* (hooded figures) offering what may be a loaf to a seated Goddess named as Cuda. There may be some reference here to a rite of sacred Mother Earth, now lost. Several of the Matres plaques show the Goddesses carrying loaves, apples, ears of corn, babies, cakes and fruit, all symbols of the fecundity and fertility of Mother Earth. It has been suggested[6] that one shown with three long loaves, each marked with a central groove, was intended to recall the female vulva, thus reinforcing the link between the Mothers and the Goddess of the Earth.

Cirencester lies about 20*km* (12½*miles*) *to the* S *of* Cheltenham, *at the junction of the* A417, A419 *and* A429 *roads. The* Corinium Museum *is in* Park Street (*tel*: 01285–655611).

Sheela-na-gig

In the church at the village of Ampney St Peter, to the E of Cirencester, there is a sheela inside the S wall of the knave, with high breasts, a large head and the vagina still visible.

Herefordshire and Worcestershire

The Giantess and the Witch

The neighbouring counties of Herefordshire and Worcestershire each have a tutelary hag who stalks the land. In the border country of Herefordshire it was the Giantess Mol Walbee, who was renowned for dropping and flinging stones, including the remains of Hay-on-Wye Castle (SO 248 463)! In Worcestershire it was Old Mother Darky, who used to hunt on Bredon Hill (an Iron Age hill fort at SO 958 402), with wolves who had been translycanthropized from small children and then changed back into human form. There are links here with the Goddess Diana riding out with her wild hunt, and with other wolf Goddesses, such as Lupis and Feronia, 'mother of wolves'. Here we have two Goddess archetypes from the wild and lonely places.

Hay-on-Wye is on the B4350 *near the* Welsh *borders*. *Bredon Hill lies to the* S *of the* A44, *about 7km* (4¼ *miles*) SW *of* Evesham.

Marden (SO 515 474)

Marden Church lies right beside the River Lugg and has a most interesting legend of a mermaid, who lived in the river and had in her possession a bell from the church, which the people tried to recover when she was asleep, but they were frightened off when she awoke. She may encapsulate in her legend the memory of a pre-Christian river spirit or deity, whose powers or following were not quenched by the building of the church on this spot. The twist to the tale is that in 1848 an ancient Celtic bronze bell was discovered in a pond at Marden! The church also contains a holy well, said to mark the place of the murdered king Ethelbert.

Marden Church lies to the E *of the* A49 *Hereford–Leominster road*.

Sheela-na-gig

Perhaps the most famous sheela in England can be seen at Kilpeck Church in Herefordshire (SO 448 305), where she sits on the right of the S door. She is one of many carvings on the corbels around the outside of the building (dating to about 1140), some of which were removed in the nineteenth century by a vicar who considered them too obscene. It is believed the sheela escaped because he thought her cavernous pudendum was her mouth!

Shropshire

St Milburga's Well (SO 568 824)

St Milburga's Well lies in an area redolent with ancient traditions and pagan associations. To the e lie the Clee Hills, an area abounding in stories of ghosts and angels, and beyond them the Wyre Forest, once a pagan sanctuary. To the w is Wenlock Edge, with its cluster of sheela-na-gig sites, and beyond that The Long Mynd and the Stipperstones – rocks dropped from the Giantess' Apron. In between lies St Milburga's Well, a place once occupied by a pre-Christian Goddess of the land.

There are a number of stories about Milburga from this place. One tradition, recorded in the early fourteenth century, has her fleeing from a neighbouring prince who 'wanted to ravish her violently': she crosses a stream, which swells and blocks his passage. In this example, the stream is a liminal place, representing the transition from the mundane world to the world of magical reality. Milburga has the power to alter that reality, and therefore she is a magical being. Later she became protectress of the nearby River Corve, which she made to flow miraculously – a memory perhaps of her original status as a river Goddess.

The second legend, which may be a variation of the first, remained in the oral tradition and was recorded in the nineteenth century. This tells how Milburga, while fleeing her enemies – this time men with bloodhounds – stumbled and fell from her white horse. Needing water for her wounds, she bade her horse strike the rock and a spring gushed forth, which is the well that lies today near the church, but not within its grounds. Milburga is thus a Goddess of the sacred waters, as she was both the means of facilitating healing, and also the beneficiary of that Goddess-healing water.

The next part of the legend is most interesting. On the opposite side of the road, some men were sowing barley in a field. Milburga caused the barley to grow green instantly, ready for harvesting by the evening, and then went on her way. When her pursuers reached this spot in the evening, they were told that Milburga was there at the time of sowing, and so they went away baffled. This legend has been interpreted[1] as Milburga originally being a grain or vegetation Goddess, moving through the landscape and changing it as she goes. The land nourishes, feeds, heals and protects her, while she causes the crops to grow and is thus a Goddess of the vegetation cycle of the wheel of the year.

It has also been suggested[2] that Milburga is linked to the fairy queen Godda, who dressed in green and rode a white horse. Stoke St Millborough, the site of the well, was originally called Godestoch in the Doomsday Book, which means Godda's Stoke, so *Godda may have been the original Goddess name for Milburga. Godda was incorporated into folklore and eventually became the semi-fictitious Lady Godiva, who rode a white horse through the streets of Coventry. There thus seem to be some very strong traditions remaining of this complex Goddess of the land, the seasons, the earth, the rivers and the healing waters.

Stoke St Millborough village lies to the w *of the* B4364 *Ludlow–Bridgnorth road. The well is situated up the hill just past the church, on the left-hand side. A gate leads down some steps to the well, which is close to some waterworks.*

Mitchell's Fold (SO 304 983)

This stone circle is beautifully sited on moorland with uninterrupted views W into Wales. It consists of 16 stones, 10 of which are still standing, and one particularly impressive one that is supposed to represent a witch (or alternatively a giant) who was turned to stone for milking a cow dry. The cow was pure white and appeared at the time of famine, allowing each person one pailful only, until the witch milked her into a sieve which never filled, whereupon the cow disappeared and never returned and the witch became petrified. We have here a legend that contains many of the elements seen elsewhere, to do with the giving of fertility and nourishment from the land, together with some negative stereotyping of witches under Christianity.

Some 5km (3 miles) to the E lies a line of quartzite outcrops called the Stipperstones, rising to 524m (1,700ft) at The Devil's Chair. Along this ridge are the Giantess' Apron cairns (SO 368 987), which a Giantess is supposed to have dropped as she strode across the land. From the Witch's Stone in the circle the hills are visible, and the stone also seems to point to nearby Stapeley Hill, a cone-shaped, rocky outcrop lying to the NE – the direction of the midsummer sunrise. Thus witch, Giantess and land are linked together in legends that may be faint memories of the tutelary Goddess of the land in these parts.

Mitchell's Fold stone circle lies between the A488 Shrewsbury–Bishop's Castle road and the A490 Welshpool–Church Stoke road. A minor road running between these two passes through Priestweston, and the circle is to the E of the village. Park by the road and walk N up a lane and across the moor.

Sheela-na-gigs

Around the area of Wenlock Edge there are a whole cluster of sheela sites. At Church Stretton, over the N (pagan) door of St Lawrence's Church is a very worn sheela. At Holdgate, to the E, there is a sheela protruding from the chancel S wall of Holy Trinity Church; young couples would visit the church to have their union made fruitful by her. And at Tugford, just S of Holdgate and N of St Milburga's Well, there are two small sheelas inside the S doorway of St Catherine's Church.

Staffordshire

Wall (SK 100 065)

Originally the Celtic settlement of Caer Lwytcoed/Cair Luitcoit, and then known as Letocetum to the Romans, Wall became a garrison fort and then a posting station (*mansio*), owing to its position on the main Watling

Street. A complex bath-house has been excavated and preserved, and at least one shrine – and possibly two – has been located. One may have been dedicated to the pagan God Cernumnos, and there is also some evidence for a second shrine dedicated to the Goddess Minerva.

In the nineteenth century, a life-size earthenware figure was discovered by workmen repairing the church, which stands about 180m (585ft) from the original *mansio*. This figure was described as 'a woman in strange dress with a man's cap like a soldier's helmet'. The statue was broken up and used for repairs to the bank of a drain (!) so we shall never know for certain, but the description does sound similar to the statue of Minerva found in Bath (see page 95). Excavations at the site have also revealed a pit containing horses' bones, that Anne Ross has suggested[1] were a foundation sacrifice to the horse Goddess Epona. Wall was sited on an ancient route, the sacred Celtic highway running from the Severn–Trent gap right through to Anglesey in Wales, so doubtless there was here a great pagan temple of the Cornovii tribe, dedicated to a native Earth Goddess who became Romanized into Minerva[2].

Wall is about 1.5*km* (1 *mile*) SW *of Lichfield* (*which has a railway station*) *and is reached by travelling either* S *from the* A461, N *from the* A5, *or* W *from the* A5127. *The site is owned by the* National Trust *and is open to the public* (*tel:* 01542–480768). *There is an admission charge. The on-site museum also contains pipe-clay* Venus *figurines.*

River Dane and Mermaid Pools

This river, which appears to be named after the Goddess Danu, flows through high moorland on the borders of Staffordshire, Derbyshire and Cheshire, a remote area that seems to have retained memories of old pagan goddesses and gods. At Ludchurch near Wincle there is a rocky chasm hidden within the woods on the slopes of the Dane Valley; this is a powerful, elemental place that takes its name from the Celtic God Lugh, foster-son of the Earth Goddess Tailtu (see Teltown, page 193).

To the E of here, on the high moorland between Buxton and Leek known as Morridge, there are two pools with interesting mermaid legends: Doxey's Pool (SK 004 629) and Black Mere (SK 040 613). The pools are quite close to each other, so there may have been some confusion over the location of the mermaid, who became attached to both. Mermaids are usually folk memories of the Goddess of the sea, but in this case the location is far inland. Other examples are known, however, at Mermaids Pool near Hayfield in Derbyshire, and Rostherne Mere in Cheshire, where the mermaid would ring a bell on the lake floor and then sit on it, singing. In the case of Doxey's mermaid, the location is not far from the river Dane, so she could be a variation of Danu herself. With the advent of Christianity she went underground, or in this case underwater. When Black Mere was drained in the nineteenth century, it was said that

she once again appeared to warn that if her pool dried up she would drown the town of Leek – still a powerful Goddess!
The River Dane can best be seen at Danebridge, S *of* Wincle *(*SJ 965 652*).* Doxey's Pool *lies to the* W *of the* A53 Buxton–Leek *road. A steep path leads up to the* Roaches*, a rocky escarpment where the pool lies.* Black Mere *is 3km (2 miles) to the* E*, on the* E *side of the* A53*, 0.75km (½ mile)* NE *of the* Mermaid Inn*, which commemorates the legend.*

Bridestones (SJ 908 622)

Near the River Dane on the borders of Staffordshire and Cheshire lie the remains of a Neolithic burial chamber, some 90m (293ft) long, with two small side chambers. It formerly had a porthole stone, also recorded at some of the Cotswold–Severn tombs, but most of it was destroyed for road building in the eighteenth century. Its interest lies in the Goddess/saint name Bride and the proximity of the site to the Timbers Brook, a tributary of the River Dane. Perhaps it was called the Bridestones at a later date in memory of the Goddess of the river in that area.
The Bridestones lie to the E *of the* A527 Congleton–Biddulph *road and* W *of the* A523 Macclesfield–Leek *road.*

Cheshire

Chester (SJ 405 663)

Known as Deva to the Romans, a legionary fortress was built here in 76–78 CE, firstly of timber and later of stone. The original town now lies beneath modern-day Chester, but parts of a large amphitheatre which could hold 8,000 people can still be seen. On the W side of the entrance is a small room that served as a shrine for Nemesis, the Goddess of fate. A replica of the original altar can be seen there. As at other Romano-British sites, the wells here were also worshipped, and a dedicatory tablet invoking the nymphs of the springs has been found.

To the S of the city near the river Dee lay the quarries from which the fortress was rebuilt. Here can be found a unique example of the Goddess in the land. A shrine to Minerva, Goddess of the crafts, was carved into the rock face itself by those working in the quarries (see page 25). She is depicted with a crown, a staff and a shield, and is accompanied by an owl. That she has remained here and not been destroyed or completely eroded through the centuries is something of a minor miracle, but apparently the shrine has always been a venerated place, with flowers and offerings left there.
Chester *(which has a railway station) lies at the meeting place of the old* Roman roads *from the* S *and* E*, and the modern-day* A41, A56, A51 *and* A55*. The amphitheatre lies just outside* Newgate *in the city. Finds from the excavations are kept in the* Grosvenor

Museum in Grosvenor Street (tel: 01244–321616). They include the altar to Nemesis; an altar to the Goddesses of healing, Hygea and Panakea; and a statuette of a Goddess with a cornucopia, who may be Juno, the Goddess of the inner face of femaleness. The quarry lies about 150m (165yd) to the S *of the Dee Bridge, on the* W *side of the road in an area called Edgars Field.*

Derbyshire

Bleaklow Moor (SK 110 965)

On the High Peak above Glossop are old traditions of a shapeless Cailleach figure, known as Th'Owd Woman or Biddy (a local version of Bridgit/Bride). She sometimes appeared in the guise of a dark horse and foal on the moor, and she may be a version of the great Celtic Earth Mother. A carving which may depict her in triple form was found on the moor, one of a number that were kept hidden there and unearthed for a special ceremony where a lamb was offered to the deity on a certain day every year. The faces are on a rectangular, concave block of millstone grit and appear to be surrounded by water weeds, symbolizing her role as a water Goddess of this place[1].

Bleaklow Moor lies about 11km (7 miles) to the NE *of Glossop (which has a railway station), and is crossed by the Pennine Way, from the B6105 at Torside Reservoir or the A57 over the Snake Pass.*

Nine Stones Close (SK 227 627)

Four great 2m (7ft) high monoliths remain here of the six that were recorded in 1847; they date from the Neolithic or early Bronze Age. A tradition has been passed down of the stones being called Grey Ladies and dancing together at midnight. There is a significant lunar alignment here to a natural rocky outcrop called Robin Hood's Stride, which consists of a horned saddle formed by two gritstone pillars[2]. The stones are in a field roughly 40 degrees NE of the Stride, and in alignment with it they present an azimuth of 220 degrees. During the major lunar standstill, the moon is neatly flanked by the two pillars when viewed from the stone circle. There is a significant association of motifs here that may have derived in whole or in part from Goddess celebrations at the site: the moon, the horned pillars, the Grey Ladies, and dancing at the site at midnight.

Nine Stones Close is on Harthill Moor, 5km (3 miles) S *of Bakewell, to the* W *of the B5056 near the village of Youlgreave. There is access from the minor Alport–Elton road.*

Nine Ladies stone circle (SK 249 633)

A ring of nine stones with an outlier lies on Stanton Moor, which also contains an early Bronze Age burial ground, and formerly other stone circles

as well. The circle has a similar legend to that of the Merry Maidens in Cornwall (see page 83): a group of maidens are turned to stone for dancing on the Sabbath, a legend that may contain echoes of ritual celebrations at the site.
The circle lies to the E *of the* B5056, N *of* Birchover. *It is reached by paths from a minor road between* Birchover *and* Stanton Lees. *Finds from the burial sites, which included incense cups, bronze knives and faience beads, may be seen in the nearby* Heathcote Museum *in* Birchover (*tel:* 01629–650313).

Arbor Low (SK 160 636)

Arbor Low consists of a henge monument with an oval bank, 76m (247ft) in diameter and raised about 2m (7ft) above the surrounding land. Around the edge lie 50 white limestone stones, resembling the hands of a gigantic terrestial clockface. Whether or not they ever stood upright is a matter of some debate. There are two entrances, at the NW and SE, and a U-shaped cove in the centre facing SSW, the direction of the maximum midsummer moonset.

The source of the stones used in the circle is likely to have been from Lathkill Dale, where the head of the river surges from a cave spring[3], a sacred place of Goddess energy. At a distance of 3km (2 miles) to the S of the circle is the village named Friden, which comes from Frigedene, meaning 'the valley of the Goddess Frig'. Frigg/Freya placenames are quite rare in Britain (see also Fretherne, page 127), so one so close to such an important megalithic site may be quite significant. Perhaps the Neolithic Goddess was still remembered here when the Norse people came and named their settlement after their own Goddess.
Arbor Low lies to the E *of the* A515 *Buxton–Ashbourne road, to the* S *of a minor road to Youlgreave. There is carparking at the farm, from where it is a short walk to the site.*

Buxton (SK 067 692)

Buxton was known to the Romans as Aquae Arnemetiae, the spa town of the Goddess Arnemetia, deriving from two springs at the bottom of the valley which gave out two different kinds of water (see also Glastonbury, page 90). The Roman remains have all disappeared and we know next to nothing about the Goddess except her name, which comes from *ar (e) nemeton*, meaning 'in front of a sacred grove'[4] (see also Bath, page 95). Later, under Christianity, the Goddess was as usual turned into a saint, in this case St Anne. The dedication to her is one of the earliest in England, and there is a medieval legend which tells of a statue – perhaps of the Celtic Goddess herself – being found in the well. This was later destroyed during Henry VIII's purges, and a chapel that had been erected on the side of the spring was also demolished in the fifteenth century. However, the Roman well survived until 1709 and was much visited for healing purposes, and many votive offerings were left there.

When the foundations of the present crescent were excavated in 1781, the remains of what appears to have been a bath for pilgrims were discovered, but it was the development of Buxton into a spa town from 1842 onwards that effectively destroyed all traces of the sacred well. Today the memory of it is marked by a drinking fountain of St Anne on The Crescent, which in its own way continues the tradition of sacred water in the town. It is well patronized by the citizens, who go to collect drinking water from there, but, as St Anne looks down on their activities, one wonders how many of them realize they are partaking of the waters of the original Goddess of the town.

Buxton (which has a railway station) is at the centre of five roads: the A5004, A6, A515 (old Roman road), A53 and A54. St Anne's Well is at the top of the town, beside the Micrarium on The Crescent. It is 'dressed' every year from the second Wednesday in July for five days.

Sheela-na-gigs

At the church in Melbourne near Derby there is a wealth of Norman carvings, including a sheela. At Haddon Hall near Bakewell (tel: 01629–812855) there is a figure above the doorway to the stables with her legs above her head, these then extending down to form arms and then hands that open her vulva.

Notes

Gloucestershire

1 See Frederick Ellis, 'An ancient Bronze Figurine from Aust Cliffs', *Transactions of the Bristol & Gloucester Archaeological Society*, vol 23, 1900, pages 323–5.

2 By Danny Sullivan in 'The Severn Bore and the River God at Little Dean', *Gloucestershire Earth Mysteries*, no 6, page 26.

3 Wheeler and Wheeler, Report on the *Excavations of the Site in Lydney Park*, 1932.

4 By Ray Spencer in *A Guide to the Saints of Wales and the West Country*, page 15.

5 See *Current Archaeology*, vol 132, pages 502–3.

6 By Martin Henig in *Roman Sculpture from the Cotswold Region*, page 39.

Shropshire

1 By Pamela Berger in *The Goddess Obscured*, pages 66–70.

2 By Chris Jenkins in 'Lady Godda: Goddess of Mercia', *White Dragon*, no 12, pages 17–18, and personal communication.

Staffordshire

1 In 'A Pagan Celtic Shrine at Wall, Staffs', *Transactions of the South Staffs*

Archaeological & Historical Society, vol XXI, page 7.
[2] See Anne Ross and Don Robins, *Life and Death of a Druid Prince*, pages 107–9.

Derbyshire
[1] See David Clarke with Andy Roberts, *Twilight of the Celtic Gods*, pages 75–6.
[2] See Craig Chapman, 'Moons, Saddles and Mountains', *Northern Earth*, no 60, pages 16.
[3] See Norman Fahy, 'Arbelows – a Geomantic Overview', *Northern Earth Mysteries*, no 46, page 4.
[4] See R.W. Morrell, 'Some Notes on St Anne's Well at Buxton', *Mercian Mysteries*, no 18, pages 21–2.

North

Merseyside

Bidston Hill (SJ 286 897)

The Wirrall peninsula lies in the industrial heartland of Merseyside, but near Birkenhead can be found some strange and enigmatic Goddess carvings (see page 80). Standing out from the urban sprawl and fertile plains are two parallel, linear sandstone ridges. On the E side stands Bidston Hill, with panoramic views from the observatory built on the top. Some figures have been carved into the soft rock, including a horse, a 'sun Goddess' and a so-called cat-headed 'moon Goddess'. The sun and moon Goddesses are about 1.5m (4ft 6in) long and lie 15m (49ft) apart: the sun Goddess is better preserved, and the outline of her body with a sun symbol at her feet can be seen clearly. The moon Goddess is more eroded, but formerly had what appears to be a moon (or sun) symbol at her feet. The horse is about 3m (9ft 6in) long and has what may also be a sun symbol on its neck. The exact date of these carvings is not known, but it has been suggested[1] that they originate with the Norse Irish, who settled here around 1000 CE, although they would have had to have been renewed (and in the case of the horse re-carved) over the years.

The carvings appear to be astronomically aligned[2], which suggests that they were constructed by a people for whom celestial Goddess-worship was an important part of their culture. The sun Goddess figure lies due E–W from feet to head, meaning that the sun rising over the horizon at both the spring and autumn equinoxes would have shone down the full length of her body, lighting up first the sun symbol at her feet, then her pubic triangle, and finally her head. The moon Goddess figure points to within one degree of where the sun rises on the horizon at the summer solstice, and the sun's rays would similarly have lit up the symbol at her feet and then travelled up the rest of her body. The horse symbol faces 180 degrees S, which is where the sun reaches its highest point each day at noon. Altogether, these carvings are an unexpected and intriguing find here on the Wirrall.

Bidston Hill lies above Birkenhead to the W of the city, between the A553 and A5027. Birkenhead is at the end of the M53 motorway, and there is a railway station here and at Bidston.

Lancashire

Peggy's Well (SD 736 426)

The River Ribble flows to the N of Clitheroe, and is associated at this site with powerful legends of the spirit of the water, who claims a sacrificial victim every seven years. The spirit of the river was called Peg O'Neill, perhaps from the Greek word *pegae* meaning a sacred pool or spring. She has also been identified as the Celtic Goddess Belisama, the Queen of Heaven, and a headless statue of her remains in an enclosure next to the river at Waddow Hall[1]. She was also the subject of a later legend, which attributed the name to a servant of the Hall who was the victim of the tyrannical mistress and subsequently drowned at this spot.

Even up until recent times the 'seven years' drowning victim' legend was widely believed. In 1908 a man drowned in the river at nearby Brungerley Bridge, and it was remarked that there had been a fatality there exactly seven years before, and another one seven years before that. This makes the next fatalities due in 1998 and 2005, so beware if you visit this site! Certainly the river runs very dangerously over the weir at this point, and at one time a bird or animal would be drowned deliberately at this spot on 'Peg's Night' every seventh year to appease the water spirit. If Peg is the memory of a water Goddess, then she is not one to be messed with! A similar legend appertains to Peg Powler of the River Tees, 80km (50 miles) to the N, who also lured people to their death.

Peggy's Well lies in the grounds of Waddow Hall, headquarters of the Girl Guide Training Centre, 0.4km (¼ mile) NW of Clitheroe on the B6478. Ask permission at the Hall.

Lund Church (SD 464 314)

A frieze of Mother Goddesses can be found in Lund Church near Kirkham. This interesting relief has three of these Goddesses on one side, and two groups of three dancing women on the right- and left-hand faces, making a nine of triple three. The frieze may have come from Ribchester 19km (12 miles) to the E (see page 142), but as 'Lund' means 'sacred grove', the church may well have been built on an original pagan Goddess site that was later Romanized.

Lund Church is situated to the N of Clifton village, which in turn is to the N of the A583

Preston–Blackpool road. (There is a railway station at Salwick, 1.5km (1mile) to the N.) *The church is generally open.*

Ribchester (SD 645 350)

This Roman fort, called Bremetennacum, stood beside the River Ribble at a major crossing-point. Here an altar stone dedicated to the God Maponus was found, which showed two Goddesses on the back wearing either a mural crown, horns or a lunar crescent on their heads. Maponus (Mabon) was the son of the Goddess Modron and a God of the hunt, so the Goddesses could perhaps represent Diana as an aspect of this.
Ribchester is on the B6245, *about 3km (2miles)* SE *of* Longridge. *The fort is owned by the* National Trust *and is open to the public (tel:* 01254–878261). *There is an admission charge. The stone is in the on-site museum.*

Yorkshire

York (SE 600 520)

Known as Eburacum to the Romans, York has proved to be a most important site. It consisted of a rectangular fort some 20 hectares (48 acres) in area, and the structure can still be seen in the streets and some parts of the city walls. Excavations are still going on, but some Goddess figurines and inscriptions have already been uncovered. Among these are a marble head – possibly part of a statuette of Venus – in a poor state of preservation, and various altars to the Matres Domesticae and the Mother Goddesses. Outside the area of the fortress and colony, there was also a temple to the Roman warrior-Goddess Bellona.
York (which has a railway station) is at the junction of the A64, A19 *and* A59 *roads. The exhibits are housed in the* Museum Gardens *(tel:* 01904–629745).

Ilkley Church (SE 116 478)

Ilkley was originally a Roman fort, called Olicana, at a crossing of the River Wharfe. A church was later built on the site, and inside it there is still an altar carving of a Goddess, probably Verbia, the river Goddess of the Wharfe (see page 24). We know her name because of an altar inscription also found in Ilkley. What makes this carving so interesting is that the Goddess is shown carrying two long, undulating serpents, one in each hand. Anne Ross has suggested[1] that there is a connection between the snakes and a water cult of the Goddess, and that 'Verbia' may mean something like 'she of the cattle': the association of river and cattle Goddesses is known from Ireland (for example, Boand – see Newgrange, page 189). On the other hand, Martin Henig says[2] that 'Verbia' means 'winding river', and if this is the case the undulating snakes in her hands

may be personifications of the river itself.
Ilkley is on the A65, 13*km* (8 *miles*) E *of Skipton (which has a railway station). The carving is in* Ilkley Parish Church, *which is in the centre of the town near a crossing of the* River Wharfe. *The altar inscription is beside a grotto dedicated to the* Virgin Mary *in the* Gardens *of the* Seminary at Middleton Lodge, *to the* N *of the town. Take the road from the church across the river and then turn left.*

Ilkley Moor/Rombalds Moor

To the S of Ilkley is Ilkley Moor and the larger Rombalds Moor. The area is covered with Bronze Age cairns, enclosures, hut circles, stone circles, cup-and-ring carved stones and inscribed stones. Two of the cairns are called the Skirtful of Stones (SE 138 451) and the Little Skirtful of Stones (SE 140 445), and were thought to have been dropped by the Giant Rombald's wife when her apron strings broke. At the time she was about to hurl them at her husband after a quarrel – an interesting variation on the Goddess of the land theme!
Ilkley and Rombalds Moors *are reached by roads and lanes from* Ilkley *(which has a railway station), and the sites by trackways across the moors.*

The Strid Gorge (SE 075 542)

The River Wharfe cuts through the Strid Gorge in the Yorkshire Dales and passes close to Bolton Abbey. According to local tradition, the Goddess of the Wharfe can appear here on May Day morning in the form of a white horse. She often presages imminent death in the river, so it might be wise to avoid visiting here on 1 May! (See also Pendeen fogou, page 85).
Bolton *Abbey is on the* B6160, *leading* N *from the* A59, 16*km* (10 *miles*) *to the* E *of Skipton. A nature trail runs alongside the* River *Wharfe and the Dales Way track can be walked* N *from* Bolton Bridge *on the* A59.

Diana's Well (SE 135 852)

At Witton Fell in Wensleydale there is an amazing well that has slipped through the net from pre-Christian times. It is far removed from any church, and its name indicates a possible Romanization of an earlier Celtic deity venerated here.

Witton Fell overlooks Wensleydale and the river Ure, with its dramatic waterfalls at Aysgarth. The hill is now thickly wooded, and beside one of the paths that run through the woods lies a shrine built to house the well, which issues forth from the hillside behind. This stone shrine was built in 1821 by the Earl of Aylesbury, who lived at nearby Jervaulx Hall and loved the place. It even contains a large stone slab inside – a perfect ritual place. The well issues from the back left-hand corner of the shrine, and then runs to the outside by means of a stone head (now overgrown)

to the left of the entrance. The well has a tradition of pin-throwing, and an old rhyme about 'Diana's water' that certainly pre-dates the nineteenth-century shrine. The local name for the well is Slaverin' Sal, which may be a folk echo of Sul or Sulis, the Celtic water Goddess[3].
Witton Fell can be reached by a lane running S *from* East Witton *village on the* A6108, *5km (3 miles)* SE *of* Leyburn. *In the wood, take the second path on the right (past some old caravans and a water company gate on the left), and after about 1.5km (1 mile) you will find the well on the left.*

Friday Well (SE 525 047)

This well was so named not because it was especially efficacious on Fridays, but after the Scandinavian Goddess Frig, who of course gave her name to Friday. There is a reference to the well in 1847 as Frigedaeg Wella, which makes the connection with Frig even clearer[4]. Within a 3km (2 mile) radius there is also the site of St Helen's Well and Chapel (SE 496 034), the name deriving from the pre-Christian Goddess *Ellen, and a former well on Harlington Common dedicated to St Ann. Altogether, this is a fascinating area of pre-Christian Goddess well dedications.
Friday Well is close to the A1(M)/A635 *roundabout junction near* Marr, *5km (3 miles)* NW *of* Doncaster. *The well (which has no surround) lies about 0.75km (½ mile) along a track running* S *from* Marr *to* Marr Grange.

St Helen's Well, Eshton (SD 931 570)

St Helen was probably a Christianization of the pagan Goddess *Ellen, and this well is one of many in Yorkshire dedicated to her. It consists of a round pool with a kerb surround, lying within a peaceful grove of trees. What makes this one unique is the presence of three stone heads submerged in the well, with just their tops showing. There is a tradition of stone head carving in Yorkshire and the north of England, and there is evidence from elsewhere[5] of an association of wells and sacred springs with a cult of the head, which the Celts believed was the seat of the soul. For example, among the finds at Coventina's Well in Northumberland (see page 151) were several small heads in bronze and a human skull, and in Wookey Hole in Somerset (see page 93) 14 human skulls were found in an underground ritual pool. The stone heads of St Helen's Well may be a special local version of this head cult.
Eshton lies to the N *of the* A65 *Skipton–Settle road, about 11km (7 miles)* W *of* Skipton. *The well is in an enclosure behind a stone wall, beside a minor road from* Eshton Hall *to* Rippa Bridge.

Bridestones, North York Moors

There are a number of sites on the North York Moors (known originally

as Blackamoor[6]) bearing the name of the old Celtic Goddess/saint Bride. The sites are either prehistoric or natural, and the name was doubtless given to them in later times by people who recognized the sanctity or power of these ancient places. These sites include the following:
1 The Bridestones consist of two groups of weathered sandstone rocks on the evocative Grime Moor (perhaps named after the Norse God Grim/Odin): the High Bridestones (SE 773 915) and the Low Bridestones (SE 874 911). They are renowned in local legend as the scene of pagan fertility rites[7], and have been described as 'sculptural, tactile, living geology'[8]. A path leading to them from Staindale passes near Hagg Wood, an interesting juxtaposition of the Cailleach with Bride, and another path approaching from the N is called the Old Wives Way, again an interesting folk memory of the Cailleach. This path runs from the tumuli at Gallows Dike (site of a medieval gallows), past the stone circle at Blakey Topping (SE 873 934) to the Bridestones. Within a few square kilometres there is thus a dramatic association of mystical rocks in the land, places of the dead, Goddess association, wheel of the year, and Bronze Age, Celtic, Norse and medieval continuity of use.
2 The Bridestones cairn circle on Nab Ridge near Bilsdale (SE 575 979) consists of about 40 small stones and is probably the retaining wall of a destroyed barrow, with a diameter of 12m (40ft). Again, note the linking of Bride with a place of the dead.
3 Bridestones stone row on Guisborough Moor (NZ 645 120–6) is a long row of 20 stones set upon a linear earthwork, the Cross Dyke, and aligned approximately N–S.
4 The High and Low Bridestones are located at Grosmont. The High Bridestones (NZ 849 046) consist of 11 megalithic stones (of which six are standing) variously interpreted as a stone row, the remains of two stone circles, or the wreckage of two four-poster settings. The Low Bridestones, about 0.75km (½ mile) to the W, consist of two possible stone rows (S – NZ 8452 0471 and N – NZ 8457 0485). Both High and Low Bridestones could have been used by the Bronze Age peoples for astronomical purposes, and were then recognized as sacred sites and named accordingly by later inhabitants of the area.
The Bridestones on Grime Moor are approached from the Dalby Forest Drive, which leads E from a minor road N of Thornton Dale on the A170, about 5km (3 miles) E of Pickering (which has a railway station), or by foot heading SE from the carpark on the A169 overlooking the Hole of Horcum, about 11km (7 miles) N of Pickering.
The Bridestones cairn circle is reached by a path (between the Carn House and Thornhill Farm turnings) leading E up the hill slope from the B1257, 3km (2 miles) S of Chop Gate.
The Bridestones stone row is situated 3km (2 miles) to the N of Commondale on a minor road S of the A171. Access is difficult.
The High and Low Bridestones lie to the S of a minor road crossing Sleights Moor from the A169 to Grosmont (which has a railway station). They are visible from the road.

Ainthorpe Rigg (NZ 708 066)

An ancient trackway called the Old Wives Road rises up the N side of Ainthorpe Rigg, crossing the moorland ridge SSE–NNW. Nearby there are prehistoric cairns and tumuli, and an alternative name for the track is the Corpseway, which is perhaps a folk memory of this. As the track rises towards the crest of the hill, it reaches a standing stone surrounded by a low, continuous circle of small unworked boulders: the Ainthorpe Rigg enclosure. There are various astronomical alignments from here[9], including the winter setting of the major lunar standstill over Brown Hill to the NW, and the winter setting of the minor lunar standstill along the N slope of Roseberry Topping to Newton Moor.

However, the most spectacular sightline from the site occurs in a NNW direction. As you approach Ainthorpe Rigg on the Old Wives Road, and then turn around to look in the opposite direction along the path, a most remarkable sight comes into view. A perfectly round, breast-shaped hill appears to rise over the horizon as you get closer to the circle enclosure, and from the site this unmistakable Earth Goddess feature is perfectly visible on the distant horizon (see Freeborough Hill, below). The site was clearly built here to get the best possible view of the hill – a place for celebrating the Earth Mother herself in the land.

The Ainthorpe Rigg enclosure can be reached from the Old Wives Road about 0.75km (½ mile) up the side of Ainthorpe Rigg, which lies beside a minor road from Ainthorpe to Danby Castle on the crest of a hill before Low Coombs Farm. This minor road runs S of the A171 Guisborough–Whitby road at Danby (which has a railway station).

Freeborough Hill (NZ 690 126)

The breast-shaped hill mentioned under Ainthorpe Rigg (see above) is a natural sandstone formation about 150m (500ft) high, which rises up from the plain below. Very Silbury-like in appearance (see page 101), its name is most revealing, deriving from the Scandinavian Goddess Freya/Frigg. From its summit, the standing stone on Ainthorpe Rigg is visible, and the whole area was clearly a ritual landscape used for celebration of the Goddess in prehistoric times. Recognizing its sacredness, later peoples gave it the name of one of their Goddesses, Freya, which gives us the clue to deciphering its past.

Freeborough Hill can be viewed from the A171 Guisborough–Whitby road, and is approached from a minor road leading to the S of this one, to the E of the turning to Moorsholm village. The hill is fenced, but is normally accessible with care.

Old Wife's Well (SE 794 940)

This ancient well also bears the 'Old Wives' name, and the reason for this becomes apparent when one looks at its location. It lies a few yards to

the E of the course of an old Roman road, parts of which are still visible, especially as a trackway across the moors to the N. This road was known as Wade's Causeway, or Wade's Wife's Causey. In Norse mythology, Wade was the son of a sea Goddess who mated with a king and then returned to the sea from whence she came. In local mythology, Wade became a mythical Giant who built the road for his wife Bel so that she could travel more easily across the boggy Moors to milk her herd of cows. As Ian Taylor says: 'For Bel/The Old Wife read Bride/the Cailleach'[10]. The Roman trackway may have been built on an earlier Celtic pathway that ran across this part of the Moor, passing near to a natural waterfall where a sacred spring to the Goddess was identified and venerated. The stone on top of the well has Nattie Fonten inscribed on it, which may be a corruption of Fons Natalis, the name of a Celtic water nymph[11].
The Old Wife's Well can be reached by a road from Stape, N *of* Pickering, *to* Egton. *It lies in a clearing beside the road. About 3km (2 miles) further on at* Wheeldale Bridge, *a section of* Wade's *Causeway heads across the moors towards Goathland.*

Other Old Wives Sites

A standing stone on John Cross Rigg near Sneaton Corner on the A171 Scarborough–Whitby road is called The Old Wives Neck (NZ 901 021). It has been suggested[12] that this distinctively shaped stone is named after Bel, the wife of the Giant Wade, as the location is only about 9.5km (6 miles) E of Wade's Causeway. At Cundall near Thirsk, about 16km (10 miles) from the SW edge of the moors, there is a low, wooded hill crowned with an earthwork, called The Old Wives Hill (SE 420 731); there is a church dedicated to St Mary immediately to the E of the hill.

At Guisecliffe on Nidderdale lies a long escarpment called The Old Wives Ridge, with rocks of fantastic shapes. A few miles to the E are two rock outcrops called Jenny Twigg and Her Daughter Tib. It has been suggested[13] that Jenny is a name attached all over Yorkshire to objects and concepts that have to do with the magical, supernatural and pagan divine. If Jenny was derived from a Celtic Goddess, then her name has been lost, although a river spirit in Lincolnshire was known as Jenny Hurn. We are dealing here with very faint echoes of goddesses, metamorphosed into giantesses and old wives, their names now lost in the mists of antiquity.

Mab Well (NZ 795 065)

This is another well that has slipped through from pre-Christian times. Mab was a Celtic queen of the fairies, whose name may be related to the Irish Goddess Queen Maeve. As fairy queen, she offered a red wine (which may have represented her own menstrual blood) to her consorts, and she was probably originally a Goddess queen of sovereignty, who by the time of Shakespeare had become the 'fairy's midwife'. She was also perhaps a river spirit, for her well lies deep within a wooded ravine near Egton on the North York Moors, where the stream tumbles over some rocks to make a small waterfall. A very old inhabitant of the village told us that as a child he and his friends had gone down there to perform what appeared to be some kind of ritual immersion in the water. This is truly an atmospheric and mysterious place.

From Egton village (which has a railway station) take the road to Glaisdale. Pass the old cemetery on the right, and at the bottom of the hill you will find a gate. Go through it, cross a field and a stream, (where the public footpath terminates) and then bear left beside a barbed-wire fence. The well lies on the other side of the fence at the bottom of the wooded ravine below, and access is very difficult.

Beverley (TA 038 392)

A very strange legend, now little known[14], attributes the origin of Beverley to an ancient ceremony that took place at a lake near the course of a stream called Hwyl, in a wood named Deira. Here a sacred shrine was kept and periodically taken out of the lake to be displayed in a pagan rite, dedicated either to the Goddess Ceres or the 'Old Lady' Hên-wen – a name elsewhere attributed to the Welsh Goddess-figure Cerridwen and clearly an aspect of the Cailleach. The shrine was called an 'ark' or 'beaver', and where it was placed was considered a mystical and holy place.

We have here perhaps a very ancient folk memory of rites of the Goddess of the River Hull, close to where Beverley stands. When the choir in Beverley Minster was restored in 1879, two old and worn steps were found which had been used as an approach to a well[15]. Could this be the site of the original sacred pool of the Goddess?

Beverley (which has a railway station) is in East Yorkshire (formerly Humberside), about 9.5km (6 miles) N of Hull. The Minster is at the junction of the Eastgate, Highgate, Moorgate and Flemingate roads in the city. The well is next to the altar and the Fridstool (an ancient choir denoting a place of sanctuary and refuge) and lies under the floor, reached by some steps leading down.

Folkton Round Barrow (TA 059 777)

This area of the rural North Yorkshire Wolds has a long continuity of prehistoric sites. At Star Carr, a few kilometres S of Scarborough, there was a Mesolithic (middle Stone Age) lakeside settlement, which was excavated and is now reburied, and at Flotmanby Wold and Folkton there are Neolithic barrow sites. The one at Folkton is a round barrow that was excavated in the 1860s and found to contain a male and female burial, with the bodies reburied in prehistoric times without their skulls. Two surrounding concentric ditches revealed more burials, and between the ditches was the grave of a five-year old child, containing three small drums, each 10cm (3½ in) in diameter, made of solid chalk from the sea-

cliffs nearby. These drums were engraved with geometric designs and stylized faces, which have been interpreted[16] as Goddess iconography. There may be a parallel here with the child burial at Arrington in Cambridgeshire (see page 121) and the 'toys' deposited to help the child gain a smooth passage to the other world and the realm of the Goddess.
Folkton lies 8km (5 miles) to the W *of* Filey *(which has a railway station) on the* A1039. *The chalk drums are in the* British Museum, *with copies in the* Mortimer Archaeological *and* Transport Museum, High Street, Hull *(tel:* 01482–593902).

Giggleswick (SD 810 643)

Outside the town of Giggleswick lies the Ebbing and Flowing Well (SD 803 654), which no longer does, but such an attribute links it with the tides and the moon (a similar quality is attributed to the well at Roche Rock in Cornwall). There is a legend that a nymph, chased up the hillside by a satyr, was turned into the spring, and the ebbing and flowing echoes her breathing. The well is also associated with St Alkeld's Church, where a stained-glass window shows sacrifices being made to the well. The church is dedicated to a Saxon Christian princess, who was strangled by pagan Danish women, and it has been suggested[17] that the 'saint' is really a Christianization of earlier pagan sacrifices to the well at the times of the new and full moons.

Closer to the church, about 90m (295ft) to the NW and now covered by the buildings of Giggleswick School, was a venerated stream called the Holy Well. From another spring close to the church, the Bankwell, a small lead figurine of a possible fertility Goddess was discovered at the end of the nineteenth century. She is bare breasted, wearing a full skirt with hatched decorations, and may be a Celtic votive offering[18]. Giggleswick Church may therefore have been built on the site of a pagan temple shrine, surrounded by holy wells and springs and dedicated to a Goddess of the moon.
Giggleswick is 1.5*km* (1 *mile) to the* W *of* Settle *(which has a railway station), on the* A65 *Skipton–Kirby* Lonsdale *road. The* Ebbing *and* Flowing Well *lies beside the road,* 1.5*km* (1 *mile) to the* NW *of the town. The fertility Goddess is now in the private possession of* Thomas Lord *of* Langcliffe.

Sheela-na-gigs

There are about half a dozen sheelas in Yorkshire. In Sheffield Cathedral, there is a complete suite of pagan carvings in the roof of the Lady Chapel, including a sheela sitting on tree roots, with arms held upwards. At Austerfield on the A614 Bawtry–Thorne road, there is a sheela in St Helen's Church. Another St Helen's Church, at Bilton in Ainsty by the B1224 York–Wetherby road, has two sheelas (one badly mutilated) seated side by side. Copgrove Church near Harrogate has a sheela located on the outside of the E wall, which was formerly on the inside of the N wall of the chancel, directly facing the altar! In her right hand she appears to be holding a sun-symbol disc, and above her right shoulder there is a large T. At Bridlington on the E coast, to the S of Scarborough, there is a sheela in a twelfth-century cloister in the Priory Church. Finally, at Croft-on-Tees on the border with County Durham there is a sheela standing on a slab inside the S entrance of the church.

Northumberland

Hadrian's Wall

This famous landmark, which runs for 117km (73 miles) from Newcastle-upon-Tyne to Bowness on Solway, marked the division of Roman Britain from the independent tribes to the N. Various forts and barracks were constructed at regular intervals along the wall, and to the S of the *vallum* (great ditch) civilian settlements and temples grew up. It is at some of these that remains of Goddess inscriptions and votive reliefs have been found.

The wall was started at Newcastle-upon-Tyne (Pons Aelius) (NZ 250 640) at a bridge over the river. From here comes a relief of Fortuna with a cornucopia and a *patera* (ritual libation dish), and one of the Three Matres. Next, at Corbridge (Corstopitum) (NY 982 648) there was a supply base and settlement which lay on a strategic crossing of two roads, overlooking the Corbridge and Tyne valley on a flat hilltop sloping S to the River Tyne. Here a Venus figurine and several Goddess reliefs were found, one showing a Goddess with a vat or tub that may represent a butter churn, making her a matron of milk and dairy produce. The Irish Goddess/saint Bride was often associated with the provision of butter, and it has been suggested[1] that an image of the Goddess Rosmerta from France also depicts a butter churn. Images of Fortuna and Ceres/Brigantia, Juno, Minerva and the Three Matres were also found.

Moving W, we come to Chesters (Cilurnum) (NY 912 701), a bridging point over the North Tyne, where an inscription was found to Ratis, the Goddess of the fortress, as well as carvings on altars and reliefs of animals such as crane, owl, serpent, horse, raven, boar and stag. Further W is the fort of Carrawburgh (Brocolitia) (NY 858 712), which has the remains of a Mithraic temple that housed in the corner a small statue of a Celtic-looking Goddess on a plinth, tentatively identified as a possible Mother Goddess. She may be related to Coventina's Well nearby (see page 151).

About midway along the wall, in a dramatically beautiful setting on one of the wildest parts, is Housesteads (Vercovicium) (NY 789 687), where a relief of the Goddess Diana, a statue of two headless goddesses (since destroyed), and several reliefs of Mother Goddesses were found. A stone was also found inscribed with the names of the Alaisigae – four war Goddesses called Bede, Finnilene, Baudihillie and Friagabi – who originally came from Gaul, where they had similar characteristics to the Norse Goddesses, the Valkyrie. About 1.5km (1 mile) further W is Chesterholm (Vindolanda) (NY 770 664), an excavated and reconstructed fort and civilian settlement. A relief of the Très Matres was found here, with a single Mother Goddess surviving, who holds a huge basket of fruit and flowers in her lap. Finally, at Birdoswald (Camboglanna) near Carlisle (NY 615 663), which is spectacularly situated above a gorge of the River Irthing, dedications to Ratis, the Goddess of the fortress, and Latis, the Goddess of the pool, were found. All these finds are indicative of a continuing and abiding reverence for the Goddesses of the Earth, nature, and fertility, set in the context of the settlements at crossings, bridges, and gorges in this wild and beautiful land.

The B6318 *road runs alongside all these sites and provides access to them. Finds from* Newcastle *are in the* Museum of Antiquities *at* Newcastle University *(tel:* 0191-222–6000). *The following sites are all open to the public, with finds in the on-site museums:* Corbridge *(tel:* 01434–623349); Chesters *(tel:* 01434–681379); Housesteads *(tel:* 01434–344363); Chesterholm *(tel:* 01434–344277); *and* Birdoswald *(April to October only, tel:* 016977–47602). *Carrawburgh's* Mithreum *is accessible at all reasonable times. The Goddess relief is in* Newcastle's University Museum of Antiquities.

Coventina's Well (NY 859 711)

In Roman times, this site at Carrawburgh was one of the most important Goddess shrines in Britain, rivalled only by Bath (see page 94), although today it is nothing but a sad and neglected swamp. It appears that it was built as a water supply in 128–130 CE and subsequently became a *temenos* – a sacred shrine to the Goddess Coventina. It remained an open-air shrine, perhaps indicating that it was a Celtic structure which was never fully Romanized. The well was excavated in 1876, and finds included ten inscribed altar stones (all except one dedicated to Coventina), pins, more than 16,000 coins, votive beads, a bronze dog and horse, brooches and glass pottery, shrine bells, and a fragment of a female skull. There were no statues of the Goddess, but there were dedications to her, reliefs that may depict her, and a bronze mask that may be attributed to her. One relief found near the well shows three Goddesses, and has been interpreted[2] as Coventina in triplicate: the Goddesses are virtually identical, each holding a water jug aloft with one hand while resting on a water vessel of some kind. Another relief, recovered from the well, shows the Goddess reclining on a water leaf, holding a branch of some aquatic plant in her right hand while resting her left elbow on an urn from which water flows. She is naked, with her breasts and nipples highlighted.

Coventina is known only from this location, apart from three other possible attributions: two altars from the Lugo area of north-west Spain and one from southern France, and it has been suggested[3] that there she may be the Goddess Brigantia in another guise. The place of Coventia in Spain is only a few kilometres from Coruna, the ancient capital Brigantium.

Whatever the origins of the cult, there is no doubt that her well at Carrawburgh was a very important shrine. Coventina is described as 'Augusta' on one altar, and 'Sancta' on another, the only native British Goddess to be so designated, and she was clearly a Goddess of healing and general well-being. The existence of her shrine here may have been the reason the Mithraic temple was built by the Romans nearby, and it may also explain the incorporation of a Mother Goddess figure within it. A third shrine (incorporating another well) dedicated to the *genus loci* was discovered in 1960, and an altar dedicated to the local nymphs was found there. Altogether, this is a place of much ancient sanctity, that badly needs resanctifying today.

The site of Coventina's Well is in a field at the bottom of a hill just N *of the Mithraic temple, and is reached by a short walk from the* B6318 *at Carrawburgh. The Mithraic temple is signposted, but not even a plaque remains to show the exact location of Coventina's Well. The only means of identifying it is the area of marshy ground with a few broken stones lying around. The reliefs recovered from the site may be seen in the Chesters Museum (tel:* 01434–681379).

Chapel Hill, Housesteads (NY 791 686)

The Housesteads fort was built on the site of an Iron Age village and an earlier Bronze Age tumulus. Two other tumuli remain on the other side of the road from the modern carpark. It has been suggested[4] that there is a landscape alignment here to a 'horned saddle' to the E and W of the hill – two twin hilltops representing the breasts of the Mother Goddess. This was a possible Bronze Age feature and the Romans continued to honour the site, which later became known as Chapel Hill. It was here that a relief to the Three Mother Goddesses was discovered (see Hadrian's Wall, page 150), as well as five altars to the Mothers found on the hill and the slope to the E[5]. Between Chapel Hill and the fort is a shallow trough with a stream known as the Knag Burn, and the whole memorable landscape contains all the elements of a ritual site. It is only from Chapel Hill that the two 'saddles' are both visible, and as one climbs up towards the fort both soon disappear. This may therefore originally have been a temple site to honour the Earth Goddess which was later sanctified by the Romans, who placed the Three Mothers relief there.

Housesteads stands beside the B6318 *road. Chapel Hill is to the left of the path that runs from the Information Centre up to the fort and museum. For Housesteads opening hours, tel:* 01434–344363.

High Rochester (NY 833 987)

This northern outpost of Hadrian's Wall, called Bremenanium, has given us a relief of three naked Goddesses and nymphs (see page 28). The scene

depicts a central Goddess, probably Venus, bathing with two attendant nymphs, one with a jug of water and the other a towel. The relief is a synthesis of classical form with Celtic style, probably carved by a native Celtic craftsperson, and is a vibrant and lively-looking depiction of a water Goddess.
High Rochester is situated beside the A68 just N of Rochester, about 9.5km (6 miles) S of the Scottish border. The Roman gate and walls can still be seen. The relief (plus another one of the Three Matres) is in Newcastle University Museum of Antiquities, (tel: 0191–222–6000).

County Durham

Lanchester (NZ 161 469)

The Roman fort of Longovicum, on the road from Hadrian's Wall, incorporated a workshop that produced at least 50 altars which have been identified in forts and civilian settlements across the Pennines in the north west of England. One of these altars, found at Lanchester, had an inscription on it dedicated to the Goddess Garmangabi, whose name appears to mean 'giving' or 'generous'. She may be a version of the Scandinavian virgin Goddess Gefjion, brought to England by the Anglo-Saxons as Gefion. She was an attendant upon Frigg, and was also known as a bestower of gifts.
Lanchester is on the A691 Durham–Consett road, and the remains of the fort lie to the S of the B6296 Lanchester–Wolsingham road. The altar may be found in the porch of Lanchester Church, which is situated on the A691 Durham–Consett road.

Cumbria

Hadrian's Wall outposts

Several outposts to Hadrian's Wall were constructed in the Carlisle area, as well as fortlets and towers on the coast of the Solway Firth. Some of these have yielded interesting native Goddess carvings.

Bewcastle (Banna) (NY 569 755) was on the Roman road running NW from the W end of the Wall. Here was discovered a relief of a Mother Goddess with a bowl of fruit in her lap, carved by a Celtic artist. A worn and headless statue of Fortuna was also found. Carlisle (Luguvalium) (NY 399 561) stood at the W end of the Wall. Excavations have produced several Très Matres reliefs, one with a male worshipper or consort, one (with two figures remaining) holding bowls of fruit, and one in which each figure is holding an offering (of bread, cake and a plant) to the Earth Mother. Drumburgh (Congavata) (NY 267 600), to the W of Carlisle, has given up a most unusual Goddess relief, depicting her with a pointed head-dress, a wreath or round stone in her right hand, and a distaff or long club resting on another round object in her left. She may be a depiction of a native British tutelary Earth Goddess of the area. Finally, from Maryport (Alauna) (NY 038 372) has come a relief portraying three naked goddesses, each with her hands in a different position. Another relief, showing a Goddess holding a vessel, may be Setlocenia (which means 'she of the long life'), as a dedication to her was found on the same site.

Bewcastle is to the E *of the* B6318 *road,* 13*km* (8 *miles*) NW *of Upper Denton on Hadrian's Wall. The relief and statue are in the City Museum, Tullie House, Castle Street, Carlisle (tel:* 01228–34781). *Carlisle (which has a railway station) is on the* A69; *the reliefs are in the City Museum. Drumburgh lies to the* n *of the* B5301, *about* 16*km* (10 *miles*) W *of Carlisle. The present location of the relief is unknown. Maryport (which has a railway station) is on the* A596, 8*km* (5 *miles*) N *of Workington. The Roman fort is to the* N *of the town beside the coast and is open to the public. The reliefs are in the on-site museum (tel:* 01900–816168).

Bride church cluster

In the coastal Solway Firth area, in which the Roman outposts are also situated (see above) is a cluster of churches dedicated to the Irish Goddess/saint Bride/Bridget[1].

At the mouth of the River Wampool lies the village of Kirkbride (NY 229 564), which was built on the site of a Roman outpost. The local church, with its Bridget dedication, dates from Norman times but incorporates some of the Roman remains in its building. About 24km (15 miles) to the SW is the village of Bridekirk (NY 116 337). The present church dedicated to St Bridget was constructed in 1868, but the churchyard also contains the ruins of an older building dating from the twelfth century. Many features from the old church were incorporated into the new one, including a twelfth-century font with runic inscription. Nearby, about 5km (3 miles) again to the SW, is the village of Brigham (NY 089 303), with an early Norman church dedicated to St Bridget. The churchyard contains a very early cross base, and a number of other pre-Norman monuments have also been found here. These three churches are in an almost straight NE–SW alignment.

Another 24km (15 miles) to the SW lies the village of Beckermet, and 0.75km (½ mile) SW of the village, also on the NE–SW axis, is the Church of St Bridget (NY 019 066), a thirteenth-century foundation that may have been built on the site of a nunnery dating from 650 CE. Two pre-Norman crosses stand in the churchyard, one of them with an unusual inscription in what appears to be eleventh-century Gaelic. There is a tradition that a well dedicated to St Bridget once existed near the church, although no trace of it now remains. There is also a Bride's Well near St Mary's Church at Stapleton (NY 504 712), about 19km (12 miles) NE of Carlisle. All these churches are evidence of a colonization of the area by early peoples, whose tutelary deity was the Goddess/saint Bride. These could either have been Irish immigrants in the fifth and sixth centuries, travelling between Ireland, the Isle of Man and south-west Scotland, or nominally Christian Vikings 300 years later, who occupied this area in early medieval times from Celtic Ireland, where they had encountered and adopted the cult of Bride/Bridget. Either way, it may be that the area was already important because of the earlier Celtic and Romano-British Goddesses worshipped here (see Hadrian's Wall Outposts, page 153).

Kirkbride is on the B5307, *16km* (10 *miles*) W *of Carlisle. Bridekirk is on a minor road 3km* (2 *miles*) N *of Cockermouth. Brigham is on a minor road,* 1.5*km* (1 *mile*) W *of Cockermouth. Beckermet is on a minor road to the* W *of the* A593, *5km* (3 *miles*) S *of Egremont. (There are railway stations at Maryport for Bridekirk, Workington for Brigham, and Braystones for Beckermet.)*

St Bees (NX 969 121)

In the same area of the Solway Firth is the monastery of St Bees, dedicated to the legendary seventh-century Irish Saint St Bega, who was supposed to have arrived on this Cumbrian coast on Midsummer Day c650 CE. She needed land to build a nunnery and approached the Lord of Egremont, who laughed at her, saying she could have as much land as was covered by snow in the morning. Despite it being Midsummer Day, a small piece of land at St Bees head was indeed covered with snow the next morning. Bega was thus a Goddess/saint who could control the seasons and the weather, which links her to St Milburga in Shropshire (see page 133). There are other pagan elements in her story: for example, oaths were formerly sworn on St Bega's Ring at St Bees Monastery, an ancient pagan custom used particularly by the Vikings.

Bega's legendary life also links her to Yorkshire. She moved to Whitby Abbey and thence to the small nunnery at Hackness near Scarborough (SE 969 906), which interestingly lies at the edge of the North York Moors with their Bride sites. Founded by St Hilda of Whitby Abbey, it was here that St Bega had a vision of the death of St Hilda and her ascension. Finally, she was laid to rest in a little church at Bassenthwaite (NY 227 287) in the Lake District. This beautifully situated church, standing by a lake below Skiddaw Mountain, dates to the tenth century, but contains traces of an earlier Norse and Saxon building. It is probable that the present site was an area sacred to pagan culture long before the Christians usurped it[2].

So what do we have here? A saint who was most probably a Goddess of the wheel of the year (she arrived on Midsummer Day, could control the seasons, and her feast day is 31 October, the old Celtic Samhain festival); who came from Ireland and is found in Yorkshire and Cumbria, in two areas redolent with Bride associations, Bride being another Goddess of the seasons (spring); and who has visionary and pagan elements to her story. Perhaps this is another branch of the Bride/Bridget trail, with the Goddess being brought from Ireland as a saint, and taken

across the Pennines from Cumbria to Yorkshire and back again.
St Bees Church is on the B5345 *5km (3 miles)* S *of* Whitehaven *(there is a railway station at* St Bees*). A statue of* St Bega *is situated within the* Mary Chapel*.* St Bega's *Church lies 11km (7 miles)* E *of Cockermouth and 8km (5 miles)* N *of Keswick on the* E *shore of* Lake Bassenthwaite*, and is reached by a minor road and a path from the* A591.

Long Meg and her daughters (NY 571 372)

This huge stone circle covers an area of 100sq m (360sq ft), with 59 stones remaining out of an original 70, of which 27 are still standing. At a distance of 18m (60ft) to the SW of the circle is a 3.5m (11ft) high sandstone outlier that has a spiral carving on the side facing the circle. The two largest stones of the circle point due E and W, perhaps denoting the spring and autumn equinoxes.

The legend of the circle is that Long Meg and her daughters were a coven of witches, who were holding their sabbat here and were turned to stone by a wizard, Michael Scot. The legend dates from at least the seventeenth century, when a local witch, Meg of Meldon, lived in the area, but, as we have seen elsewhere (for example, at Merry Maidens in Cornwall and Mitchell's Fold in Shropshire, see pages 83 and 134), legends of women turned to stone for pagan practices are quite common[3]. What is especially interesting here is that the tall outlier with the spiral carving (Long Meg) is reputed to bleed if a piece is ever broken off. We have here many of the elements of Goddess: the bleeding woman, the mystic spiral, the group of witches, the turning to stone, and the ritual alignment.
The circle lies 8km (5 miles) to the NE *of* Penrith*, to the* W *of the* A686 *on a minor road* 0.75*km (½ mile)* N *of* Little Salkeld.

Sheela-na-gig

A sheela was discovered in 1926 built into the E wall of Pennington Church, to the W of the A590 Barrow-in-Furness road. She was subsequently removed and 'deliberately and secretly built into the church beside the altar, thus propitiating both new and old gods'[4]. She was known locally as Freya, obviously a folk memory of the old Scandinavian Goddess worshipped in the area, which was heavily settled by Norse people. She is carved on to a block of stone about 1m (3ft) long, and has a deeply incised vulva which shows signs of having been well rubbed. She was considered locally to be a 'fertility figure', and at some point prior to 1991 she was taken out and exhibited at a village festival, following which several local women became pregnant, including the vicar's wife! She is now on display in Kendal Museum (tel: 01539–721374).

Isle of Man

The history of this island, owing allegiance to the Crown of Britain but politically independent, is a most interesting one. Christianity came here early from Ireland, from about the fifth century onwards, but in the ninth century the Vikings arrived and the island reverted to paganism, until the Norse themselves were Christianized some two centuries later. There is on Man a fascinating mixture of paganism and Christianity, and of several cultures and different races of people. The island is named after the Celtic sea God Mananan/Mannin, but further back in the mists of time there is a trace of a primal Goddess known as Teeval – the 'untouchable maiden of the sea' – and as Morann, the mother of Curoi, who was an avatar of Mannin[1]. Throughout the Middle Ages the island was known as Inis Seanta, the 'sacred isle', and is sometimes today called Ellen Vannin, Manx for the Isle of Man.

North Barrule mountain (SC 443 909)

There is a tradition that a witch called Berrey Dhone dwelt here, either on or inside the mountain, and the imprint of her heel can still be seen in the crevice between Cronk yn Lhaa and the neighbouring peak of Barrule. It has been suggested[2] that Berrey was a mountain hag, a version of the Cailleach Bheur, an ancient folk memory of the Goddess who shaped the hills.

North Barrule lies to the S *of the* A18 *road, about 3km (2 miles) from* Ramsey, *and is best approached by a road leading* S *from* Ramsey *through* Ballure Glen, *or by a minor road leading* S *off the* A18 *at* Gooseneck. *There is a steep climb to the top.*

Bride Sites

The most northerly parish of the island is named Bride (NX 449 012), and the parish church, built in 1869, replaces an earlier one built adjacent to a hill where a tumulus once stood, the stones of which are incorporated into the church tower. Further S, there are the remains of St Bridget's Chapel at Eyreton Farm near Crosby (SC 318 803), a seventh- to eighth-century keill (early Celtic church). Later, a twelfth-century nunnery dedicated to St Bridget was established on the outskirts of Douglas (SC 371 753). It was subsequently dedicated to St Mary, showing the close link between the Celtic Goddess/saint and the Christian saint.

Bride parish is 6.5km (4 miles) to the N *of* Ramsey *on the* A10. *St Bridget's Chapel is 5km (3 miles) to the* W *of* Douglas, *on the* N *side of the* Al. *The remains of the nunnery may be found to the* S *of* Douglas, *reached by a turning off* Castletown Road.

Notes

Merseyside

[1] By Janet and Colin Bord in *Mysterious Britain*, pages 50–1.

[2] See Ali Fitchet, 'Bidston Observatory', *Northern Earth Mysteries*, no 38.

Lancashire

[1] See John Billingsley, 'The Lady of the Dark Waters', *Northern Earth Mysteries*, no 54, page 13.

Yorkshire

[1] In *Pagan Celtic Britain*, pages 279.

[2] In *Religion in Roman Britain*, page 17.

[3] See Edna Whelan and Ian Taylor, *Yorkshire Holy Wells and Sacred Springs*, pages 40–1.

[4] See Rob Wilson, *Holy Wells and Spas of South Yorkshire*, page 16, and personal communication.

[5] See Anne Ross, *Pagan Celtic Britain*, pages 140–9.

[6] Jon Barker, 'The Goddess of Blackamoor' (personal communication).

[7] See Ian Taylor, 'Bride and the Old Wife – 1', *Northern Earth Mysteries*, no 53, page 4.

[8] Martin Collins, *Classic Walks on the North York Moors*, page 95.

[9] See Ian Taylor, 'Bride and the Old Wife – 2', *Northern Earth Mysteries*, no 54, page 2.

[10] In 'Bride and the Old Wife – 1', *Northern Earth Mysteries*, no 53 page 4.

[11] See Edna Whelan and Ian Taylor, *Yorkshire Holy Wells and Sacred Springs*, page 14.

[12] By Peter Walker in *Folk Tales from the North York Moors*, page 165.

[13] By Guy Ragland Phillips in *Brigantia*, pages 135–7.

[14] See Robert Charles Hope, *The Legendary Lore of the Holy Wells of England*, pages 186–7.

[15] See Rev William Smith, *Ancient Springs and Streams of the East Ridings of Yorkshire*, pages 177–185.

[16] See Marija Gimbutas, *The Language of the Goddess*, page 71.

[17] By Guy Ragland Phillips, op cit, pages 117–120.

[18] See Alan King, 'Romano-British Metalwork from the Settle District of West Yorkshire', *Yorkshire Archaeological Journal*, 1970, pages 410–17.

Northumberland

[1] By Hilda Davidson in 'Otherworld Cattle', *At The Edge*, no 1, page 2, and Séamus Ó Catháin in *The Festival of Brigid*, pages 12–13 and 25–127.

[2] By Anne Ross, *Pagan Celtic Britain*, pages 109 and 280, and Miranda Green in *Celtic Goddesses*, page 100.

[3] By Allason-Jones et al in *Coventina's Well*.

[4] By John Billingsley in 'The Saddle – A Sacred Landscape?', *Northern Earth*,

no 57, page 13–18.
[5] See drawing by William Stukely, 1725.

Cumbria
[1] See Mike Haigh, 'The Cumberland Bride Church Cluster', *Northern Earth*, no 57, pages 20–1.
[2] See Alex Langstone, *Bega and the Sacred Ring*, pages 14 and 36.
[3] See Samuel Pyeatt Menefree, 'Meg and Her Daughters: Some Traces of Goddess Belief in Megalithic Folklore' in S. Billington and M. Green (eds) *The Concept of the Goddess*, pages 78–90.
[4] From *Barrow News*, 14 September 1929, quoted in Andy Roberts, 'An Encounter with Freya', *Northern Earth*, no 56, pages 12–13.

Isle of Man
[1] See Mona Douglas, *Christian Tradition in Mannin*, page 10.
[2] By Walter Gill, quoted in Margaret Killip, *The Folklore of the Isle of Man*, pages 62–3.

Wales

WALES IS DIVIDED HERE INTO TWO AREAS: south and north, and then into counties. The county boundaries are those established under the most recent (1996) local government reorganization, with the former counties in brackets where there is a difference.

South

Monmouthshire (formerly Gwent)

Caerwent (ST 469 905)

Known as Venta Silurum, this town was the capital of the Silures tribe, and was founded in c75 CE when the tribe had come under Roman administration. It may have been a healing cult centre, and stretches of the original walls and foundations of some of the houses and shops remain, as well as a small octagonal Romano-Celtic temple, which lies outside the E wall. Many finds have been made, including bronze brooches, mirrors and heads, and one particularly impressive Mother Goddess figurine. She is 26.6cm (10½ in) high with a large, pear-shaped face, and dates from the first to the fourth century CE. She holds a small round fruit in one hand and what has been variously interpreted as an ear of corn, a palm leaf or fir tree in the other, all symbols of fertility. She is a very Celtic-looking Goddess, and seems to have more in common with earlier native Earth Goddess depictions than with formalized Roman ones.
Caerwent is on the A48, *8km* (*5 miles*) W *of Chepstow* (*which has a railway station*). *The Goddess and other finds are in the* Newport Museum and Art Gallery, John Frost *Square*, Newport (*tel*: 01633–840064).

St Anne's Well, Trelleck (SO 503 051)

This well, dedicated to the Goddess/saint Anne, is the only remaining one of nine that were originally in the area, each one renowned for curing a different illness. The well is still in very good condition, and if a pebble is dropped into the water, fast-rising bubbles mean that the wish will be granted.
Trelleck lies 8km (*5 miles*) S *of Monmouth on the* B4293. *The well is in a field beside*

a lane to the SE *of the village. In a field to the* SW, *beside the main road, lie three standing stones called* Harold's Stones.

Blaenau Gwent (formerly in Gwent)

Llanhilleth Hills (SO 230 020)

Mynydd Llanhilleth used to be the haunt of the Old Woman of the Mountain, who sounds like an ancient Cailleach Goddess of the land. In her later manifestation she wore a four-cornered hat, ash-coloured clothes and an apron thrown across her shoulder (the Giantess' Apron), and carried a pot or wooden can. She roamed the hills and led travellers astray, even when they knew the road.

The Llanhilleth Hills *lie to the* S *of* Abertillery *and* E *of* St Illtyd, *off the* A4063 *road.*

Vale of Glamorgan (formerly South Glamorgan)

St Anne's Well, Llanmihangel (SS 981 719)

This is a quite amazing place, containing as it does a well dedicated to the Goddess/saint Anne/Anu with a sculpture of Anne, in which the healing waters issue forth from her breasts and vagina (see page 71)! The well and sculpture was first mentioned in 1888[1] but the location was subsequently lost, until rediscovered as part of the research for this book[2]. The well is outside the nearby church and is situated in the middle of boggy ground, surrounded by vegetation. It consists of a square basin with three rough steps leading down to the well, the water probably about 1.25m (4ft) deep. On the outside of the wall of the well, on the opposite side to the steps, there is a rectangular slab with the relief of Anne. Her head and shoulders are still above ground and are covered in very fine moss and ground ivy, a healing herb, trails down over her. Her left breast is largely missing, it would appear from age rather than destruction, but the right breast is intact. A lead pipe leads out of the breast from which the water flows, and down below, buried under some silt, it also issues forth from her vagina. She is a real guardian of the well, a tacit reminder of the female healing powers of what was undoubtedly originally a pre-Christian site.

Llanmihangel *is* 5*km* (3 *miles*) S *of the* A48 *at* Cowbridge, *and is reached by minor roads. The whole site of the church and well is overlooked by* Plas Llanmihangel, *a large gothic* Victorian Manor House.

Swansea (formerly in West Glamorgan)

Gower Peninsula caves

The Gower peninsula is covered with Neolithic and Bronze Age standing stones, cairns and burial chambers, and, hidden from view along its S coast, are a number of caves with traces of prehistoric occupation and ritual. The Goats Cave/Paviland Cave (SS 437 858) yielded a human skeleton, dating from the upper Paleolithic (about 28,000 years ago). The body had been buried with some personal possessions and amulets as protection against evil spirits and, most significantly, had been painted with a red ochre, the colour of the life blood[3]. In Paleolithic times the site had been a river valley, which was subsequently flooded by the rising sea, so the body had been buried in a natural cave that may have been symbolic of the womb of Mother Earth.

About 5km (3 miles) to the SE lies the Culver Hole Cave (SS 467 844), which in its turn yielded something from a much later period. A small bronze figurine of a nursing mother or Goddess was found here, probably dating from the Romano-Celtic period. Her placing in this underground cavern may have been a deliberate offering to the Goddess of the underworld – the same ritual motivation as at Paviland, but about 26,000 years separates the two deposits.

The Gower peninsula lies to the W *of* Swansea *(which has a railway station). The caves are accessible at low tide by scrambling around the rocks, and this only with extreme care. The Culver Hole figurine is in the* National Museum of Wales, Cathays Park, Cardiff *(tel:* 01222 397951).

Arthur's Quoit (SS 491 905)

Among the many megalithic remains on the Gower peninsula is a chambered tomb (dolmen) with a huge 30 tonne capstone, known as Arthur's Quoit or Maen Ceti. Formerly, young maidens would visit the site at midnight on full-moon nights, crawl around the stones three or seven times, and leave offerings of barley and honey cakes. This may be a folk memory of pagan rites to the Earth Goddess performed here in prehistoric times.

The site is situated on open moorland to the NE *of* Reynoldston, *which lies to the* N *of the* A4118.

Carmarthenshire (formerly Dyfed)

Llyn y Fan Fach (SN 804 219)

In the Black Mountain lies a lake with a mythological tale that may contain a faint echo of a Goddess motif. A fairy bride – the Lady of the lake – made a marriage with a local farmer's son, and brought a herd of otherworldly cattle with her out of the lake. When the farmer broke the conditions of the marriage by touching her three times, she returned into the lake with her cattle. Cows are often a symbol of the nurturing earth Goddess (see Mitchell's Fold, page 134) and in this case she is also a heal-

ing Goddess, as she taught her three sons herbal remedies using local plants and their descendants became physicians in the area.
Llyn Y Fan Fach is 8km (5 miles) s of Myddfai. It is reached by minor roads to Llanddeusant and Blaenau, and then a track to the lake.

Pembrokeshire (formerly Dyfed)

Preseli Hills and Carn Ingli

The Preseli Hills, from where the Bluestones were quarried and taken to Stonehenge (see page 99), was probably always a sacred Goddess landscape. There are a pattern of landscape alignments linking standing stones, stone circles and stone rows to hills in the area, marking significant solar and Celtic festivals[4]. A stone circle, Gors Fawr (SN 134 294), was known by a 'local shepherd' to be a place 'where you could tell the time of day or year by simply using the alignments of stones'[5]. According to a local folklorist and historian, the old people kept watch at Gors Fawr and, by using the alignments, could predict the spring and autumn equinoxes, and winter and summer solstices. The whole area was thus a ritual calendar to time the celebration of the festivals associated with the wheel of the year (see also Loughcrew, page 191). At nearby Parc-y-Meirw stone row (SM 998 358) the stones were aligned on Mount Leinster in the Wicklow Hills, 145km (91 miles) away in Ireland, in order to predict eclipses of the sun or moon[6]. A 'wandering white lady' was supposed to be seen near the site, perhaps a mythologizing of the Goddess of the moon, celebrated here in the moon eclipse alignments.

One of the outliers to Gors Fawr circle was known to be a place to rest your head if you wanted to have visionary insights. One of the outlying hills of the Preselis, Carn Ingli (SN 058 374) – literally, 'hill of angels' – was also known as a place where, if you spent the night, you would become a poet, a lover or a madman! There are a number of 'spirit paths' – alignments of sites of the dead – that converge on Carn Ingli. It has also been suggested[7] that there is a landscape figure seen when standing on the plateau W of Carn Ingli, looking E at the peak from position SN 056 374. Her feet point to the N, with her head and flowing hair pointing S. Her hands are clasped, and she seems to be about four months pregnant, her arms and legs being formed by ancient walling. If she was seen by our ancestors in this way, she may have been the shape of the Goddess of the sacred mountain itself (see also Callanish stone circle and Hag Mountain, pages 182 and 183).
The Preselis are crossed by the B4329 road. Gors Fawr is to the W of a minor road running parallel to the A478. Carn Ingli is to the S of the A487 Newport–Cardigan road, and is reached most easily from Bedd Morus standing stone (SN 038 366) and then a 3km (2 mile) walk. Parc-y-Meirw is in a hedge beside a minor road near Llanychaer, to the N of the B4313 Fishguard–Narberth road.

Pentre Ifan (SN 099 370)

Pentre Ifan consists of the denuded remains of a Neolithic burial chamber or dolmen, standing close to the Preseli Hills (see page 163), which are visible from the site. It consists of a 5m (16ft) long capstone supported by three 2.5m (8ft) high uprights, and originally covered by a mound 40m (130ft) long. To the NE of the chamber is a large stone, originally upright, that served a ritual purpose associated with a fire pit to its S. The site was known as The Womb of Cerridwen[8], the Welsh Mother Goddess who possessed the Cauldron of Inspiration. Folk legend remembers that it was a place where initiates would pass into the dark chamber within, and the spirits of the dead used to be seen dancing around the site in the guise of fairy folk.

Pentre Ifan is beside a minor road to the S *of the* A487 *Newport–Cardigan road and is signposted.*

Nevern churchyard (SN 083 401)

This churchyard has become famous as a 'Goddess site' because of its bleeding yew tree. A red substance exudes from its trunk, which has been interpreted as the menstrual blood of the Earth Mother. This belief is held in some other parts of the world[9], although there are no relevant legends associated specifically with this place. This is thus an example of a contemporary belief, arising out of the Goddess-revival movement, rather than an ancient association. There is also a worn figure on the outside wall that has been interpreted[10] as a sheela-na-gig figure. The churchyard also contains some ogham and inscribed stones.

Nevern churchyard lies on the B4582 *road, 3km (2 miles) to the* E *of* Newport.

River Alun (SM 752 254)

This river, which flows through St Davids by the cathedral, takes its name from the river Goddess Alauna, who also gave her name to the Breton river Alaunus. It may also exist in the name of another river, the Alun, a tributary of the Dee, which itself takes its name from Deva, yet another Goddess. The River Alun was renowned for its fish that 'in the sacred stream came occasionally to the banks and regarded human beings without fear'[11]. They would also 'wink' at married women, and it has been suggested[12] that such fishes were regarded as water spirits (aspects of the Goddess) associated with fertility, healing and divination. The location of the cathedral would also seem to suggest that it was built near to an already sacred Goddess river.

St Davids *is on the* A487 *in the* W *of* Pembrokeshire. *The river runs through the cathedral city and at various points is crossed by small bridges.*

St Non's Well (SM 751 243)

This site was formerly a pagan place, and some remains of a stone circle can be seen in the field above the well. Tradition tells how St Non came to this spot in the sixth century when there was a fierce storm raging, but found sunlight and blue skies within the stone circle. She gave birth to the legendary St David, and a holy well with healing powers is dedicated to her there. The site was a centre of pilgrimage for people from all over Europe in the Middle Ages and today continues to be well cared for, with a statue of 'Our Lady' in a niche next to the well. This is a site that was undoubtedly sacred to the Goddess before Christianity, and one that continued to be revered in acknowledgement of a female spiritual presence.
St Non's Well and Chapel lie 0.75km (½ mile) s of St Davids at the end of the lane to St Nons Bay, signposted from St Davids.

St Bride's Bay

South of St Davids Head is St Bride's Bay, which forms a huge sweep along the coast. At the s end is the village and Church of St Brides (SM 802 109), built on the site of a sixth-century monastery (stone coffin burials can still be seen sticking out from the cliff face in places). Before that, Nab Head was occupied in the Iron Age, and as far back as the Mesolithic (middle Stone Age) era when the bay was dry land. Its name comes from the Celtic Goddess/saint, and it is clearly the place where early Irish immigrants landed, bringing Bride with them.
St Bride's Bay is 8km (5 miles) w of Haverfordwest off the B4327 towards Dale, or the B4341 to Broad Haven and then turn w.

North

Powys

Pennant Melangell (SJ 024 265)

This remote church near Lake Bala is the foundation of the saint Melangell, who may be related to the Goddess Oestre, whose totem animal was a hare. Melangell, the daughter of an Irish king, fled here to avoid marriage, a motif paralleled by the Welsh saints Winifred and Dwynwen, and one that may hint of a pre-Christian women-only sanctuary like that of Bridget in Kildare, Ireland (see page 195). ('Coincidentally', the nearby parish here is dedicated to Saint Ffraed, the Welsh form of St Bridget.)

Having shielded a hare who was being hunted, Melangell became their patron saint, and they were called in the area *ŵyn bach Melangell*, 'Melangell's little lambs', and were considered sacred. The legend is

depicted on carvings on the rood screen in the little church, which also incorporates a reconstructed twelfth-century shrine to Melangell, and an inner sanctum positioned behind the altar which houses her eighth-century grave. The whole foundation stands within a circular churchyard, which was originally a Bronze Age site, and is at the foot of a beautiful breast-shaped hill, also indicative of its pre-Christian status. Altogether, it is an incredibly peaceful and sacred place, redolent with echoes of an original Goddess sanctuary.
The church can be reached by a turning to the W *of the* B4391 *at* Llangynog, 16*km* (10 *miles*) SE *of* Bala, *which then runs through remote mountain scenery for* 3*km* (2 *miles*) *to the church.*

Llan (SH 884 008)

There is a memory here of the ancient Earth Mother. In this tiny village there is a mound on which an early-fifteenth-century church was built, and which was doubtless an earlier sacred site. The mound was known to be breast-shaped, and the Welsh saying '*Llanbrynmair llun bron merch*' preserves the memory of this (*bron*=breast). The site is close to the river Afon Twymyn, and on the hill of Newydd Fynyddog above are two stone circles, Lledd Croen Yr Ych (SH 903 008) and Cerrig Caerau (SH 904 005). The former has a curious legend that attributes it to the grave of a long-haired ox, which was separated from its mate and died of grief. It was then skinned and its hide stretched on the ground and surrounded by the circle of stones. This legend may be a reference to shamanic sacred sleeping at the site, as it was an ancient tradition for a seer to sleep in an ox or other animal skin[1]. The memory of using the ancient site for visionary dreaming to connect with the Earth Mother may subsequently have been transferred to the hillock at Llan, with its breast-shaped mound.
Llan is on the B4518, 3*km* (2 *miles*) S *of* Llanbrynmair, *which is on the* A470, 16*km* (10 *miles*) E *of* Machynlleth. *Another* 0.75*km* (½ *mile*) *further* S *from* Llan *the road is crossed by a minor road that runs back to the* A470 *at* Talerddig. *From this minor road, tracks lead* N *to the stone circles on* Newydd Fynyddog.

Denbighshire (formerly Clwyd)

Cadair Bronwen (SJ 075 346)

'Branwen's Seat' is a mountain peak in the Berwyn range that has probably been named after the character in the Second Branch of the *Mabinogi*. Branwen appears as Brân's sister, but in an earlier incarnation as Bronwen she may have been a Goddess in her own right[2]. With its nipple-like cairn, the mountain peak is very prominent, especially from the cairn circle of Moel-ty-Uchaf (SJ 056 372), which is beautifully positioned to align with the mountain in a SE direction, denoting the midwinter solstice sunrise.

Thus Cadair Bronwen may well have been an early Bronze Age sacred mountain of the Earth Goddess, later given the name of a Celtic Mother Goddess archetype.

Cadair Bronwen (784m/2,548ft) is reached by a path that runs SE *for 16km (10 miles) from Ty Uchaf at a turning (at a phone box) 5km (3 miles)* N *of Llandrillo on the B4401 Corwen–Bala road. The cairn circle of Moel-ty-Uchaf is positioned dramatically on a hilly ledge about 1.5km (1mile) along the track, with stunning views to Cadair Bronwen in one direction and Snowdonia in the other.*

GWYNEDD

Lake Bala/Llyn Tegid (SH 890 310 to 930 350)

This legendary lake, 4km (2½ miles) long and 0.5km (⅓ mile) wide, is surrounded by green hills and mountains. In *The Tale of Taliesen* it was the home of the Goddess Cerridwen, the shape-shifting Goddess of rebirth and regeneration who owned the Cauldron of Inspiration. The Irish cauldron described in *The Tale of Branwen* also came from a lake, and there is abundant archaeological evidence for the ritual deposition of cauldrons in lakes and marshes during the last millennium BCE. The lake was evidently thought of as a liminal place between the worlds, and there is a link with the Goddess Aine in Ireland, who made her home below Lough Gur (see page 204).

Lake Bala lies to the SW *of Bala itself. The A494 road runs along the* W *bank, and the B4403 road and the Bala Lake Railway along the* E *bank.*

Harlech Castle (SH 581 312)

This late-thirteenth-century castle is mentioned in the Welsh mythic tale of the *Mabinogi* as being the seat of the family of Llyr, members of whom included Branwen and her brother Brân. Branwen is a divine queen who may originally have been an ancestor Goddess, and her tale contains many strange and other-worldly elements. She was betrothed to the king of Ireland and sailed from here with her husband Matholwch, but was humiliated and became the cause of the war between the Welsh and Irish tribes. She eventually returned to Wales and died, broken hearted, at Aber Alaw. She may originally have been the tutelary Goddess of this place.

Harlech (which has a railway station) is on the A496 Barmouth–Blaenau Ffestiniog road. The castle (tel: 01766–780552)lies in the town centre, overlooking the dunes and bay.

Caer Arianrhod (SH 424 546)

Caer Arianrhod, the dwelling of the Goddess Arianrhod, is a rock 1.2km (¾ mile) off the W coast of North Wales. It is all that remains of the land where the Goddess and her women attendants dwelt. Arianrhod means 'silver wheel' and she was the most powerful of the mythic children of the Mother Goddess Danu. She may have been a matriarchal moon Goddess, or a Goddess of the wheel of the year. It was said that she lived a wanton and immoral life, and eventually the land was inundated and all were drowned, but this may be later patriarchal disapproval of a free and independent Goddess-woman who shared her land with other women and had powerful magic powers.

Caer Arianrhod is visible from the coast S *of Caernarfon, to the* W *of the* A499 *coastal road.* A *good viewpoint is from the hill fort of* Dinas Dinlle (SH 436 563).

Flintshire (formerly Clwyd)

St Winefride's Well (SJ 185 763)

This is one of the most famous wells in Britain, and still a place of Catholic pilgrimage, including an annual festival that attracts thousands of people to Holywell. The well dates to at least the seventh-century CE and probably further back into Celtic times. The legend of St Winefride (Gwenfrewi in Welsh) tells of her beheading by a spurned suitor. Where the head fell, the holy well sprung up. Her head was replaced by St Bruno and she became abbess of Gwytherin. Her well was said to have healing properties, and there are two other significant associations: one, that for three days after her death the well gave forth milk, a memory perhaps of the pre-Christian Mother Goddess worshipped here; and the other, that stones and moss in the well that are stained red are said to be her blood and hair. The day of her beheading was 22 June, the time of the summer solstice, so Gwenfrewi/Winefride may also be the Christianization of a pagan sun Goddess.

Holywell is on the A55, 24*km* (15 *miles*) W *of* Chester. *The well is at the* N *end of town beside the* B5121 *Greenfield road.*

Aberconwy (formerly Gwynedd)

Druids Circle, Penmaenmawr (SH 722 747)

The remains of a Bronze Age stone circle lie on the NE slopes of Moelfre, consisting of 30 stones arranged in a circle 26m (85ft) across. Excavations revealed that young children were buried here, possibly as foundation sacrifices. The circles have long been associated with the worship of two Goddesses, Cerridwen and Andras, the latter a possible corruption of Andraste, the Goddess invoked by Boudica when she fought against the Romans. The site is close to Anglesey, the centre of Celtic Druidic worship, so 'Andras' may be a memory of continuity of the place from the Bronze Age into Celtic times.

Penmaenmawr is on the A55 on the N coast of Wales, 1.5km (1 mile) to the E of Conwy and 8km (5 miles) W of Bangor. The Druids Circle is reached via a path signposted from Craig Lwyd, which climbs to the stones 360m (1,170ft) up on the hillside above.

Anglesey

Barclodiad y Gawres (SH 328 708)

Anglesey contains a large number of megalithic sites within its 48sq km (30sq miles). One of the most spectacular is Barclodiad Y Gawres, whose name means 'The Giantess' Apronful', in memory of the Earth Goddess who dropped the stones that made up the original mound. Another, smaller, cairn with the same name and legend can be found at the pass of Y Ddeufaen (SH 716 716), about 80km (50 miles) to the E beside the old Roman road that runs from Bont Newydd to Roewen in Denbighshire (formerly Clwyd). It is clearly connected with Barclodiad Y Gawres, as the legend tells of it being dropped by a Giantess on her way to Anglesey.

The Giantess' mound of Barclodiad Y Gawres has long been removed, but is now replaced by a modern concrete dome that is grassed over to resemble the original as much as possible. Within the mound is a passage, some 7m (23ft) long, leading to a central burial chamber, with three other chambers leading off to the E, W and S. Cremated remains with bones and antlers were found. The central area of the tomb was used not for burial, but for ceremonial and ritual purposes. A 'witch's brew' of frog, toad, snake, mouse, hare, eel, wrasse and whiting was poured over a ritual fire and then quenched with a cover of limpet shells and pebbles. Five of the stones within the passage grave were found to be decorated in the manner of similar tombs in Brittany and Ireland. One stone is covered with zigzags, chevrons and losenges, and another with four spirals. These carvings have been interpreted as representations of the Mother Goddess watching over the dead[3], and the folk legend of the Giantess' Apron may be a memory of that same Mother Goddess association. In addition, the entrance of the tomb faces out across the flat Anglesey plain in a NE direction (the midsummer solstice sunrise) towards two distinctive hilltop shapes: Parys mountain (147m/478ft) and Mynydd Bodafon (178m/579ft). Perhaps the tomb was deliberately positioned here to view the breasts of the Earth Goddess.

Barclodiad Y Gawres stands on the headland at Treastell Bay, beside the A4080 (there is a carpark). It is normally locked, but the key is available from the Heritage Centre in the nearby village of Aberffrau. (There is a railway station at Bryn Du.)

Bryn-Celli-Ddu (SH 508 702)

The name means 'hill in the dark grove', and the site stands near to the River Braint, which may have been named after the Goddess/saint Briget[4].

It consists of a chambered cairn, begun as a circle-henge, and then incorporated by a mound 26m (85ft) across, with a double kerb of stones around its edge. The passage leads into a chamber, inside which is a stone with a spiral on it and a free-standing pillar that has been interpreted[5] as a representation of the Mother Goddess, watching over the bones spread at her feet. Certainly the mound (although originally extending further W) has the appearance of the womb of Mother Earth, with the entrance passage flanked by two portal stones as the vaginal passage and labia. Outside at the rear is a replica of a stone originally discovered near a ceremonial pit, covered with meander carvings of wavy lines and spirals. Standing in the flat Anglesey countryside, the site is as dramatic and powerful today as when it was built some 5,000 years ago.

Bryn-Celli-Ddu is to the W of the A4080 near Llanddaniel Fab. The original of the 'Pattern Stone' is in the National Museum of Wales (Tel: 01222 397951).

Llanddwyn 'Island' (SH 386 627)

This 1.5km (1 mile) long promontory contains the remains of a church and holy well dedicated to St Dwynwen, a Celtic saint who carries an earlier Goddess association. Like Uncumber and Melangell (see pages 105 and 165), she fled from an enforced marriage; like Bega (see page 155) and Melangell, she founded a nunnery in a wild and remote place; and like Milburga (see page 133) and Melangell, she is successfully protected by the land. Like the other saints, she also has magical powers: in Dwynwen's case, she gives her would-be suitor Maelon a magic potion to 'freeze him' and then later unfreezes him, and she has the power to answer all requests on behalf of lovers while never marrying herself. She also has oracular powers: lovers would visit her holy well to make their vows, and prophetic fish in the well would foretell the destiny of anyone wishing to marry. People would also bring sick animals to be healed at her shrine in the church. She seems to be a Christianized version of a Goddess of love and healing – an Artemis-Diana figure – a strong, independent female who has power over men's lives, and who has her own separate sanctuary in the land, where people would come for help and inspiration. As a daughter of Anglesey, known as the 'Mother of Wales', she is also a tutelary Goddess archetype rooted in the land.

Llanddwyn 'Island' can be reached through Newborough Forest, S of the A4080 at Newborough crossroads. There is a charge for cars to enter the woods, but parking can then be made by the shore, with a walk across to the peninsula. A path leads to the ruined church and site of the well, and an old cottage on the 'Island' has a small display.

Bedd Branwen (SH 376 843)

This is the traditional burial place of Branwen, who died broken hearted on the banks of the River Alaw after returning from the wars fought over her in Ireland. The site consists of a Bronze Age barrow dating from around 1400 BCE, which stands on the floor of a valley in the centre of a slight natural rise in the bend of the river. It has a large standing stone protruding from the centre. The site was excavated in 1813 and 1967, and was shown to be a multiple burial mound with urns containing cremated bones and incense cups. The site thus dates from at least 2,000 years before the time of Branwen, but was clearly recognized as an important burial mound at the time that Branwen's resting place became associated with it.

Bedd Branwen can be approached from Glanalaw, reached by a track to the E of a minor road S of Llanddeusant, which lies to the E of the A5025 that runs down the W side of the island. Ask permission at Glanalaw.

Sheela-na-gig

A well-preserved sheela can be found in the Old Parish Church to the SE of Llandrindod Wells on the A483 Newton–Builth Wells road, not far from the Welsh border. At Penmon Priory on the E coast of Anglesey, there is a sheela on the inside wall (formerly on the outside W wall of the S transept). There is also a holy well nearby, dedicated to St Seiriol.

Notes

South Wales

[1] *Archaeologia Cambrenisis*, 1888, page 409.
[2] Information supplied by Mrs M. Henderson in personal communication.
[3] See Aubrey Burl, *Rites of the Gods*, page 25.
[4] See Gaynor Francis, *The First Stonehenge*.
[5] Michael Howard, 'Circle of Stars', *The Cauldron*, no 76, page 18.
[6] See Roger Worsley, *The Pembrokeshire Explorer*.
[7] By Laurence Main in 'A Sleeping Angel, Goddess and Giant', *The Ley Hunter*, no 122. page 34.
[8] See W.Y. Evans-Wenz, *The Fairy Faith in Celtic Countries*, pages 155–7.
[9] See John Allegro, *Lost Gods*, page 129.
[10] By Roger Worsley, op cit, page 87.
[11] Francis Jones, *The Holy Wells of Wales*, page 110.
[12] By Julie Trier in 'The Sacred Springs and Holy Wells of St David's Peninsula – 1', *Source*, vol 2, no 4, page 20.

North Wales

[1] See *The Ley Hunter*, no 115, page 22.
[2] See Miranda Green, *Celtic Goddesses*, pages 55–6.
[3] By Frances Lynch in *Prehistoric Angelsey*, page 40, and Aubrey Burl in *Rites of the Gods*, page 89.
[4] See Anne Ross, *Pagan Celtic Britain*, page 47.
[5] By Mick Sharp in *A Land of Gods and Giants*, page 70.

Scotland

SCOTLAND IS DIVIDED INTO TWO AREAS: Lowlands and Inner Hebrides, and Highlands and Western Isles (Outer Hebrides). The boundaries are those established by the 1996 local government reorganization, with the former regions in brackets where there is a difference.

Lowlands and Inner Hebrides

Dumfries and Galloway

Birrens (NY 219 752)

The northern territory of the Brigantes tribe extended into the lowlands of Scotland. Their great tribal Goddess was Brigantia, who appears on a stone relief found at the Roman military site of Birrens (Blatobulgium). She is depicted wearing a mural crown and carrying a spear and a globe of victory, with an amulet around her neck picturing Minerva's symbol of a gorgon's head. She was thus an important tutelary deity for the original Celtic tribe and then for the Romans, who may have honoured her as a Goddess who had given them victory in the area. Other finds from Birrens include the head of a Goddess, and altars to (1) Fortuna, (2) Minerva (inscribed with dolphins and a raven) and three Rhineland Goddesses, (3) Harimella, (4) Ricagambeda and (5) Viradecthis.
Birrens fort is in the Annandale valley (Mein Water), 1.5*km* (1 *mile*) s *of* Middlebie *on the* B725. *The Brigantia stone relief and altars* (1) *and* (4) *are in the* National Museum *of* Antiquities *of* Scotland (*tel*: 0131 225 7534). *From the end of* 1998 *they will be in the newly built* Museum *of* Scotland. *The head of the local Goddess and altars* (2) (3) *and* (5) *are in* Dumfries Museum (*tel*: 01387–253374).

Dumbarton and Clydebank (formerly Strathclyde)

Dumbarton Rock (NS 400 745)

The river Clyde was probably named originally after the Goddess Clota, the name also appearing in the old Irish Claud ('the washer, or strongly flowing one') and in the Gaulish Clutoida[1]. No specific ritual deposits have been found, but the area was occupied by the Dumnonii tribe. If we are seeking clues as to their ceremonial centre, then it may have been at Dumbarton Rock, an isolated volcanic outcrop in a striking location overlooking the Clyde, on the outskirts of Dumbarton. The name means 'Dun of the Britons' (dun=fortified homestead), and the site is thought to be the later capital of the British kingdom of Strathclyde from the fifth to eleventh centuries CE. A legend, which reinforces the sacred nature of the rock, tells of it being dropped by some witches, who threw it after St Patrick as they were chasing him out of the country – a possible folk memory of the conflict between this pagan centre and the incoming Christianity.

Dumbarton Rock is on the E *side of the mouth of the River Leven, where it flows into the Clyde on the* S *outskirts of* Dumbarton (*which has a railway station*).

North Ayrshire (formerly Strathclyde)

Isle of Arran

This island in the Firth of Clyde has a wealth of prehistoric remains, including the standing stones and stone circles of Macrie Moor (NR 900 324). At one time, the whole of the island was one single parish of Bride[2], and there was a convent at Narachan (NR 937 504) and a church at Kilbride (NS 032 323) dedicated to her. Later, it was divided into two parishes, St Bride (E) and St Molios (W): they met at the river that gave its name to Lochranza ('the loch of the rowan-tree river'). The rowan has long been associated with the Goddess Bride/Brighid, and in the same area the whitebeam rowan, a tree particular to Arran, can be found. In Glen Rosa, to the NW of Brodrick and overshadowed by Glen Shant Hill ('the sacred glen hill'), Allt na Bride ('the stream of Bride') can also be found. From this point Cioch na h'Oige ('the pap of the maiden') can be viewed, itself another probable Bride as Goddess association.

The Isle of Arran is reached all year round by ferry from Ardrossan *on the* E *mainland to Brodick, the capital, and from* Claonaig Bay *to the* W *of the* Mull *of* Kintyre *to* Lochranza (*summer service only*).

Argyll and Bute (formerly Strathclyde)

Ballochroy and Kintraw (NR 730 523 and 830 050)

These two megalithic sites on the W coast of Scotland have been identified[3] as significant solar observatories that align with the hills of the Paps of Jura – the breasts of the Earth Goddess on the island of Jura to the W (see page 175). At Ballochroy on the Mull of Kintyre there are three standing stones and a cairn in a line on a level patch of ground. The centre stone is a thin slab, one of its faces having the appearance of being deliberately flattened and smoothed. The sightline from here is to Corra Beinn, the most northerly peak of the Paps of Jura, about 30km (18½ miles) NW across the sea. This marks the position on the horizon where the midsummer solstice sun would have set in about 1800 BCE, the slope of the mountainside being almost the same as the apparent path of the setting sun. The other two stones could have marked the extreme positions of the sun's final brief reappearance and disappearance to the right of the mountain.

At Kintraw, about 50km (30 miles) further N, is another solar observatory relating to the Paps of Jura, this time the S peak of Beinn Shiantaidh, about 43km (26½miles) to the SW. Once again, on a level piece of ground there is a cairn and a standing stone about 4m (13ft) high, but now leaning 25 degrees from the vertical. From here the sun would have set behind Beinn Shiantaidh at the winter solstice, once again disappearing behind the mountain to re-emerge briefly before its final setting. There may have been a specially constructed platform above the stone to facilitate the observations and/or ceremonies.

At these two sites there is a good indication that prehistoric peoples built their megalithic monuments in order to observe the passage of the sun at significant times of the year in relationship to the Earth Mother, the name of which has come through to us as the Paps of Jura. There are a wealth of other prehistoric remains in the area, including standing stones, stone circles, cup-marked stones, and a hill fort at Dunadd (NR 837 936) used for inauguration ceremonies.

The site at Ballochroy *is beside the* A83 *road, which runs along the* W *coast of the* Mull of Kintyre. *The site at* Kintraw *is beside the* A816 *road, which runs along the* W *coast of* Argyll *between* Lochgilphead *and* Oban.

Isle of Islay

Known as the Queen of the Isles, Islay (pronounced 'Isle-a') is the most southerly of the Inner Hebrides, and one of the largest of the islands. Its old name was Ile, sometimes given as Eila; legend says that it was named after an ancient Goddess of that name, although other tales turn her into Yula, a Danish princess who is said to be buried E of Port Ellen in the shadow of Cnoc Hill, near Kildalton (NR 389 461)[4]. Two standing stones that mark the spot can be seen there, and nearby is the site of Kilbride Chapel, dedicated to St Lasar, an obscure sixth-century female saint who was doubtless an avatar of Bride. Off the SE coast of the island are three small islets called Eilean Craobhach, a'Churrin and Bhride, whose names mean respectively the Isle of Trees, Cairns and Bride. These islets lie opposite the early Christian site of Kildalton chapel and Celtic cross, but are an indication that the area was sacred long before the coming of Christianity.

Islay was also the centre for the Lords of the Isles, who had to stand on a sacred stone with the impression of a foot hollowed in it in order to be given the right to rule the land, originally the dispensation of the Goddess of sovereignty. This stone stood on the islet of Eilean Mor in Loch Finnigan (NR 388 680), and was said to be the burial place of the queens and children of the Lords of the Isles. Recently, excavations have shown[5] that a natural mound, Cnoc Seannda, near the shore of the loch, contains a stone chamber that may be a Neolithic barrow into which the bones of an animal were ritually deposited. From this mound, a single standing stone (about 1.5m/5ft high) can be seen aligned to the rounded hills of the Paps of Jura (see below). In fact, the stone stands in the cleavage of the Paps, and beyond it evidence has been found of a stone row (now buried). The whole terrain of barrow, standing stone and stone row, all pointing to the breasts of the hills of the Earth Goddess, forms a fascinating ritualistic prehistoric landscape.

Islay is reached by ferry from Kennacraig on the Mull of Kintyre to Port Ellen in the S of the island, or to Port Askaig in the NE. Loch Finnigan is 5km (3 miles) W of Port Askaig, to the N of the A846. Kildalton and the three islets are 11km (7 miles) E of Port Ellen on the A846, and then a minor road.

Isle of Jura

The Isle of Jura lies to the NE of Islay, the two islands separated by the narrow Sound of Islay, and to the W of the Kilmartin area of Argyllshire (see Ballochroy and Kintraw, page 173). Its famous hills, the Paps of Jura, are the focus of the S half of the island, and include the peaks Corra Beinn (An Oir, its mystical name, means 'the mountain of gold') and Beinn Shiantaidh (similarly, Siontaidh means 'the holy mountain'), to which so many of the sacred sites on the neighbouring islands and mainland are aligned. It, too, has an Eilean Bhride off its E coast (NR 554 698), and in addition an association with the Cailleach, the ancient Goddess of the land. Legend says that she washed her clothes in a whirlpool, the Corryvreckan, which lies off the N coast of the island (NM 685 023). In some tales she carried a creel of rocks on her back, and as she waded through the Sound of Mull her strap broke and one by one the rocks fell to form islets in the sea. She is thus the ancient Earth-shaper Goddess, with the same motif as the Giantess' Apron. She is also known to ride across the land in the form of the 'night mare', a proto-Celtic horse-goddess.

Jura is reached by the Feolin Ferry from Port Askaig on Islay. The main road, the A846, runs up the E side of the island, from where the Paps of Jura are visible to the W and Eilean Bhride to the E. At Ardlussa in the N the road becomes a track, which then runs N to Kinuachdrach harbour. 5km (3 miles) further on, between the N tip of the island and the small island of Scarba, is the Gulf of Corryvreckan.

Isle of Mull

The Isle of Mull, with an area of about 40sq km (25sq miles), lies to the N of Jura, close to the mainland. It was once part of the ancient kingdom of Dalriada and before that was occupied by the Neolithic peoples, who left a stone circle and standing stones all over the island. These have recently been shown[6] to be part of another ritual landscape, focused on a mountain called Ben More (976m/3,169ft), which lies in the centre of the island and seems to have been a sacred mountain peak. Seven settings of standing stones on northern Mull were investigated: Glengorm (NM 435 571), Quinish (NM 413 552), Maol Mor (NM 435 531), Dervaig north (NM 439 520), Dervaig south (NM 438 516), Balliscate (NM 500 541) and Ardnacross (NM 542 491), and a pattern emerged of orientation to the maximum southernmost moonrise (in its 18.6 year cycle), whereby watchers would have been able to follow the track of the moon across the distant horizon until it set. Five of the seven stone rows were placed on the limits of visibility of Ben More, and all within a 10 degree (Quinish 20 degree) orientation of the mountain. At Glengorm, the only site where an exact orientation is known as the result of excavation, the alignment upon Ben More is precise. At Ardnacross, excavation uncovered a copper bracelet with chevron carvings, found in a ritual pit near one of the rows. Chevron carvings have been elsewhere interpreted as symbols of the Goddess, so once again we can see a linking of a sacred mountain, megalithic stones, alignment to solar/lunar events, and the Earth Goddess in the land.

Mull has other interesting places. There is an old Drover's Road on the island, where the cattle were brought in from the outer islands and taken across to the mainland. This road runs from Croaig in the N to Grass Point in the SE, and about halfway along its route is Teanga Brideig, 'the stream of Bride's tongue of land'. The bridge over the stream is guarded by a holly tree, where the drovers traditionally asked the Goddess/saint for protection and blessing for their cattle[7]. Another Goddess honoured on the island in the guise of a saint is Tobar Mhoire (Tobermory), at the well of Mary (NM 500 505). On the festival date of Lughnasad/Lammas pilgrimages were made to the well, particularly by women in the hope that they would be fruitful. It seems that the old Earth Goddess and the newer Celtic guardian saints co-exist quite happily on this island.

Mull is reached by ferry either from Oban on the E *mainland to Craignure and Tobermory on* Mull, *or across the* Sound *of* Mull *from* Lochaline *on the* N *mainland to* Fishnish Point *on* Mull. *Mary's* Well *is to the* W *of* Tobermory *on the* N *of the island, near a ruined chapel.*

Isle of Iona

Iona is a small island 5km (3 miles) long by 1.5km (1 mile) wide, just off the SW of Mull. Its fame eclipses its size, as it is a major centre of early

Celtic Christianity, brought to the islands by St Columb in the sixth century. A monastery was established here, which in the thirteenth century became a Benedictine order that lasted until the Reformation. The monastic remains were rebuilt in a twentieth-century revival that turned the island into an all-male, Gaelic-speaking, strictly Presbyterian community. It has since widened its scope, but remains a bastion of Christianity.

However, there are interesting hints here and there of the earlier paganism that St Columb replaced. An earlier alternative name of the island was Ioua, which is the name of an ancient Goddess of the moon, and old chants carrying her name can still be found. This association with the moon Goddess ties in with one of the oldest places on the island, called Tobar na h'oige, 'the fount of youth'. This well or pool is on an isolated hill called Slibh Meanach, near to an old fortress called Dun-I (NM 284 252). It is said that this well sprang from the sacred cauldron of the De Dannan (people of the Goddess Danu), and at the magic times of dawn, dusk and full moon it became a fount of vision and healing[8].

Later, under Christianity, it became the rule that the only women allowed on the island were nuns. However, a small islet off Iona was called Eilean nam Ban, which means 'the isle of women'. Anne Ross has suggested[9] that this legend seems to be an echo of the old pagan theme of small sacred islands that were inhabited entirely by women dedicated to the cult of the Goddess (see also Caer Arianrhod, page 167). In the medieval Nun's Refectory (NM 284 240) on the island, seated in a lintel above a window is a badly weathered carving of a sheela-na-gig, looking rather pregnant and with her arms akimbo, gesturing towards her pudenda. It seems that even on the male-exclusive Christian establishment of Iona, the Goddess-spirit could not be obscured entirely.

Iona is reached by passenger ferry from Fionnphort *on the* Ross *of* Mull. *The path from the ferry on Iona leads to the nunnery church, to the* S *of which is the refectory. The hill of* Slibh Meanach *and* Dun-I *is to the* N *of the abbey. The island of* Eilean nam Ban *lies to the* E, *between* Iona *and the* Ross *of* Mull.

Sheela-na-gig

In Muckairn Parish Church on the mainland, 16km (12 miles) E of Oban, there is a weathered sheela on the S wall, which is believed to have come originally from the nearby thirteenth-century Killespickerill Church.

Perthshire and Kinross (formerly Tayside)

Glen Lyon (NN 379 427)

Far off the beaten track in the Grampian mountains of Tayside can be found an amazing survival[10] of an old Goddess/pagan rite. Glen Lyon is a magical place where the old Celtic tradition lingers on, probably because of its very isolation. There is a glen leading off a glen leading off Glen Lyon called Glen Cailliche (the Hag's Glen), and on the high moor between the mountains of Ben Achaladair and Ben à Chuirn a burn called Allt Cailliche (the Hag's Stream) rises, eventually pouring into Glen Lyon. Here, in the shadow of Beinn à Cailliche (the Hag's Mountain), standing above the burn, is a pile of stones that at first glance one might just pass by. But this is Tigh nam Cailliche (the Hag's House) and if one looks more closely at the stones, they seem to have a curious anthropormorphic shape, a rough-and-ready depiction of humanoid figures, although in fact they are natural waterworn stones from the burn. The largest (about 46cm/18in tall) is the Cailliche, and there is also the Bodach (old man) and the smaller Nighean (daughter). Recently another three 'children' have appeared, perhaps in response to the legend that says that every 100 years or so the Cailliche Goddess bears another child. Although the babies of the family are very small, the stories say that they are growing, and one day they will be as big as the others!

What makes it all so fascinating is that, in a ritual going back probably thousands of years, the stones are brought out from the Cailliche's stone house by a local shepherd every Beltane, washed in the local burn, and then placed to guard the flocks all summer, before being returned to the house at Samhain for winter. Formerly, the little house had a thatched roof which was renewed annually on May Day eve, but it now has a stone roof. The Cailliche and her family were evidently thought of as having the power to protect the well-being of the animals, and this is reinforced by an old legend that tells of a time in the past when a giant and his pregnant wife arrived at the Glen at Beltane in thick snow. The homeless couple had a house built for them by local crofters, so they stayed there forever and 'blessed the glen and all its flock and stock and progeny provided the correct ritual was carried out'[11]. And so the ritual continues to be carried out, the last remnant of an ancient rite that honours the Goddess of winter, who transmogrifies into the Goddess of spring every year at Beltane and watches over the cattle and the land.

Tigh nam Cailliche lies in a remote part of Glen Cailliche. *From the village of* Fortingall, *8km (5 miles)* W *of Aberfeldyon on the* B486, *take the road that runs for 44km (28 miles) up Glen Lyon to Loch Lyon reservoir. From a* N *branch of the Loch called Glen* Meran, *walk* W *into Glen Cailliche. The* Old Hag's House *lies about 3km (2 miles) further on above the burn that runs through the glen.*

Highlands and Western Isles

Highlands

Isle of Skye

Strictly speaking, Skye is one of the Inner Hebrides, although administratively it falls within the area of the Highlands and Islands. It is an island (although now joined to the mainland by a bridge) some 600sq km (234sq miles) in size, with a deeply indented coastline. It also has some of the wildest and grandest hills and mountains in all the islands, and has retained in its legends memories of a whole mythic landscape of the Goddess. The name Skye comes from the Gaelic and translates as 'the winged isle'[1]. It is named, perhaps, after the Goddess warrior-woman Sgathach/Skiach/Scathac (pronounced 'skyah'), whose name means 'winged' or 'shield'. She is the tutelary Goddess of the island, but in fact the mythic history of the place goes back even further than her.

Legends say[2] that when the world was new, there was a great heather-clad plain between Glen Brackadale in the W and the Red Hills in the E. In this dark and lonely place the Cailleach Bhur, the Hag or Old Woman of winter, dwelt on Ben Wyvis. She gave her name to the mountain Ben-na-Cailleach (NG 601 233) in the Red Hills and to Biodanan Cailleach (the Peak of the Hag) and Fearan nan Cailleach (the Land of the Hag) (NG 375 385) above Glen Brackadale. The legend says she was in conflict with spring, who fought with her, but she was stronger than him and he could do nothing. He appealed to the sun to help, and the sun flung his spear at Cailleach Bhur as she walked on the moor. Where it struck the ground, a blister, 9.5km (6 miles) long and wide, burst forth as the Cuchullin/Cuillin mountain range, a glowing molten mass.

For a time no living thing inhabited the Cuchullins, but then came Sgathach, a Goddess warrior-woman, who dwelt in the mountains. She was challenged by Cuchullin, the hero of Ulster, who came across to Skye and fought a long battle with her. Eventually they both ate of the hazels of knowledge and realized that neither could overcome the other, so they made peace and Cuchullin returned to Ireland, leaving Skye as the realm of Sgathach and her daughter.

What we have here is the nearest thing in Britain to a creation myth. The Cailleach Bhur is the Goddess of the land, the Earth-shaper who becomes part of the creation of the mountains. Sgathach is sovereignty, the Goddess whose land it is and who defends it against patriarchal usurpation. Their marks can be seen all over the land, in the mountains and by the lochs. The Cailleach lay her clothes out to dry on The Storr (NG 495 540), a 726m (2,358ft) mountain in the N; and she left her footprint at Rudha nan Clack (the Point of Stones) near Drynoch (NG 406 316), where standing stones mark the spot. Wherever we look in Skye, we can see the places of the Goddess from the beginning of time.

Not only can the Goddess of winter be found on Skye, but the Goddess of spring as well. In one version of the myth, the Cailleach Bhur, who washes her clothes in the Corryvreckan (see the Isle of Mull, page 176), becomes the fairest maid in the land, the youthful Goddess of spring, when she puts on her plaid. And just as the Cailleach dwelt in the high places of the mountains, so the Goddess Bride, the Goddess of spring, has her special places in the land too. At Kilbride (NG 590 203) there is a standing stone and holy well next to the ruined St Bridget's Church. The stone is called Clach na Annait (the Stone of the Mother) and the well Tobar na Annait (the Well of the Mother), which may refer to the Mother Church, but which may also carry a reference to an older Mother Goddess. Bride's epiphany, the oyster-catcher bird called 'the servant of Bride', can still be seen sometimes hovering over the place. Skye is truly an isle with many magical Goddess associations.

Skye is reached by road from the A87 *to the Kyle of* Lochalsh, *and then across the new road (toll) bridge to Kyleakin, or by train from* Inverness *to the Kyle and then across the bridge by shuttle bus. It can also be reached by ferry from* Glenelg Bay *to* Kylerhea *(summer service only) and by ferry from* Mallaig *to* Ardavasar/Armadale, *this link also serving the train from* Glasgow *and* Fort William.

On the island, the A850 *runs* W *to* Broadford, *to the* W *of which is the red granite mountain of* Ben-na-Cailleach. *From here, the* A881 *runs* SW *to* Kilbride *with its ruined church, well and stone, finally terminating at* Elgol. *Here boats may be hired to cross the sea loch of* Scavaig, *and then there is a narrow neck of land before you reach* Loch Corvisk *(the Cauldron of* Water*), which lies in the shadow of the* Cuillins. *In the* N *of the island,* 9.5*km* (6 *miles*) N *of* Potree *is the mountain called* The Storr. Drynoch *is on the* A863, *which runs up the* W *coast, and* Rudha nan Clack *is to the* W *of the road. From* Uig *on the* NW *of the peninsula, ferries may be taken to* Tarbert *on* Harris *and* Lochmaddy *on* North Uist.

Ballachulish (NN 080 570)

A rare wooden image of what may be an Earth Goddess was found in a peat deposit near Ballachulish. This is an oak figurine, which may date from as early as the seventh century BCE, with a striking facial expression, hag-like features, eyes inlaid with pebbles and clear sexual organs. Her hands point towards her pudenda in a manner reminiscent of many of the sheela-na-gig figurines, although millennia separate the two. She was found with traces of wickerwork, suggesting that she was originally kept in some kind of wicker shrine. It has been suggested[3] that she may have been an image of the ancient Earth-shaping Goddess, the Cailleach.

Ballachulish *is on the* W *coast of* Scotland, *about* 16*km* (10 *miles*) S *of* Fort William. *The figurine is in the* National Museum *of* Antiquities, *but is not currently on display. However, it is intended to put her on display when the new* Museum *of* Scotland *opens at the end of* 1998.

Cave of Raitts, Lynchat (NH 777 019)

This *souterrain*, which may be late Iron Age in origin, consists of a horseshoe-shaped cave 20m (65ft) long, 2.5m (8ft) wide and 2m (7ft) high, with the roof formed of large stone slabs. Its function is unknown: storage, refuge and ritual have all been suggested, but the legends associated with it refer to more ancient mythology. Built by giantesses, who dug out the cave and carried the earth down to the River Spey in their aprons, it is another variation of the Giantess' Apron motif – the earth-shaping Goddess of the land.

The souterrain lies 100m (110yd) to the N *of the new* A9 *at* Lynchat, *between* Kingussie *and* Aviemore *(both of which have railway stations).*

Inverness

The capital of the Highlands has two interesting hills in its locality. In the town there is Tomnahurich, the hill of the fairies (NH 656 442), a 66m (215ft) hill, where the fairy queen held court and the little people dwelt. The latter would do homage to 'Cynthia', who may be the memory of a Goddess figure. In addition, 13km (8 miles) to the SE of the city is the 562m (1,827ft) hill called Beinn nam Cailleach (NH 725 325), where the Old Hag has once again been carving out the land.

Inverness (which has a railway station) lies at the junction of the A9, A82 *and* A96 *roads. Tomnahurich hill is 1.5km (1 mile) to the* SW *of the city beside the* A82, *and is surmounted by a cemetery.* Beinn nan Cailleach *lies to the* S *of the* A9 *Inverness–Aviemore road.*

Aberdeenshire (formerly Grampian)

Aberdeenshire recumbent circles

Aberdeenshire has the greatest concentration of stone circles in Britain, and there are a couple of dozen or so still extant in various degrees of preservation. They are all recumbent circles: that is, part of the circle consists of a large stone lying sideways (the recumbent) flanked by two uprights. In one case after another, these have been shown to have been placed deliberately as a kind of window in order to view the key times of the moon's 18.6 year cycle, including the major southern moonrise and moonset and the minor southern moonset. Many of the stones also have significant use of white quartz and some have cup-marks or other artwork. The symbolism of all of this suggests that these places were used for ceremonies to celebrate the Goddess, and the Cailleach, whose name was corrupted to Fulziemont, is remembered as the old woman mountain of Wheedlemont at Rhynie, one of the earliest stone circle areas in Aberdeenshire.

The sites themselves are listed fully elsewhere[4], but some worth noting include Yonder Bognie Wardend (NJ 601 458), with its recumbent aligned to the smoothly rounded Colyne Hill at the major southern moonrise; Backhill of Drachlaw (NJ 673 464), its stones with veins of quartz, and an enormous Carlin stone nearby (NJ 674 465), the name another corruption of Cailleach; Loanhead of Daviot (NJ 747 288) with 12 cup-marks on one stone and a major southern moonset alignment; Easter Aquorthies (NJ 732 208), its recumbent flecked with white quartz aligned on the major southern moonset; and Sunhoney (NJ 716 058), with a lavishly cup-marked recumbent aligned on a saddle between two hills at the minor southern moonset. There are many other sites, including Midmar Kirk (NJ 699 064), built into a churchyard, and the beautiful elfin-like ring of North Strone (NJ 584 138), with major southern moonrise alignment. They all repay a visit, to get a sense of the sacredness of a megalithic landscape focused around the cycles of the moon.

Aberdeen is on the A92 on the NE coast of Scotland. The sites cover an area of some 50sq km (30sq miles) in the hinterland to the W and N of the city.

Western Isles

Isle of Lewis

Callanish stone circle (NB 213 330), sometimes called the Stonehenge of the North, is a magnificent site on the W side of Lewis overlooking Loch Roag. It consists of a circle of 13 tall stones and is 13m (42ft) across, with one off-centre stone and the remains of a small burial cairn. Radiating out from this circle are four 'arms', forming the shape of a Celtic cross. To the N there is a double avenue of stones 83m (90yd) long, with 19 stones still standing; to the E, W and S are single rows with four stones (15m/16yd long), four stones (12m/13yd long) and six stones (27.5m/30yd long) respectively. Nearby there are other small circles, such as Cnoc Ceann – Callanish II (NB 226 326) and Garynahine (NB 230 303), and other researchers[5] have brought the sites up to 19 in number, several of which incorporate alignments that record the horizon positions of moonrise and moonset at the standstills.

Most of the sites, including Callanish I, lie in an area in which the hills of Pairc in south-eastern Lewis and the hills of North Harris are particularly noticeable, and suitable for observation of the rising and setting moon at its southern extreme. The Pairc hills in particular form the profile of a sleeping woman, called in Gaelic Cailleach na Mòinteach (the Old Woman of the Moors), but known locally as the Sleeping Beauty or Sleeping Woman. At the major southern standstill of the moon (every 18.6 years), the moon appears to rise out of her legs, creep low along her body, silhouetting first one part then another, hang low over her breasts, and then disappear behind a nearby hillock, only to reappear inside the circle of stones at the foot of the tallest central one and at the head of the burial cairn[6]. This spectacular sight (last observed in 1987) is pure megalithic magic: a perfect blending of astronomy, ritual, landscape and Goddess.

There are also other ways of viewing the relationship between the ancient sites and the mountain: from the head of the Sleeping Beauty, the midsummer solstice sun rises out of the sea at North Tolsta over a volcanic boulder called the Black Rock, and then across a number of sacred sites to the Goddess mountain herself[7]; from Achmore stone circle (NB 321 291), the summer growth on the hills gives the Sleeping Beauty a ripe pregnant form at Lughnasad[8]; and from Callanish, the full moon sets into a V-shaped notch in the Harris hills at Glen Langadale (Clisham range) at the southern standstill[9]. There is also a legend that at the time of famine a white cow appeared at the site from the sea and told women to take milk pails to the circle, where they received a pailful each night. The bounteousness of the Earth Mother, the sea Goddess, the power of the moon, and the shape of the Earth Mother herself all link together at this place in a great celestial harmony.

The NW of the island has a fascinating example of the continuity of tradition into modern times. At Melbost Borve there is a well (NB 411 573) which, although supposedly built in the 1920s, is dedicated to Bridgit. Her presence here on a Protestant island may be a memory of an old legend of the Calleach transformed into the Goddess of spring. The Old Hag of the hills retired to a miraculous well, and at the first glimmer of dawn she drank from the waters and emerged as a beautiful new Goddess, whose magic turned the grass green and brought out the summer flowers[10]. She is commemorated nearby at Rubha na Caillich, and Bridget can be found nearby at Teampull Brighde, an early Christian foundation that may have been built on an earlier Goddess site.

Lewis is reached by ferry from Ullapool to Stornaway, and by air from Glasgow and Inverness. Callanish stone circle and Visitor Centre (tel: 01851–621422) is 25km (16 miles) to the W of Stornaway, standing on a plateau off the A858. Tobar Brighde (St Bridget's Well) is in a field at the W end of Melbost Borve, which lies to the W of the A857 Butt of Lewis road.

South Harris

The hill of West Stocklett (NG 104 950) lies beside an ancient funeral path running across the island of South Harris, from Ardvey in the E to the old graveyard at Seilebost in the W. Within historical times the dead were carried along this path, and there are flat stones along the route where the coffins were rested. This funeral path may be on a much more ancient route used as a pathway by the Neolithic people, who formerly occupied the W side of the island. The hill itself is in the shape of a sleeping or dead Hag, and is thus described by Jill Smith: 'She is amazing – grey hair

streams from her head, which has a sharply delineated nose, sunken mouth and chin and a dark shadowy eye. Her scraggy neck sinks down and her bony rib cage and old woman's breast and nipple rise up; her belly is sunken and her lower part seemingly covered in a skirt or garment'[11]. This hag-shaped hill, known as Hag Mountain, was probably another representation of the Earth Goddess Cailleach to the Neolithic peoples, who constructed a sacred path to run alongside her.
Harris is reached by the A859 S *from* Lewis, *or by ferry to* Tarbert *from* Uig *on* Skye *and* Lochmaddy *on* North Uist. *Ardvey lies at the head of the sea loch* Stockinish, *about* 3*km* (2 *miles*) S *of the* A859 *and* 13*km* (8 *miles*) S *of* Tarbert. *From here the funeral path runs across the island, and the hill of* West Stocklett *lies about halfway along to the* E *of the track. The full walk takes about two hours in either direction.*

Sheela-na-gig
St Clement's Church, on the SE tip of South Harris, has a sheela set into the tower in the centre of one wall. She is seated, with a child or animal held above her knee.

North Uist

Moving S from Harris, the next island is North Uist, which has many lochs and inlets, and dedications to two Goddesses, one Gaelic and one Norse. On the slopes of Beinn a'Charra hill, a Norse Goddess is commemorated in the name of a 2.7m (9ft) high standing stone called Clach Bharnach Bharaodag (NF 787 691), which means 'the limpet stone of Freya'. The Gaelic/Celtic Goddess can be found on an islet called Vallay off the NW coast, where there are some Bronze Age standing stones called Leac nan Cailleacha Dubha (NF 785 763), which means 'the stones of the old black crone'. Local legend attributes them to two witches accused of stealing milk, who were buried up to their necks and then trampled to death by cattle. It has been suggested[12] that this violent story hides a mytho-religious content, in which we may see a reversal of the former practice of a rite of the Goddess (the giving of milk) twisted under Christianity/patriarchy into a horrendous punishment for the pagan 'witches'.

The 'black' element may come from the racism of the Christian church, equating 'black' with 'evil', because many of the early Goddesses who came from the East and Africa were black: indeed, there is still an unofficial cult of the Black Madonna in many churches in Europe today. Alternatively, it may be a reference to the Cailleach as Goddess of winter and long nights. Either way, there are more examples from other places in the Western Isles: on Boreray there is a cairn enclosing a long cist, from which project three stones in a line called Cailleacha Dubha (NF 857 816), and on Lewis there was formerly a building known as Tigh nan Cailleachan Dubh (House of the Old Black Crone), which appears to have been a Benedictine convent! On Vallay, with its old black crone standing

stones, no less than three chapels were built as well. The old religion and the Goddess were obviously still felt to be very powerful in these islands.
North Uist is reached by ferry from Uig on Skye and from Tarbert on South Harris to Lochmaddy. From Lochmaddy, take the A865 anti-clockwise along the N coast of the island. Vallay is reached by a ford across the sands from Botarua. Boreray is an uninhabited island to the NE of Vallay, with no regular access. From Botarua, an unmetalled road (the Committee Road) runs S to rejoin the A865 at Ardheisker. About halfway along this road is a track leading up the hill to the Freya standing stone.

South Uist

At the S tip of the island is Pollachar, the Bay of the Standing Stone, and a Bronze Age standing stone can be found here overlooking the Sound to Eriskay and Barra (see below). Interestingly, the settlement here is called Kilbride after the Goddess/saint – a direct example of the continuity of a religious site. In the E of the island is the mountain of Beinn Mhor (620m/2,034ft, NF 810 310). This is the dwelling place of the Loireag, a woman not of this world, who is said to supervise the working of the cloth and every process associated with it. She sounds like a tutelary Goddess of the land, who brought the tradition of weaving to the women (see also Barra, below). In the N of the island there is a 38m (124ft) high statue on the slope of Reuval, 'the Hill of Miracles' (NF 777 407), dedicated to the 'Lady of the Isles'. She may now be the Christianized figure of Mary, but she is only really a modern-day version of the ancient Goddess of the Isles of the Hebrides, Domnu, who came from Ireland and whose lands were Domon and Erdomon, the Outer and Inner Hebrides. The veneer of Christianity lies very thin in these islands[13].
South Uist is reached by ferry from Oban to Lochboisdale, or by the A865 running S from North Uist and Benbecula. Pollachar and Kilbride are at the S end of the A865/B888. Beinn Mhor lies to the E of the A865 at Loch Ollay. Reuval statue is reached by a track to the E of the A865, S of West Geirnish.

Barra

The islands of Barra and Vatersay are the most southerly inhabited islands of the Outer Hebrides. Barra, which is only about 48sq km (30sq miles) in area, has many associations with the Sidhe (pronounced 'Shee'), the other-worldly fairy folk of the Highlands and Islands[14]. On Barra, the gifts of the Sidhe to the people were most often those of music, smithcraft or spinning, which links them strongly to the Goddess Bridget, who is matron of, or linked with, these crafts. As late as the sixteenth century, a songwriter of the Hebrides, Mari Nic Iain Fhin, was reputed to have received her gift from a fairy lover. At Sgalary on the E side of Barra is a well (NL 698 994) frequented by a Sidhe woman dressed in green; she gave a set of pipes to a young man, who became master of his craft. And at Dun

Borve on the W side of the island (NL 677 012) there is a dwelling where the Sidhe women gave aid to the women of the island with their spinning. From hollow hills, like Creag Goraich in the N of the island, the sound of Sidhe music could be heard, which was a good omen for whatever task was being undertaken. The Sidhe came from the other world, and would once have represented aspects of the Goddess herself.

Barra is reached by ferry from Oban to Castlebay, and by passenger ferry from Ludag on South Uist to Eoligarry on Barra. One road, the A888, makes a 22km (14 mile) circuit of the island, and at North Bay a track goes N past the mountain of Heavel, which has a marble statue of the 'Lady Star of the Sea' on its S flank.

St Kilda

St Kilda is a group of small islands 48km (40 miles) to the NW of Barra. The main island, Hirta, was occupied until 1930, when the inhabitants were evacuated at their own request. Old legends tell of an Amazonian woman walking across the sea from the W to the islands with her greyhounds on a leash. Her home was the Amazon Woman's House, a beehive hut structure in Gleann Mor, in the remote NW part of Hirta (NA 085 000). It was also said that her form could be seen in the land, visible from the island of Soay, off the NW tip of Hirta[15]. She was clearly an ancient and powerful sea and Earth Goddess of these islands, perhaps a tutelary aspect of Artemis/Diana, the huntress.

St Kilda is owned by the National Trust and permission is required to visit. There are occasional organized trips: contact the Western Isles Tourist Information Centre (tel: 01851–703088).

Orkney and Shetland

Britain's most northerly groups of islands have a wealth of prehistoric sites, but do not seem to have the same degree of legendary material relating to a primal Earth Goddess as we have seen on other Scottish islands. It has been suggested[16] that the orientations of the tombs, as well as some of the inscriptions and carvings, can be compared with other identified Goddess sites, such as Malta. The holm of Papa Westray south chambered cairn, lying just off the Orkney island of Papa Westray (HT 509 518), has stones carved with dots, arcs, lozenges and zigzags, similar to those found in Irish chambered tombs. Similar motifs have been found at other ancient sites. However, little Goddess material seems to have entered the folklore, probably because of the Norse influence. By the time the Vikings arrived in the tenth and eleventh centuries, they had all but eliminated the Goddess from their pantheon, and any earlier Goddess associations seem to have been eliminated as well.

For the rest, there are beautiful stone circles on Orkney (the Ring of Brodgar (HT 294 133)and Stones of Stenness (HY 306 125), with Viking legends of the full moon and betrothals through the holed stone of Odin, chambered cairns as ceremonial places for the dead, and a tomb (Maes Howe) with a midwinter solstice sunset alignment, which is the mirror-image (HY 318 127) of Newgrange in Ireland (see page 189). There is one other curiosity: a stone circle on Fetlar island in Shetland (HU 622 923) has a legend of a group of trolls or maidens turned to stone for dancing on the Sabbath – a legend that takes us right back to the Merry Maidens in Cornwall (see page 83), some 1,000 or so miles away to the S. Perhaps the priestesses of the Goddess were there after all thousands of years ago.

Orkney is reached by ferry from Scrabster near Thurso to Stronmess; Shetland by ferry from Kirkwall in Orkney to Scalloway, or from Aberdeen to Lerwick. Both Orkney and Shetland are also accessible by air from Glasgow, Inverness, Aberdeen and Edinburgh. Fetlar is reached by ferry or air from Tingwall on mainland Shetland.

Notes

Lowlands and Inner Hebrides

[1] See Anne Ross, *Pagan Celtic Britain*, page 47.

[2] See Helen McSkimming, 'Arran – Isle of Apple Trees', *Dalriada*, vol 7/4, pages 21–5.

[3] See John Edwin Wood, *Sun, Moon and Standing Stones*, pages 84–97.

[4] See Helen McSkimming, 'Islay the Green Isle', *Dalriada*, vol 8/3, pages 14–23.

[5] See John Billingsley, 'A Sacred Landscape at Loch Finlaggan', *Northern Earth*, no 62, pages 18–21, and Bob Trubshaw, 'Loch Finlaggan', *Mercian Mysteries*, no 23, pages 14–16.

[6] See Ruggles, Martlew and Hingle, 'The North Mull Project 1–4', *Archaeoastronomy*, vol 14, pages s137–149; vol 16, pages s51–575; vol 17, pages s1–13; and vol 18, pages s55–64.

[7] See Helen McSkimming, 'Mull', *Dalriada*, vol 8/2, pages 24–9.

[8] See Helen McSkimming, 'Iona, the Sacred Isle', *Dalriada*, vol 2/7, pages 3–5.

[9] In *The Folklore of the Scottish Highlands*, pages 100–1.

[10] First discovered by Anne Ross and revealed in a lecture at *The Ley Hunter* Moot, 1991. Subsequently written up by David Clarke as 'The Hag's House', *The Ley Hunter*, no 120, pages 1–4.

[11] David Clarke, *A Guide to Britain's Pagan Heritage*, pages 145–8.

Highlands and Western Isles

[1] See Helen McSkimming, 'Skye the Winged Isle', *Dalriada*, vol 7/3, pages 8–14.

[2] See Otta F. Swire, *Skye – the Island and its Legends*, pages 20–3.

[3] By Anne Ross in *Pagan Celtic Britain*, page 297.

[4] By Aubrey Burl in *A Guide to the Stone Circles of Britain, Ireland and Brittany*, pages 92–111 and 135–140.

[5] See Gerald and Margaret Ponting, *The Stones Around Callanish* and *New Light on the Stones of Callanish*.
[6] See Margaret Ponting and Ron Curtis, 'Moon Watching at Callanish 1987', *The Ley Hunter Moonwatch Supplement*, 1988, pages 17–19.
[7] See John Sharkey, *The Road Through the Isles*, pages 175–6.
[8] See Jill Smith, 'Turning the Circles', *Dalriada*, vol 10/2, pages 10–13.
[9] See Margaret Ponting and Ron Curtis, op cit.
[10] See John Sharkey, op cit, page 176.
[11] From 'The Hag Mountain Funeral Path on South Harris', *The Ley Hunter*, no 123, pages 9–10.
[12] By John Sharkey, op cit, page 143.
[13] See Helen McSkimming, 'South Uist – Isle of the Bent Grass', *Dalriada*, vol 8/4, page 2.
[14] See Helen McSkimming, 'Barra', *Dalriada*, vol 8/1, pages 11–15.
[15] See John Sharkey, op cit, page 157.
[16] By Cristina Biaggi in *Habitations of the Great Goddess*.

Ireland

IRELAND IS TREATED HERE AS A WHOLE, irrespective of present-day political divisions into Northern Ireland and the Republic of Ireland. It is divided into the historic four provinces: Leinster (SE), Munster (SW), Ulster (NE) and Connacht (NW). Sites are listed by county in the Province. It should be noted therefore that Ulster includes not only the six counties of Northern Ireland but also Donegal, Cavan and Monaghan, which constitute the historic Ulster Province.

Leinster

County Meath

Newgrange (O 007 727)

The greatest megalithic tomb in Ireland, probably in the whole of Britain and Ireland, Newgrange is famous the world over. Its name in Gaelic is Brú na Bóinne, meaning 'the home of the Goddess of the River Boann', and it was built on the highest part of a ridge overlooking a bend in the river Boyne, which was named after the Goddess Boand. Her name may mean 'she of the white cows', which makes her a tutelary nurturing Earth Goddess. It has been said of her that she was 'the Primary Goddess of ancient Ireland, the personification of the mystical sprirituality within Life, symbolized in the sacred river, from which everything is derived'[1]. Together with her consort Elemar, she was the first legendary inhabitant of the mound of Newgrange. He was supplanted by the Dagda, the father-God of ancient Ireland, who by means of trickery seduced Boand – who conceived and gave birth to their son Aongas on the same day. The myth may encode early memory of the takeover of Goddess sites by the patriarchal sky God religion.

Newgrange itself is a huge chambered mound, 92m (300ft) in diameter, and 13.5m (44ft) high. Some 180,000 tonnes of stone were required to build it, and its top was originally covered by a coat of shining white quartz pebbles. It is surrounded by 12 standing stones (out of a possible 36 originally), including one recumbent one in front of the entrance that is covered in spiral patterns, and a ring of kerbstones, including one on the opposite side (no 52) that is covered in spiral, lozenge and interlocked horseshoe patterns, which have been interpreted[2] as symbols of the generative vulva of the Goddess. It has also been suggested recently[3] that they may represent entropic images generated by shamans and shamankas in trance states at the site.

These two stones align with the entrance passage of the tomb, above which is a lintel (roof box) that allows the rising sun to enter only on the days of the midwinter solstice – a ritual of rebirth and regeneration for the dead. The entrance shaft of light is projected into the end recess, where reflected light from the floor illuminates a distinctive triple spiral carving on a stone to the right of the recess. Today the shaft of light shines into the entrance of the recess only, but at the time the tomb was built the sun rose about one degree further S and would have shone right into the back of the recess chamber at the moment of sunrise. This would have been a dramatic enactment of the fusion of sun alignment and spiral carving in a language of the Goddess, that can still speak directly to us 7,000 years after the tomb was built.

Recently, it has also been suggested[4] that a legend of chequered lights at the mound refers to an even more elaborate phenomenon at the site. This theory postulates that the mound was constructed around an intricate mechanism to allow the suspension of a burnished gold mirror, which would reflect the downward beam of light from the roof box and direct it back along the passage and out into the valley below to illuminate the River Boyne – the Goddess herself. In this manner, the old legend of the union between the river Goddess and the Dagda who lived in the mound would take on a physical and quite literal representation. The theory sounds far fetched, but a 1/25th scale model of the site has been built and has shown it to be possible. However, it is equally possible that rituals were enacted which involved the participants moving from the mound out over the land, carrying flaming torches down to the River Goddess herself to pay homage to her. Whatever the precise nature of the rituals of Newgrange, it is certainly a dramatic and powerful Goddess site.

Newgrange and the Boyne Valley lie to the S *of the* N51 *Drogheda–Navan road, about* 10*km (*6 *miles)* W *of Drogheda. There is an admission charge to the site (tel:* 041–24488*), which includes a guide who demonstrates the winter solstice alignment from inside the tomb.*

Dowth and Knowth (O 022 738 and N 990 730)

Close to the famous site at Newgrange (see above) are two sacred mounds in the Boyne Valley. Dowth, 3km (2 miles) to the NE, is 86m (280ft) in diameter and 15.5m (50ft) high. It is closed at present and scheduled for long-term excavation, but we know that it is aligned on the midwinter solstice sunset, making it a 'synchronized counterpart of Newgrange'[5]. Its Gaelic name is Dubad, which appropriately means 'darkness'. A second passage aligns on the cross-quarter days of 8 November (old Samhain) and 4 February (old Imbolc), and there is artwork of triangles, lozenges and meanders at the site.

The mound at Knowth (Cnogba) has the same dimensions as that at Dowth. It is currently undergoing excavation and reconstruction, so once again the interior is not accessible, but we do know that its passages are aligned E–W to the spring and autumn equinoxes. A large number of kerbstones are engraved with meanders and possible lunar cycles (eg no 5), and finds here have included two 'maceheads', one of which has an anthropomorphic head with a wide-open mouth and spiral eyes that has been interpreted[6] as a stylized rendering of the head of the tomb Goddess, the Goddess of death and regeneration. There are other satellite tombs and standing stones, and the whole area was obviously a ritual landscape focused around the sacred Goddess-river Boann/Boyne.

Knowth is reached by a turning just S *of the* N51 *that leads to* Newgrange. *The mound, together with its* 17 *satellite tombs, is open for guided tours* (*tel*: 041–24824). *At present, Dowth is closed and fenced off.*

LOUGHCREW (N 586 775)

Much less well known than the Boyne Valley complex (see above), Loughcrew, some 32km (20 miles) to the W, is a still partially functioning solar calendar centred on a hill named after a Goddess – Slieva na Calliagh, the Hill of the Cailleach. This 280m (910ft) hill is covered with 20 or so cairns and chambered tombs, which were supposed to have been dropped from the Old Hag's apron. The principal tomb, Cairn T, has a stone set on its side where she sat and surveyed the view, with a panorama extending over 18 counties. This Goddess of the land has an amazing ritual landscape calendar of cairns following the wheel of the year. She is the hub of the wheel, and its spokes are the entrances to the many chambered cairns on two hills: Carnbane East and West. Carnbane means 'the white cairn' and may be a reference to the original covering of the tombs with white quartz, similar to the one at Newgrange.

Here at Loughcrew there is a wealth of artwork that has been interpreted as sun symbols[7] and/or cunnic female symbols[8]. On Carnbane East, the spectacular Cairn T is aligned to the spring/autumn equinox sunrise, when the sun enters the chamber and illuminates the back stone, which is covered with an array of symbols. The light moves slowly across the stone, illuminating one symbol after another in a dazzling display of rosy golden light, until it narrows, focuses on a specific sun/Goddess symbol and then disappears. The alignment, with its symbolism, takes into account the four-year cycle of the sun at the equinox (there being 365¼ days in each year).

Other cairns have other alignments. Cairn L on Carnbane West, which is similarly decorated with carvings, is aligned on the 8 November (old Samhain) and 8 February (old Imbolc) dates to receive the rays of the ris-

ing sun, which enter and touch a white standing stone inside. From the entrance of this cairn and surrounding ones, the hill of Carnbane East is outlined, with Cairn T looking unmistakeably like a nipple on the breast of the Mother Goddess – a sight that was presumably intended by the megalithic builders. Some of the cairns (eg Cairns F, H and I on Carnbane West) act as solar 'predictors', being aligned to the rising sun on the days leading up to the festivals, and some (eg Cairns S and U on Carnbane East) focus on the setting sun on the cross-quarter days[9]. The whole complex is a fascinating and spell-binding ritual Goddess landscape.
Loughcrew lies 5*km* (3 *miles*) SE *of Oldcastle and* 16*km* (10 *miles*) W *of Kells, on the* N3. *There is free access to the site, although* Cairn T *is normally locked and a key must be obtained from a house at the base of the hill* (*tel*: 049–41256).

Tara (N 920 597)

The hill of Tara is probably the most sacred hilltop in Ireland. It has been suggested[10] that Tara ('Teamair' in Gaelic) was named after the proto-tutelary Goddess *Tea, whom legend tells us came to Ireland from the East and married an Irish king. The site was occupied in prehistoric times, and has the remains of burial chambers, passage graves and ritual earthworks, which have yielded rich remains including two gold torques, bronze daggers and a necklace of copper, jet, amber and faience beads. However, it was in the first century CE that Tara became the seat of the High Kings of Ireland, and a 1.5m (5ft) high granite stone here, the Stone of Destiny (Lia Fail) is said to have been a royal inauguration stone, originally brought to the site by Tea. On this hill, the kings of Ireland were required to mate symbolically with the Goddess of the land, or sovereignty, during the ritual banquet (*feis temrach*) at their coronation. The site of the so-called Banqueting Hall (Teach Miodchuarta) still remains as an avenue of parallel earthworks, and may have been a ritual entrance to the whole site along which the living and the dead were borne.

The Goddess of death and fertility celebrated here was Mebd/Maeve, the Goddess/queen of Connacht, and a divine female who was both ruler-Goddess and battle-queen[11]. She mated with nine kings, and no man could rule at the royal court unless he slept with her, thus validating his kingship. Her choice of consort determined the kingship of all Connacht and Ulster in the N of Ireland. Other supernatural beings – Goddess archetypes – associated in the legends with Tara are Etáin, who was imprisoned at her husband's court with her lover Midhir, but escaped by their shape-shifting into swans and flying away; and Gráinne, who, with her lover Diarmud, eloped on her wedding day and gave her name to an earthwork on the hill, Rath Grainne.

Tara has a long continuity as a ceremonial site from the Bronze Age into the Christian era, and hovering over it all are the shadows of the Goddesses Tea and Mebd/Maeve. About 1.5km (1 mile) S of Tara is Rath

Maeve, a hill fort contemporary with Tara and also named after the Goddess.

Tara is reached from a minor road W *of the* N3, *38km (23 miles)* NW *of Dublin and 9.5km (6 miles)* SE *of Navan. There is a Visitor Centre and an admission charge (tel: 046–25903).*

Teltown/Taillten (N 801 741)

Tailtu, the harvest Goddess and foster-mother of Lugh, the God of light, gave her name to this most celebrated place, where she cleared the forests and then died from her labour[12]. She represents the sacrifice of Mother Earth and her death is a metaphor for the coming of agriculture and the pastoral cycle, enacted in the festival of Lughnasad, the 'festival of the first fruits'. Lughnasad was supposedly inaugurated in her honour by her foster-son Lugh, and here at Teltown the Great Games of Ireland were held on 1 August into medieval times, and then as a rural festival right up until the eighteenth century. Pagan marriages lasting a year and a day could also be made nearby at Cnocán a'Chrainn (the Hillock of the Tree). The precise location of Tailtu's festival is a matter of speculation, but it may have been the Rath Dubh, a raised circular earth rampart about 100m (325ft) in diameter, which still exists on the Hill of Tailtu near a bend in the river.

Teltown lies 2.5km (1½ miles) to the NW *of Donaghpatrick, which is to the* N *of the* N3, *about 6.5km (4 miles)* SW *of Kells and 9.5km (6 miles)* NW *of Navan. The Rath Dubh lies to the* S *of a minor road from Donaghpatrick to Oristown (on the* R163), *to the* N *of the River Blackwater that runs beside the* N3.

Hill of Ward (N 737 637)

This hilltop fort, comprising a central enclosure surrounded by four pairs of banks and ditches, was named after the Goddess Tlachtga, about whom few details are known, but who is believed to be buried under the hill. It was an important site, especially at the festival of Samhain Eve, when fires were lit and rituals performed.

The Hill of Ward is situated 1.5km (1 mile) W *of Athboy and 13km (8 miles)* W *of Navan, to the* S *of the* N51.

County Westmeath

Hill of Uisnech (N 290 490)

This hill marks the mythical centre of Ireland, where the Goddess of all Ireland, Ériu, had her seat. A large limestone rock on the W side of the hill was known in ancient times as Ail Na Mireann, meaning 'the stone of divisions', which marked the point of the meeting of all Ireland's ancient

Provinces – the 'navel of Ireland' itself. Here Ériu, who was a Goddess, a Giantess and a magician, held sway. Sometimes she appeared as a beautiful woman, and sometimes she shape-shifted into a crow. Here the invading Milesians had to negotiate a truce with her before they could occupy the land. She was the primal Goddess of the land and of sovereignty in Ireland.

King Tuathal built a fortress-palace here in the second century, and a yearly meeting of all the chiefs in Ireland took place on the feast of Beltane. These pagan rites with bonfires and feasts continued well into historical times. 'Through them the Goddess reoccupied and saw her whole land, and by the embers, promised to return next day with an entire summer's sunshine'[13].

Many of Ireland's sacred sites are joined together in solar alignments that run through Uisnech. For example, the midsummer solstice sun rises over Slieve Gullion in Ulster and Sleive na Cailliighe at Loughcrew (with which it is inter-visible), and sets over Rathcroghan in Connacht (see pages 198, 191 and 201). Also, Emain Macha in Ulster, Uisnech, and Cnoc Aine in Munster (see pages 197 and 204) are all in a direct line, linking together the great Goddesses of Ireland: Macha, Eriu and Aine.

The Hill of Uisnech lies 16km (10 miles) SW *of Mullingar, to the* N *of the* R390 *and near the village of* Killare. *Twenty Irish counties may be seen from its 212m (690ft) summit.*

County Louth

Faughart (J 072 118)

Supposedly the birthplace of St Bridget in the fifth century, an old church can be seen here on the site of an ancient monastery she is believed to have founded. The indications are that this is a Christianization of an earlier pagan site dedicated to the Goddess Bride[14]. On the hill above the town there are prehistoric stone tombs, and the shrine set up to St Bridget attracted annual pilgrimages in February and July, close to the dates of the pagan Imbolc and Lughnasad festivals. There are legends about the saint in the area, including one of St Bridget's cow that was milked by a poor woman. The cow then took her calf down Carlingford Lough and out to sea, where two rocks bear their names to this day. Another legend tells how St Bridget was pursued by a determined suitor on horseback, a story parallel to that of St Milburgha in Shropshire (see page 133).

At this spot at Faughart, Bridget plucked out her eyes to avoid being recognized, and the stream is still part of the holy round performed here in her honour. Offerings to her healing powers can sometimes be found on nearby bushes, and there is also a holy well dedicated to her. The whole area is redolent with a feeling of the continuity of Goddess ritual and spiritual observance.

Faughart is 3km (2 miles) NE *of Dundalk (which has a railway station), on the* N1. *At Ballymascanlan, 1.5km (1 mile) to the* E *on the* R173, *is the Proleek Dolmen, comprising a 40 tonne capstone on three upright stones.*

County Kildare

Kildare (N 729 124)

This is the renowned centre of the Goddess/saint Bride/Bridget. Its Gaelic name, Cill Dare (Church of the Oak), is an indication of its pre-Christian origins, and it is here, in the grounds of what is now the Church of Ireland Cathedral, that St Bridget's fire was tended by 19 holy women, a continuation of an earlier celebration of the Goddess. Each woman took her turn to guard the fire at night and keep the flames going, and on the nineteenth night the abbess (previously priestess) would tend the fire and incant: 'Brigid, guard your fire. This is your night'. No man was allowed to enter the area, which was surrounded by a hedge[15] – a sacred place of the Goddess, who was so powerful she could only be turned directly into a saint of the same name. The sacred fire lasted right up until the sixteenth-century dissolution of the monastries.

As well as the foundations of Bridget's 'fire temple' in the churchyard, the cathedral hides another secret. On the sixteenth-century tomb of Bishop Wellesley, set below the left-hand corner of the top slab and neatly juxtaposed above a crucifixion panel, is a sheela-na-gig! She has her legs parted and her pubic hair showing. Although sixteen centuries separate her from the pagan Bride shrine here, her presence is an ironic reminder of the power of this all-female, Goddess-celebrating place.

Kildare is on the N7 *Dublin–Limerick road, and St Bridget's Cathedral is in the centre of the town. The foundations of St Bridget's fire temple, which were restored in* 1988, *are in the churchyard. Bishop Wellesley's tomb is in the cathedral. Lying* 1.5*km* (1 *mile*) *to the* S *of the town, near Tully House, are the ruins of Tully Church and a holy well dedicated to St Bridget.*

Carbury (N 687 340)

Another legend of the Goddess Boann (see Newgrange, page 189) links her to this town, where her husband, King Nechtan, had in his garden a very special well that no woman was allowed to approach. Boann ignored this, and not only went to the well but walked around it three times widdershins (anti-clockwise) – a pagan ritual challenge to the law of patriarchy. Nechtan's well rose up in horror and chased her off, so she became the River Boyne and was swept out to sea[16]. She was probably a very ancient eponymous Goddess, whose very existence proved so strong that it was encoded in the myth of Nechtan's well.

Carbury is on the R402, *7km (4¼ miles)* E *of* Edenderry, *overlooking the central plain of the* Boyne *valley. The well is now lost, but the source of the sacred river lies nearby at* Edenderry.

DUN AILLINNE (N 820 078)

This Iron Age ring fort crowns Knockaulin Hill (180m/585ft), which excavation has shown to be a ritual and ceremonial site going back to the Neolithic period. It was also the royal seat of the kings of Leinster, and there are traces of ancient roadways leading to it on the hillside. As with so many of these holy hilltops in Ireland, the site was named after a Goddess, the shadowy Almha/Almu (pronounced 'Alva'), one of the Tuatha de Danaan. She continued to be acknowledged into the Middle Ages as a 'beautiful woman'.
Dun Aillinne lies 0.75*km (½ mile) to the* W *of* Kilcullen, *on the* N9 *Naas–Carlow road.*

Sheela-na-gigs
County Dublin Several sheelas are in the National Museum in Dublin, but not all are on display. They include sheelas that came from Drynam (County Dublin), Carne Castle (County Westmeath), Birr (County Offaly), Sier Kieran Church (County Offaly), Ballylarkin Church (County Kilkenny), Cavan Church (County Cavan), Lavey Church (County Cavan), Ratoo Round Tower, Ballyduff (copy only – original missing; County Kerry), Lixnaw Castle (County Kerry), Burgesbeg churchyard (County Tipperary), Clonmel (County Tipperary) and Newtown Lennan (County Tipperary). Other sheelas in County Dublin are at Malahide Abbey and Stepaside, where a stunted cross has a pagan fertility figure cut in high relief, her hands pointing towards her hidden pudenda.
County Meath At Dowth Old Church; Rosnaree, built into a wall by an old watermill on the banks of the River Boyne; and Drogheda Museum, from a house in the town.
County Longford At Abbeylara, inside the wall of the Cistercian tower – it is badly weathered.
County Westmeath At Athlone in the Castle Museum, from the Convent of St Peter's Port; Moate Castle yard; and Taghmon Church.
County Offaly At Clonmacnois monastery, in the Nun's Chapel on the River Shannon (named after the Goddess Sinaan) – it was here that the Viking King Turgesius' wife pronounced pagan oracles from the high altar! Also at Doon Castle, in the S angle of the E wall.
County Kildare At Blackhall Castle, which is near Dun Aillinne, and in Kildare Cathedral.
County Laois At Cullahull Castle, high up on the S wall of the peel tower.
County Kilkenny At Toomregon outside the Protestant church, originally from a nearby monastery.

Ulster

County Armagh (Northern Ireland)

Navan (H 847 452)

The site of Navan hill fort is part of the ritual landscape that includes Haughey's Fort, a neighbouring hilltop site, the Bronze and Iron Age sacrificial pools, the King's Stables (findings of deer antlers and a human skull made into a mask) and Lough na Shade (offerings of a bronze trumpet, horns and skulls). The whole area has a long continuity of use from the Neolithic period, through the Bronze and Iron Ages, and into the early Christian period. Excavations at Navan hill fort have revealed an Iron Age ritual temple-like structure, with a huge central 'totem pole', the whole covered with a cairn 3m (10ft) high and 38.5m (125ft) in diameter. This perhaps functioned as an other-world sanctuary, the home and burial place of the tutelary Goddess of the site.

Navan was the legendary ancient capital of Ulster and the hill-fort palace of Ulster's Gaelic kings, who traced their lineage from Macha. The site is known as Emain Macha in Gaelic, meaning roughly 'twins of Macha', referring to the legend of Macha, a divine bride, who was forced to run a race against the king's best horses even though she was pregnant. She appealed to the king and all his men in the court, but was ignored. She won the race, but the effort killed her just after she had given birth to twins. As she died, she cursed the Ulstermen, which caused them to become weak and helpless for five days and four nights at a time, a period that may relate to the dark side of the moon. Macha is a complex, many-layered entity, embodying concepts of war, rulership and fecundity[1]. As one of the triple Goddesses of the Morrigan, she both controls the fates of men in war (and harvests human heads), and functions as a sovereignty Goddess of the land (her name means 'field' or 'plain'). Legend also tells how she was challenged by the five sons of Dithorba over her right as a woman to rule, so she enslaved them and forced them to build Emain Macha, before she was later defeated. These myths seem to be symbolic renderings of an ancient matriarchal religion in Ireland and its subsequent overthrow by the patriarchy.

Navan/Emain Macha is to the N *of the* A28, *about* 3*km* (2 *miles*) W *of the city of* Armagh. *There is an admission charge, and an impressive* Visitor Centre *with interpretive displays* (*tel*: 01861–525550).

Armagh (H 872 454)

The city was named Ard Mhacha in Gaelic, which means 'Macha's height', because of the association of Macha with Navan fort nearby (see above). In the Protestant cathedral there is a female figure carved with rounded

breasts and a bow lifted behind her head. She may be a depiction of the great warrior-Goddess Macha herself, although it has also been suggested[2] that she may be a counterpart of a harvest Goddess of plenty carrying sheaf and sickle.
Armagh is at the junction of A28, A29 and A3 roads. St Patrick's Protestant Cathedral is in the city centre, between Vicars Hill and Castle Street (off Market Square).

Slieve Gullion (J 025 203)

At 583m (1,893ft), this is the highest mountain in Armagh, and on the summit, with its spectacular views, is the prehistoric passage-tomb of the Celtic hag-Goddess Calliagh Birra's House. It has been suggested[3] that the chambers of the cairn were deliberately shaped to evoke the Goddess as hag. The cairn is nearly 30m (98ft) in diameter, with its SW entrance aligned to the midwinter solstice sunset, and facing the passage tomb complex at Loughcrew (see page 191), 60km (37 miles) away, both ritual sites linked by the Goddess Cailleach. There are a series of alignments running from Slieve Gullion to other ancient sites in County Armagh, and it seems that we have here another sacred hilltop of the Goddess. A nearby lake, to the N along the mountaintop of Slieve Gullion, is known as Calliagh Birra's Lough and is reputed to be bottomless, and she herself is said to live in a deep chamber at the bottom of the mountain. At the base of the hill, 0.4km (¼ mile) to the SE is a rocky hillock, on top of which is Cailleach Bearea's chair, where local people used to sit as part of a ceremonial visit, recalling her chair on Loughcrew hill[4] (see page 46). This is a site intimately linked to the Earth-creating Goddess of the land.
Slieve Gullion is a prominent mountain to the SW of Newry, reached from S of the A25 or W of the A1. From the B113, a drive leads through the thickly wooded mountain park, followed by a track to the summit. It is open from Easter to the end of September (tel: 013967–71144 or 01693–848084).

County Tyrone (Northern Ireland)

Knockmany (H 547 559)

This is another holy hilltop, the summit of which is crowned by another prehistoric grave, known as Annia's Cove. It is a small, passageless tomb, but is worth visiting for its decorated stones, three of which are covered with spirals, cup-marks, serpents, concentric circles and other motifs. The name may derive from either the Goddess Aine or from Anu, guardian of the dead[5], and it has been suggested[6] that the elaborate symbols on some of the stones may denote the Neolithic eye-Goddess.
Knockmany lies 3km (2 miles) to the NW of Augher through Knockmany Forest, and is approached by a track leading from the carpark. The tomb is locked, but admission

can be gained (before 4pm on weekdays) by contacting the Environment and Heritage Service *in Belfast in advance (tel:* 01232–235000).

County Donegal (Irish Republic)

Grianan Ailigh (C 366 198)

The third of the major holy hilltop sites in the historic province of Ulster is named after Grianne, the ancient sun Goddess of Ireland. It has been suggested[7] that she was the twin of the Goddess Aine (see Cnoc Aine, page 204), who represented the summer sun, while Grianne represented the winter sun. This is given some credence by Grianan Ailigh's position in the far N of Ireland, while Cnoc Aine lies to the S. On the top of the mountain is a reconstructed Iron Age *cashel* (stone-walled fort) known as the Sun Palace and held sacred right through into the Christian era.
The Grianan of Ailigh is on a 244m (793ft) hill at Carrowreagh, 8km (5 miles) W *of (London) Derry. It is accessed from a minor road running* S *of the* N13/A2 *at Bridge End.*

County Fermanagh (Northern Ireland)

Lower Lough Erne

This lake system is an area of outstanding natural beauty, consisting of the Upper and Lower Loughs, connected by a 16km (10 mile) long river. The loughs are full of islands and islets: it is said that there is one for every day of the year. Lough Erne takes its name from the Goddess-maiden Erne, who fled here from Rathcroghan (see page 201). The Lower Lough was known for its tutelary spirit, the 'Lady of the lake', who walked through the mists on the lough, surrounded by light and carrying wild flowers[8]. She sounds very much like a water Goddess, and also a Goddess of the harvest, as her appearance signified good weather and good crops, and she may have been a folk-memory of the Goddess Erne. So powerful is the belief in her that a 12 day Festival still takes place every July in the Irvinestown area to celebrate her legend.

The Lower Lough also has two particular islands – Boa Island (H 088 620) and White Island (H 163 601) – that have some enigmatic carved stones, probably pagan in origin. The ones on Boa Island include a double-faced Janus idol, and a figure with one eye (from the neighbouring Lusty Island). The ones on White Island are perhaps more Christian in appearance, but include a sheela-na-gig, placed on her side next to the doorway of the church. Boa Island itself, Inis Badbhda in Gaelic, is named after the Celtic Goddess Badbh, one of the triple Goddesses of the Morrigan, a war-Goddess who combined destruction, sexuality and prophecy[9]. Her name literally means 'battle-crow' or 'scald-crow', and in

Irish myth she represented destruction, chaos and death. We have here, on this very beautiful lough, a Goddess island of death and the other world, symbolized by a pagan idol looking both ways at the threshold of death and life.

Lower Lough Erne lies to the NE *of Enniskillen. Irvinestown is about 32km (20 miles)* N *of Eniskillen, on the A35. For details of the Lady of the lake festival, tel: 013656–21177. White Island is to the* W *of Irvinestown opposite Castle Archdale, from where boats may be hired for the ten-minute journey across. Boa Island is in the* N *end of the lough and is joined to the shore by bridges, over which crosses the A47. The figures are at the* W *end of the island, on the* S *shore in the ancient Caldragh graveyard.*

County Cavan (Irish Republic)

Lough Macnean Upper (H 060 381)

On the S shore of the lough at Killinagh is a monastic site with the ruins of a twelfth-century church. Here there is a holy well, Toberbride, dedicated to Bridget/Bride, and in a field adjacent to the churchyard lie the ruins of a megalithic tomb known as St Bridget's House. Near the lake shore is St Bridget's Stone, a large boulder with two smaller ones, containing 16 *baullauns* – cup-shaped marks into which rounded pebbles would be placed. These were known as 'cursing stones', and if moved widdershins (anti-clockwise) a successful curse could be placed on someone. There is here an eclectic mixture of pagan and Christian, all under the aegis of the Goddess/saint Bride.

The monastic site can be found on a promontory 2.5km (1½ miles) W *of Blacklion,* N *of the A4/N16 Enniskillen–Sligo road. Situated 6.5km (4 miles) further* S *is the Burren, with its barren limestone country and other remains of megalithic tombs.*

Sheela-na-gigs

County Antrim At Belfast's Ulster Museum is a figure from Ballygawley hilltop church (County Tyrone), which was on the probable site of a Celtic shrine or sanctuary.

County Derry At Maghera Church, on the N side of the tower.

County Fermanagh At Aghalurcher, there is a strange carving with legs wrapped around her face, but vagina showing. Also on White Island (see Lough Erne, page 199).

County Cavan At Toomregon, outside the Protestant church, but originally from a nearby monastery.

Connacht

County Sligo

Knocknarea (G 626 346)

This 308m (1000ft) mountain, with marvellous views over the surrounding countryside and sea, is crowned by a huge megalithic tumulus called Maeve's Lump (Miosgán Méadhbha) after the Goddess/queen of Connacht (see Tara, page 192). It measures over 61m (200ft) in diameter, is over 10m (33ft) high, and is thought to contain a passage-grave which, if ever excavated, could be as richly decorated and impressive as Newgrange (see page 189). Its prehistoric importance is indicated by the attribution of a legend in which it became Maeve's burial tomb. It is certainly part of a ritual landscape: 6.5km (4 miles) to the SE of the mountaintop is the passage-tomb cemetery of Carrowmore (G 665 335), which originally contained close on 100 monuments (of which about 60 remain), including chambered tombs, passage-graves, standing stones, ring forts, cairns and a holed stone – an extensive site, dating back as far as 4000 BCE.
Knocknarea and Carrowmore are about 5km (3 miles) SW *of* Sligo *(reached via the* N15, N16 *and* N4 *roads), on the shore of* Sligo Bay. *The* R292 *ring road from* Sligo *runs around the peninsula to* Sligo Airport, *and gives access to both mountain and monuments.*

Slieve Daeane (G 704 295)

To the SE of Knocknarea is another mountain, Slieve Daeane, and to the S of its summit is a passage-tomb named after the Cailleach, called Cailleach Bhearra's House. It is another example of the attribution of holy hilltops and megalithic tombs to the Goddess of the land.
Slieve Daeane lies 5km (3 miles) to the NE *of Collooney, which is at the junction of the* N17 *and* N4 *roads,* 9.5*km* (6 *miles*) S *of Sligo.*

County Roscommon

Rathcroghan (M 795 831)

This area has many associations with the Goddess/queen Maeve, who was born here of Crochen, maid of the sun Goddess Etain. She may thus have been a later manifestation of a much earlier primal Goddess. Maeve is frequently referred to in the early Irish texts as dwelling in Rathcroghan Palace, where she 'extended the friendship of her upper thighs' (as the Irish epic puts it!) in scenes of ritual king-making and feast drinking.

The area is composed of a limestone plain stretching from Roscommon to Castlereagh, which contains a cave, the Cave of Cruacha

(Cave of the Cats), and a *souterrain* (underground chamber) that were considered to be the entrance to the other world. This liminal place was probably originally a sacred entrance into the Goddess' realm: Sinech, whose name means 'having large paps', dwelt here in early Irish myth, and the Goddesses (such as the Morrigan) and Gods emerged from here into the material world. Nearby there are ancient barrows, tumuli and mounds, the most prominent of which is called Rath Crúachain, the name derived from the Goddess Crochen Croderg, whose name may mean something like 'the blood-red cup'. She was the maid of the sun Goddess Etain, and her mound was given a distinctive nipple-shaped cairn on its summit in prehistoric times. The whole area has been described[1] as having 'an ancient aura which harks back to the earliest human practices, the worship of landscape features [which was] the most ancient form of Goddess worship.'

The Rathcroghan crossroads are on the N5 *about 5km* (3 *miles*) NW *of Tulak. The cave lies 1.5km (1 mile) to the* S *of the crossroads and is reached via a lane leading off the Rathcroghan–Lissalway road, near the township of Glenballythomas. The other sites are all within a 1.5km* (1 *mile*) *radius of the cave.*

Bride's Well / Tobar Bhride (M 941 447)

This famous well rises from deep within a limestone outcrop, and is surrounded by a wall with a gate and steps leading down to the water. A well house, built in 1625, through which the water flows, is fashioned like a cow byre, and there is a modern statue of St Brigid nearby. The well house has a bench and walls on which votive offerings have been placed, and there is space inside for the pilgrim to visit Bridget's sacred waters. The site continues to be visited on the last Sunday in July by supplicants who circumnavigate the well and receive a Catholic blessing, clearly a Christianization of a much more ancient Lughnasad tradition. The well has long been celebrated for the efficacy of its waters, and was renowned for curing barrenness. There is also a legend of sacred fish in the water, linking it with the River Alun in South Wales (see page 164).

The Bride's Well is on Brideswell Common in the village of Brideswell, which lies on the Athlone–Newbridge road, 8km (5 *miles*) W *of Athlone.*

County Mayo

Croag Patrick (L 904 801)

'The holiest mountain in Ireland', this is St Patrick's territory, where every year on the first Sunday in August some 60,000 pilgrims climb to the top to honour the Christian saint. Originally, however, it was a pagan mountain of the Mother Goddess. Patrick had to wrest it from a great bird, Corra (in Gaelic, Caorthineach – 'the devil's Mother'), and a great monster serpent, both totem animals of the Goddess. It was a Lughnasad festival mountain, where the harvest of the Goddess was celebrated, and even up until the mid-nineteenth century only barren women were permitted to climb to the top to be fertilized by the Mother mountain herself.

Recently, outlines of a prehistoric fort and hut circles have shown up on the summit: these date from the Bronze Age and show that the mountain was a pagan site long before the introduction of Christianity. It has also been suggested[2] that it has a solar alignment: when viewed from the Boheh stone, an inscribed cup-and-ring stone some 6.5km (4 miles) away, the setting sun appears to roll down the side of the mountain in April and August.

Croagh Patrick lies 8km (5 miles) to the W *of* Westport, *near the* N *coast of* Mayo. *A path runs to the top of the mountain from* Murrisk *on the* R335 Westport–Louisburgh *road.*

County Galway

Clonfert Monastery (M 963 218)

This monastery stands near the River Shannon, named after the Goddess Sinaan, who went to seek inspiration from the magic powers of the well of Coelrind/Connla, but the well overwhelmed her and she became the river that bears her name. This legend is very similar to that of Boann (see Carbury, page 195). The monastery contains a fifteenth-century chancel arch, decorated with a mermaid carrying a mirror and inscribed with a vaginal moon symbol, and a sheela-na-gig, who has her legs splayed wide and her arms pointing to her pudenda, with her fingers inserted into her vagina[3]. Perhaps the Goddess of the river lingered late in this monastery by her river.

Clonfert is situated 14.5*km* (9 *miles*) SE *of* Ballinasloe, *reached by a minor road* E *of the* R355 *or* N *of the* R356. *The church is usually locked.*

Sheela-na-gigs

County Roscommon At Cloghan Castle, on a slab inserted sideways as a quoin.

County Galway At Clonfert Abbey (see above), and at Ballinderry Castle, on a keystone in the doorway arch. The latter is carved on a background of Celtic knotwork, threads, circles and a wheel ornament of six spokes, and it has been suggested[4] that these are specifically Goddess-inspired images.

Munster

County Limerick

Cnoc Aine and Lough Gur (R 677 364 and R 640 405)

Cnoc Aine hill is named after the Goddess Aine, who was the tutelary Goddess of Munster and was associated with fertility in women and cattle. Her name derives from the root *an*, meaning 'bright', so she was apparently a sun Goddess, who assumed the form of Lair Derg (the 'red mare') whom none could outrun[1]. She may also have been a moon Goddess, for local people used to gather here at night especially to watch the moon[2]. The two aspects – sun and moon – are linked together in her special festival of Midsummer Night, when, right up until the late nineteenth century, local farmers would carry torches of straw in procession around the hill and then wave them over the cattle and fields for protection. Sometimes Aine herself was seen leading the procession, and in later times her spirit was said still to haunt the hill in the form of the queen of the fairies. Annual fairs continued to be held on the hill on 11 August and 11 November, the nearest days to the old Celtic Lughnasad and Samhain festivals.

Nearby, about 5km (3 miles) NE of the hill, is the legendary lake Lough Gur, where Aine was supposed to have disappeared and where she can still be seen sometimes combing her hair above the lake. Legend says that under the lake lies the enchanted castle of her son Geróid, and to the E of the lake in the area called Knockadoon is the chair (*suideachan*) where she sits – a motif similar to that of the Cailleach's Seat at Loughcrew and Slieve Gullion (see pages 191 and 198). In reality, the lough is extremely rich in megalithic remains, dating from the Neolithic period onwards. Many finds were discovered when the lake was drained during the nineteenth century, including bronze horns, axes, a sword grip and stone discs, undoubtedly part of a ritual deposit.

Beside the shores of the lough is a stone circle, the Lios, consisting of an earthern bank, some 46m (150ft) in diameter, enclosing about 100 large stones. Excavation revealed large quantities of broken pottery, evidently smashed in some kind of ritualistic ceremony, perhaps at Beltane or Lughnasad, when the entrance of the circle is aligned to the sunrise across the lough. The circle continued to be revered until quite recent times: a garland of flowers would be left at the largest stone in the circle, perhaps in honour of the Goddess[3]. Around the area of the lough are other stone circles, standing stones, tombs and stone forts. The centre of the lake houses a *crannog*, an artificial lake-dwelling dating from the Iron Age/early Christian period. Finally, beside the lake is a hill called Cnoc Fennell, a place of the mythic Oenach midsummer races. The name Fennell apparently refers to a sister Goddess to Aine (Fennell is from *fin*, meaning 'white') or is an aspect of Aine herself. Aine was a well-loved and respected Goddess, remembered in the myths and legends, the customs and offerings, and in the old saying 'Aine was the best-hearted woman that ever lived'.

Cnoc Aine hill lies to the NW *of Knockainy village,* N *of the* R516 *Hospital–Croon road, 16km (10 miles)* W *of Tipperary. Lough Gur is at Hollycross on the* R512 *Limerick–Kilmallock road, 19km (12 miles)* SE *of Limerick. Cnoc Fennell lies to the* N *of the lough.*

County Clare

Liscannor (R 063 883)

This fishing village on the N of Liscannor Bay has two interesting associations. Near to the village on the headland is a holy well dedicated to St Brigid, which formerly was visited by crowds of people at the Celtic Lughnasad festival. These included Aran islanders, who used to row over for the festival, and there was singing at the well throughout the night and horse racing on the sands below[4]. The festival is now Christianized and takes place on 15 August.

To the W and N of the village are the magnificent Cliffs of Moher, towering 215m (700ft) above the Atlantic ocean. The southernmost outcrop is called the Hag's Head, named after Mal, who chased the legendary Celtic hero Cúchulainn all over Ireland and fell to her death here. The headland is a simulacrum of the seated Hag. She may be a version of the Cailleach, and the juxtaposition of Bride and Cailleach here is a clue to the earlier presence of the Goddess.

Liscannor is on the R478, *6.5km (4 miles)* W *of Ennistymon. Daigh Bhride (Bride's Vat) is a spring in a grove on the headland, situated about 77m (250ft) above a slope which stretches up from Liscannor Bay to the Cliffs of Moher. The Cliffs and the Hag's Head are reached by a minor road to the* W *of the* R478.

County Kerry

Slieve Mish Mountains (Q 750 070)

This mountain range at the neck of the Dingle peninsula is associated with two of the ancient triple Goddesses of Ireland, Ériu and Banba (the third was Fódla). According to the Irish text *Lebor Gabála*, Banba met the invading troops of the Milesians here. Her name means 'land unploughed for a year', so she was probably one of the vegetation Goddesses. Slieve Mish itself means 'mountain of a month', and the word *mis* is also related to *mistae*, meaning 'menstrual flow', so Ériu and/or Banba may have been earlier lunar Goddesses, presiding over the whole cycle of the year[5].

The mountains are visible from the R559 running W of Tralee to Dingle. From the town of Camp a path runs to the westernmost and highest peak, Caherconree, which has a stone fort and legend of the Cuchullain and Blanaid, the wife of the king of Munster.

Croag Skearda (Q 609 069)

The Dingle peninsula is associated with the Cailleach Daingin, one of the three ancient Cailleachs of these SW peninsulas, and in the peninsula is a mountain on whose remote heights lie a cluster of Cailleach sites. Near the townland of Cnoc Ghvalann (Gowlin) is a place called Bothán na Cailligh (the Hag's Cabin), where the ghost of the old woman can be seen at nights. A little further E in the mountain, above the gap and mountain tarn of Beárna na Gaoithe, there is a tradition of two crone Goddesses – the Cailleach Dhuibhneach and the Cailleach Laighneach – who lived in a cave called Cró na Cailligh (the Hag's Field). The former was the local Giantess, the latter an interloper from Leinster. They lived together, then quarrelled, and one threw the other over the mountain[6]. This mythological legend contains echoes of a tutelary Goddess of the land celebrated by the people in this isolated area, who perhaps were in conflict with peoples who moved in from the E with their own Goddess of the land.

Croag Skearda lies to the E of the Connor pass, which rises dramatically from Dingle across the mountains to its 405m (1,316ft) summit and down to Brandon Bay.

The Hag's Glen (V 836 873)

MacGuilly Cuddy's Reeks (Na Cruacha Dubha, 'the black peaks') contain the highest mountains in Ireland, including Carrauntuohill at 1,051m (3,414ft). Along the N side of the range is the Hag's Lake (Loch Calee) and the Hag's Glen (Coom Callee), named after the Cailleach. In this case, the legend tells of the Cailleach who cared for a young child, an interesting variation on the theme, showing the Crone in a nurturing or Mother Goddess role. It is said that there is a rock on the E side of the glen showing the marks of their feet. The Cailleach association was given another twist, because within historical times (end of the eighteenth to the mid-nineteenth centuries) an actual old woman called the Cailleach dwelt there, perhaps an old wise crone living close to the land that bore the ancient Goddess' name.

The Hag's Glen is reached via a minor road running SW from Beaufort Bridge, which is on the R562. Follow the signs to Carrauntuohill, which lead eventually to a farmhouse where vehicles may be parked. Walk from there into the glen.

Paps of Anu (W 125 855 and 134 855)

The Gaelic name for these hills is Dá Chích Annan, which means 'the breasts of Anu', Mother Goddess of all Ireland and associated especially

with Munster. The hills are two very breast-like shapes, with nipple-shaped cairns built on the summits. They lie on the NW side of the Derrynasaggart mountains, and are a distinctive feature from the area S of Killarney. The pass that leads over the hills by the Paps has a well that was visited on May Day eve and dedicated to Crobh Dearg (Red Claw), a deity associated with the three sisters of Kerry and Cork – Latiaran, Lasair and Inghean Bhuidhe – all of whom are probable memories of a pre-Christian Goddess tradition[7] (see Cullen, below).
The Paps are to the N *of the* N22 *Killarney–Macroom road, about* 16*km* (10 *miles*) SE *of Killarney. A good view may be had from the* N22 *past Poulgorm Bridge,* 13*km* (8 *miles*) SE *of Killarney.*

Beara Peninsula (also in County Cork)

This western peninsula is named after the Cailleach Beara, the old hag-Goddess, who was reputed to come from here, where she is remembered as the great shaper of the land. Her form may be found as a ridge of metamorphic rock overlooking Coulagh Bay, where she was transformed, having lived through at least seven lives[8]. She in her turn may be linked with the Goddess Etain, who was ruler of Beara Island[9] (V 440 700), and lived in the sacred hill of Eochaid Airem, or at the entrance to the underworld, Bri Leith. She was a powerful sun and horse Goddess of the Tuatha de Danaan and, after magical transformation, she wed the king of Ireland, and then the fairy King Midir, thus making her a Goddess of sovereignty.
The Beara Peninsula stretches for 48*km* (30 *miles*) *beside Bantry Bay – the* N71 S *from Kenmare to Bantry gives access. Coulagh Bay is at the* W *end of the peninsula. Beara Island lies to the* S *of the peninsula, accessible by ferry from Castletownbere Quay.*

County Cork

Cullen (W 228 967)

This remote village lying to the NE of the Paps of Anu (see above) has a well dedicated to a mysterious saint, known only at this place, called Latiaran. In local mythology she was one of a trio of sisters, the other two being Lasair (meaning 'flame') and Inghean Bhuidhe (meaning 'yellow-haired girl'). The meaning of Latiaran is unknown, but legend tells of her carrying an apronful of hot embers, so all three of them could have been memories of a pre-Christian triple Goddess of fire. Elsewhere in County Cork and County Kerry, other beings were associated with the trio, such as Crobh Derag (Red Claw), who gave her name to a well at the pass of the Paps of Anu, and St Cobnait, who was matron saint of Ballyvourney to the S of the Derrynasaggart mountains.

At Cullen, Latiaran's Well was much visited on the Sunday before 25 July, a local Lughnasad festival[10], and at nearby Dromtarriff, Inghean

Bhuide's feast day was 6 May, the old Beltane. Lasair's feast day has been lost, but her name ('flame') gives a clue, as Imbolc (1 February) was the festival of a fire goddess, Bride/Brigit. Also, a legend tells of Lasair's association with the latter. In gratitude for Brigit's gift of milk to feed her and St Patrick, Lasair 'gave' her church and all her followers to Brigit, who is still venerated there[11]. The legend appears to refer to the cult of Lasair (linked with ewes) being replaced by that of Brigit. Thus, these three saints may originally have been triple aspects of the local fire Goddess, linked to the pre-Christian quarter days of Imbolc, Beltane and Lughnasad.
Cullen is on a minor road to the N *of the* N72, *about 8km (5 miles)* E *of* Rathmore. *The well lies beside the old ruined church in the graveyard.*

Glandore (W 227 354)

Off the coast of this seaside resort is Tonn Cliodna, the wave of Cliodna/Cleena. Cliodna was one of the Tuatha De Dannan, followers of the Goddess Danu, and she herself was said to be the guardian Goddess of the O'Keefes of Cork[12]. She dwelt in the other world, where there was feasting, sport and merrymaking with no evil, death, ageing or decay, and she possessed three brightly coloured magical birds which could lull humans to healing sleep with their song[13]. She fell in love with a mortal man and they ran off together, but Cliodna was (in one legend) swept back to her own country by a miraculous wave, or alternatively (in another) drowned by a wave sent by the God Manannan. To this day she is thought to rule the biggest ninth wave of every nine waves, and she also takes the form of a swooping seabird[14]. She also became a fairy queen of Munster, and offered the gift of loquacity by giving the Blarney Stone to the human race. A sacred hill in Cork, Carrig Cliodna, is also named after her.

Close to Glandore is Dromberg (W 247 352), a beautifully positioned recumbent stone circle with 17 stones standing, aligned to a notch in the surrounding hills at the midwinter solstice sunset.
Glandore is on the R597, *to the* S *of the* N71 *Skibbereen–Clonakilty road*. *Dromberg is situated* 2.5*km* (1½ *miles*) *to the* E *of the town*.

County Tipperary

Mother Mountain (R 872 618)

This evocatively named mountain (Mauher Slieve, or Mathair Shliabh in Gaelic) is one of a number of mountains in the area called The Twelve Mountains of Eblenn. Eblenn was a Goddess, a daughter of Guaire from Brugh na Boine (see Newgrange, page 189). She married a king of Cashel, then ran away with his son. Until the early twentieth century, she continued to be honoured by local people at Lughnasad celebrations in her

mountains[15].
The Mother Mountain lies to the W *of the* R497 *Nenagh–Tipperary road and to the* N *of the* R503 *Limerick–Thurles road, at Kilcommon.*

Slievenamon (S 298 303)

The name of this mountain (at 729m/2,363ft, one of the highest in Ireland) means 'mountain of the women', after the legend that tells of the women who raced there to decide who would wed Finn MacCool. The sun Goddess Grianne was the winner, but the mountain is also known as Slieve mna mBab, after a more ancient Goddess, the eponymous Banba, one of the three primal ruling Goddesses of Ireland.
Slievenamon lies 11km (7 miles) NE *of Clonmel on the* N24. *The small village of Kilcash, on a minor road to the* N *of the* N76, *lies under the* S *escarpment of the mountain.*

Sheela-na-gigs
County Clare At Ballyportry Castle; Bunratty Castle near Limerick, set by the S window in the hall of the Great Keep; Clenagh Castle near Shannon Airport, on a quoin on the SE wall; Killaloe, upstream from Limerick, a headless figure at St Flannan's Well; Clonlara canal bridge, originally from Newton Castle, a fierce hag-like creature, known locally as The Witch's Stone; Rath Old Church, SE of Corofin, on an ornamental panel; and Killinaboy Church, NW of Ennis, above the S doorway – the name of the church comes from Cillinine Baoith, meaning the daughter of Boath, the great Goddess Boand (see Newgrange and Carbury, pages 189 and 195).
County Kerry At Kilsarkan Church, E of Farrnafore, above the S window – the genital area shows signs of rubbing.
County Cork At Cork City Museum, from Tracton Abbey; Ballinacarriga Castle, E of Dumnaway, inside the chapel, high on the E wall; Ballyvourney shrine, on the N22 Killarney–Macroom road, over a window at the E end of the S wall – still an active Catholic shrine, dedicated to St Gobnait, the female saint of the bees, who may be related to a Goddess archetype; Castle Windenham, near Castletownroche, originally at the holy well, now in the castle tower; and Aghadoe Castle, Killeagh. on the old dovecote.
County Limerick From Caherelly Castle near Lough Gur (see page 204), now in the Hunt Museum in Limerick – perhaps a representation of the Goddess Aine; at Dunnaman Castle, near Adare, high on the wall of the peel tower, obscured by ivy; and Tullavin Castle, near Croom, on the S face of the tower.
County Tipperary At Ballyfinboy Castle, S of Borrisokane, on a cornerstone; Ballynahinch Castle, alongside the River Suir, on the E wall of the peel tower; Fethard Abbey, to the S of the town; Fethard Old Wall, a fierce hag-like creature overlooking the medieval bridge; Kilitane Church, SE of Fethard, a replica – the original was stolen in 1990; Kilitane Castle well

house, called locally The Guardian of the Well – the figure holds 'Goddess symbolism' such as the sickle in her left hand and a serpent(?) in her right; Holycross Abbey, beside the River Suir SW of Thurles; Leighmore, near Urlingford, above the N door of the church on the site of a monastery; and Shanrahan, near Ballyporeen, on the W wall of the old church tower.

Notes

Leinster

[1] Jack Roberts, *The Sacred Mythological Centres of Ireland*, pages 5.
[2] By Marija Gimbutas in *The Civilization of the Goddess*, pages 300–1.
[3] By Jeremy Dronfield in 'Subjective Vision and the Source of Irish Megalithic Art, *Antiquity*, vol 69, no 264, pages 539–49.
[4] By Hugh Kearns in *The Mysterious Chequered Lights of Newgrange*.
[5] Martin Brennan, *The Stars and the Stones*, page 82.
[6] By Marija Gimbutas, op cit, page 213.
[7] By Tim O'Brien in *Light Years Ago*, pages 40–52.
[8] By Anthony Weir in *Early Ireland: A Field Guide*, page 194.
[9] See Martin Brennan, op cit, pages 108–18.
[10] By Gary Brindle in 'If the Stones Could Talk', *Dalriada*, vol 9, no 2, page 6.
[11] See Miranda Green, *Celtic Goddesses*, pages 40 and 80.
[12] See Maire MacNeill, *The Festival of Lughnasa*, pages 207–8.
[13] Michael Dames, *Mythic Ireland*, pages 209 and 213–42.
[14] See Pamela Berger, *The Goddess Obscured*, page 74.
[15] See R.J. Stewart, *Celtic Gods, Celtic Goddesses*, page 96.
[16] See Patrick Logan, *The Holy Wells of Ireland*, page 48.

Ulster

[1] See Miranda Green, *Celtic Goddesses*, pages 40–1 and 76–8.
[2] See Jorgen Andersen, *The Witch on the Wall*, page 118.
[3] By Michael Dames in *Mythic Ireland*, pages 55–6.
[4] See Maire MacNeill, *The Festival of Lughnasa*, pages 160–1.
[5] See Marija Gimbutas, *The Language of the Goddess*, page 211.
[6] By O.G.S Crawford in *The Eye Goddess*, page 91.
[7] By Patricia Monaghan in *The Book of Goddesses and Heroines*, page 140.
[8] See Janet and Colin Bord, *Sacred Waters*, page 111.
[9] See Miranda Green, op cit, page 41–3.

Connacht

[1] By Jack Roberts in *The Sacred Mythological Centres of Ireland*, page 32.
[2] By Michael Viney in 'The Magic of the Rolling Mayo Sun', *Northern Earth*, no 63, pages 6–8.
[3] See Jack Roberts, *The Sheela-na-Gigs of Britain and Ireland*, page 28.
[4] Ibid, page 13.

Munster

[1] See Patricia Monaghan, *The Book of Goddesses and Heroines*, page 11.
[2] See W.Y. Evans-Wenz, *The Fairy Faith in Celtic Countries*, pages 79–80.
[3] See Janet and Colin Bord, *The Secret Country*, page 39.
[4] See Marie MacNeill, *The Festival of Lughnasa*, pages 275–86.
[5] See Michael Dames, *Mythic Ireland*, page 237.
[6] See Marie MacNeill, op cit, pages 207–8.
[7] Ibid, pages 270–5.
[8] See Jack Roberts, *The Sacred Mythological Centres of Ireland*, pages 46–7.
[9] See Patricia Monaghan, op cit, page 115.
[10] See Marie MacNeill, op cit, page 271.
[11] See Mary Condren, *The Serpent and the Goddess*, page 231.
[12] See Lorraine McDonald, 'The People of the Mounds', *Dalriada*, vol 8, no 1, page 5.
[13] See Miranda Green, *Celtic Goddesses*, pages 87 and 176.
[14] See Patricia Monaghan, op cit, page 80.
[15] See Maire MacNeill, op cit, pages 214–15.

Appendices

Appendix 1

A newly discovered Neolithic site with Goddess stones

Researcher and writer Terence Meaden has recently recognized a hitherto-unidentified site in Wessex in southern England, a major Goddess-celebrating centre covering a large area. It consists of many megaliths forming circles, sanctuaries, sacred enclosures, standing stones and stone rows. Finds include deliberately shaped and natural stones that appear to have been Goddess cult objects and figurines. The stones that he has so far identified, together with the names he has attributed to them, include:

Site 1: Ring-stone Down A holed stone, and two pyramidal megaliths.
Site 2: South Temple A small stone circle, plus a probable concentric damaged one at the spur of a hill ridge, together with large free-standing stones.
Site 3: North Temple Badly damaged sacred temple area, with stone rows, and station stones to the sun and moon. Finds include a pubic triangle stone with pecked-out vulva, and a crude stone head.
Site 4: The Cuntistones Numerous megaliths centred on an altar stone and vulva gap, aligned to a lunar marker and to Site 7. Finds include a Goddess head, a pubic triangle with vulva and vagina, a flint Goddess figurine with vulva, and fertility charms.
Site 5: Quoits Circle A stone circle with a centre stone, and a long stone row with lunar alignment.
Site 6: Delphi Earth-womb Temple A forty-tonne focal stone, vulva stone, cervix stones and other megaliths, forming an outstanding open-air temple.
Site 7: Megaliths One moon alignment, a midsummer solstice sunrise and a midwinter solstice sunset.
Site 8: Moonstone Field A triangular station stone, and finds of a Goddess head, torso and pubic triangle, with pecked-out vulva.

At the time of writing the site is confidential, although full details will be published by Terence Meaden (Souvenir Press, London 1998). He says there is absolutely no doubt that this is a significant sacred site, and comments: 'All the sites constitute one vast religious area glorifying Goddess. Only once have I detected any sign of a masculine contribution, and that is ambivalent. It appears to have been in use for more than 1,000 years'.

Appendix II

Named British and Irish Goddesses and their locations

E=England W=Wales S=Scotland I=Ireland

*Indicates Goddesses suggested by linguistic clues, for whom there is no written verification.

AINE Knoc Aine and Lough Gur (I – Munster) Grianan Ailigh (I – Leinster)
*ALAUNA River Alun (W – South Wales)
ALMHA/ALMU Dun Aillinne (I – Leinster)
ANDRAS (TE) Druids Circle (W – North Wales)
ANNE Whitstone (E – Cornwall) Chertsey (E – Surrey) Hempsted (E – Gloucestershire) Llanmihangel (W – South Wales)
ANU Knockmany (I – Ulster) Paps of Anu (I – Munster) Grianan Ailigh (I – Leinster) (see also DANU)
ARIANRHOD Caer Arianrhod (W – North Wales)
ARNEMETIA Buxton (E – Derbyshire)
ATARGATIS London (E – London)
BADBH/BANBA Lower Lough Erne (I – Ulster) Slieve Mish (I – Munster) Slievenamon (I – Munster)
BEDE Hadrian's Wall (E – Northumberland)
BELLONA York (E – Yorkshire)
BAUDIHILLE Hadrian's Wall (E – Northumberland)
BOAND Newgrange (I – Leinster) Carbury (I – Leinster)
BRANWEN Bedd Branwen (W – North Wales) Cadair Bronwen (W – North Wales) Harlech (W – North Wales)
BRIDGET/BRIDE Landue (E – Cornwall) Morvah (E – Cornwall) Bridestow (E – Devon) Glastonbury (E – Somerset) Brean (E – Somerset) St.Briavels (E – Gloucestershire) London (E – London) Bridestones (E – Staffordshire) Bridestones (E – Yorkshire) Bride Churches (E – Cumbria) St Bride's Bay (W – South Wales) Bryn-Celli-Ddu (W – North Wales) Arran (S – Lowlands) Islay (S – Lowlands) Mull (S – Lowlands) Skye (S – Highlands) Lewis (S – Highlands) Faughart (I – Leinster) Kildare (I – Leinster) Lough Macnean (I – Ulster) Bride's Well (I – Connacht) Liscannor (I – Munster) Cullen (I – Munster)
BRIGANTIA Hadrian's Wall (E – Northumberland) Birrens (S – Lowlands)
CAILLEACH North Barrule (E – Isle of Man) Islay (S – Lowlands) Glen Lyon (S – Lowlands) Skye (S – Highlands) Ballachulish (S – Highlands) Inverness (S – Highlands) Aberdeenshire (S – Highlands) North Uist (S – Highlands) Loughcrew (I – Leinster) Slieve Gullion (I – Ulster) Slieve Daeane (I – Connacht) Liscannor (I – Munster) Croag Skearda (I – Munster) Hags Glen (I – Munster) Beara Peninsula (I – Munster)
CERES Beverley (E – Yorkshire) Cirencester (E – Gloucestershire) River Thames (E – London) Hadrian's Wall (E – Northumberland)
CERRIDWEN Beverley (E – Yorkshire) Pentre Ifan (W – South Wales) Lake Bala (W – North Wales) Druids Circle (W – North Wales)

CLIODNA Glandore (I – Munster)
CLOTA Dumbarton Rock (S – Lowlands)
CUDA Cirencester (E – Gloucestershire)
*CUNTI Kennet River (E – Wiltshire)
DANU Dane Hills (E – Leicestershire) River Dane (E – Staffordshire) (see also ANU)
DEA NUTRIX Canterbury (E – Kent)
DEA REGINA Chedworth (E – Gloucestershire)
DIANA (see also LUNA) Frithelstock Priory (E – Devon) Eggardon Down (E – Dorset) Maiden Castle (E – Dorset) Richborough (E – Kent) Dover (E – Kent) London (E – London) Hornchurch (E – Essex) Mucking (E – Essex) Woodchester (E – Gloucestershire) Chedworth (E – Gloucestershire) Cirencester (E – Gloucestershire) Ribchester (E – Lancashire) Diana's Well (E – Yorkshire) Hadrian's Wall (E – Northumberland)
DOMNU South Uist (S – Highland)
*DOURA Dover (E – Kent)
EBLENN Mother Mountain (I – Munster)
*EILA Islay (S – Lowlands)
*ELLEN St Helen's Well, Eshton (E – Yorkshire)
EPONA Westbury (E – Wiltshire) Uffington (E – Berkshire) Wandlebury (E – Cambridgeshire)
ERIU Uisnech (I – Leinster) Slieve Mish (I – Munster)
ERNE Lower Lough Erne (I – Ulster)
ETAIN Tara (I – Leinster)
EUROPA Lullingstone Villa (E – Kent)
FENNELL Lough Gur (I – Munster)
FINNILENE Hadrian's Wall (E – Northumberland)
FORTUNA Marlborough (E – Wiltshire) Royston (E – Hertfordshire) Cirencester (E – Gloucestershire) Hadrian's Wall (E – Northumberland) Birrens (S – Lowlands)
FRIAGABI Hadrian's Wall (E – Northumberland)
FRIG/FREYA Frithelstock Priory (E – Devon) Fretherne (E – Gloucestershire) Froyle (E – Hants) Friden (E – Derbyshire) Friday Well (E – Yorkshire) Freeborough Hill (E – Yorkshire) Pennington (E – Cumbria) North Uist (S – Highlands)
GARMANGABI/GEFION Lanchester (E – County Durham)
*GODDA St Milburga (E – Shropshire)
GRAINNE/GRIANNE Tara (I – Leinster) Grianan Ailigh (I – Ulster) Slievenamon (I – Munster)
HARIMELLA Birrens (S – Lowlands)
HYGEA Chester (E – Cheshire)
*INGHEAN BHUIDHE Cullen (I – Munster)
*IOUA Iona (S – Lowlands)
ISIS London (E – London) Thornborough (E – Buckinghamshire)
JUNO Chester (E – Cheshire)

*LASAIR Cullen (I – Munster)
*LATIRAN Cullen (I – Munster)
LATIS Hadrian's Wall (E – Northumberland)
*LOIREAG South Uist (S – Highlands)
LUNA (see also DIANA) Bath (E – Bath) London (E – London)
MACHA Navan (I – Ulster) Armagh (I – Ulster)
MAEVE/MEBD Mab's Well (E – Yorkshire) Tara (I – Leinster) Knocknarea (I – Connacht) Rathcroghan (I – Connacht)
MATRES London (E – London) Arrington (E – Cambridgeshire) Lincoln (E – Lincolnshire) Ancester (E – Lincolnshire) Cirencester (E – Gloucestershire)
MINERVA Bath (E – Bath) London (E – London) Thornborough (E – Buckinghamshire) Nene Valley (E – Cambridgeshire) Cirencester (E – Gloucestershire) Wall (E – Staffordshire) Chester (E – Cheshire) Hadrian's Wall (E – Northumberland) Birrens (S – Lowlands)
MODRON Madron (E – Cornwall)
MORRIGAN Rathcroghan (I – Connacht)
NANTOSUELTA East Stoke (E – Notts)
NEMESIS Chester (E – Cheshire)
NEMETONA Bath (E – Bath)
PANAKEA Chester (E – Cheshire)
RATIS Hadrian's Wall (E – Northumberland)
RICAGAMBEDA Birrens (S – Lowlands)
ROSMERTA Hadrian's Wall (E – Northumberland)
SABRAAN/SABRINA Aust (E – Gloucestershire) Little Dean (E – Gloucestershire)
SCATHAC/SKIACH/SGATHACH Skye (S – Highlands)
SELENE Bath (E – Bath)
SETLOCENIA Maryport (E – Cumbria)
*SILLINA Nornour (E – Scillies)
SINAAN Clonfert (I – Connacht)
SINECH Rathcroghan (I – Connacht)
SULIS (MINERVA) Bath (E – Bath)
TAILTU Teltown (I – Leinster)
*TEA Tara (I – Leinster)
TLACHTGA Hill of Ward (I – Leinster)
VENUS Richborough (E – Kent) Canterbury (E – Kent) Chart Sutton (E – Kent) London (E – London) St Albans (E – Hertfordshire) York (E – Yorkshire) High Rochester (E – Northumberland)
VERBIA Ilkley (E – Yorkshire)
VIRADECTHIS Birrens (S – Lowlands)

Bibliography

Allason-Jones, Lindsay and McKay, Bruce *Coventina's Well* Chesters Museum, 1985.
Allegro, John *Lost Gods* Michael Joseph, 1977.
Andersen, Jorgen*The Witch on the Wall* Allen & Unwin, 1977.
Ashbee, Paul *Ancient Scilly* David & Charles, 1974.
Atkinson, R.J.C. *Stonehenge* Pelican, 1979.
Austen, Hallie Inglehart *The Heart of the Goddess* Wingbow Press, 1990.
Baring, Anne, and Cashford, Jules *The Myth of the Goddess* Penguin, 1991.
Baring-Gould, S. *A Book of Dartmoor* 1900, reprinted Wildwood House, 1982.
Berger, Pamela *The Goddess Obscured* Robert Hale, 1988.
Berresford Ellis, Peter *Celt and Saxon* Constable, 1993.
— *Celtic Women* Constable, 1995.
Biaggi, Cristina *Habitations of the Great Goddess*, Knowledge, Trends and Ideas, 1994.
Billington, S. and Green, M. (eds) *The Concept of the Goddess* Routledge, 1996.
Bord, Janet and Colin *Earth Rites* Granada, 1982.
—*Mysterious Britain* Granada, 1974.
—*The Enchanted Land* Thorsons, 1995.
—*Sacred Waters* Granada, 1985.
—*The Secret Country* Paul Elek, 1976.
Branston, Brian *The Lost Gods of England* Thames & Hudson, 1974.
Brennan, J.H.*A Guide to Megalithic Ireland* Aquarian, 1994.
Brennan, Martin *The Stars and the Stones* Thames & Hudson, 1983.
Brewer, Richard J. *Corpus Signorum Imperii Romani* vol 1, fasc 5, Oxford University Press, 1986.
Briggs, Katharine M. *Folklore of the Cotswolds* Batsford, 1974.
Broadhurst, Paul *Tintagel and the Arthurian Mythos* Pendragon, 1992.
Burl, Aubrey *A Guide to the Stone Circles of Britain, Ireland and Brittany* Yale University Press, 1995.
—*Prehistoric Avebury* Yale University Press, 1979.
—*Rites of the Gods* Dent, 1981.
—*The Stonehenge People* Dent, 1987.
Cameron, Kenneth *English Place Names* Batsford, 1988.
Castleden, Rodney *The Stonehenge People* Routledge, 1987.
Chippindale, Christopher *Stonehenge Complete* Thames & Hudson, 1983.
Clarke, David *A Guide to Britain's Pagan Heritage* Robert Hale, 1995.
Clarke, David with Roberts, Andy *Twilight of the Celtic Gods* Cassell, 1996.
Cleal, Walker and Montague *Stonehenge in its Landscape* English Heritage

Archaeological Report, 1995.
Cles-Reden, Sibylle von *The Realm of the Great Goddess* Thames & Hudson, 1961.
Coles, Bryony & John *Sweet Track to Glastonbury* Thames & Hudson, 1986.
Collins, Martin *Classic Walks on the North York Moors* Haynes, 1990.
Condren, Mary *The Serpent and the Goddess* Harper Collins, 1989.
Cooke, Ian *Journey to the Stones* Men-an-Tol Studio, 1987.
—*Mother and Sun: the Cornish Fogou* Men-an-Tol Studio, 1993.
Coulston, J.C. and Phillips, E.J. *Corpus Signorum Imperii Romani* vol 1, fasc 6, Oxford University Press, 1988.
Coxhead, John *Devon Traditions and Fairy Tales* Raleigh Press, 1959.
Crawford, O.G.S.*The Eye Goddess* Phoenix House, 1957.
Crow, James *Housesteads* Batsford, 1995
Cunliffe, B.W. and Fulford, M.G. *Corpus Signorum Imperii Romani* vol 1, fasc 2, Oxford University Press, 1982.
Dames, Michael *The Avebury Cycle* Thames & Hudson, 1977.
— *Mythic Ireland* Thames & Hudson, 1992.
—*The Silbury Treasure* Thames & Hudson, 1976.
Devereux, Paul *Places of Power* Blandford, 1990.
— *Symbolic Landscapes* Gothic Image, 1992.
Dixon-Kennedy, Mike *Celtic Myth and Legend* Blandford, 1996.
Douglas, Mona *Christian Tradition in Mannin* Times Press, 1965.
Eddy, David, J. *A Brief History of the Obby Oss* Acorn Press, Padstow.
Eisler, Riane *The Chalice and the Blade* Unwin Hyman, 1987.
Ellis Davidson, H.R. *The Lost Beliefs of Northern Europe* Routledge, 1993.
— *Gods and Myths of Northern Europe* Penguin, 1964.
Evans-Wentz, W.Y. *The Fairy-Faith in Celtic Countries* 1911; Colin Smythe, 1977.
Fradenburg (ed) *Women in Sovereignty* Edinburgh University Press, 1992.
Francis, Gaynor *The First Stonehenge* Christopher Davies, 1986.
Gadon, Elinor *The Once and Future Goddess* Harper Row, 1990.
George, Demetra *Mysteries of the Dark Moon* Harper, 1992.
Getty, Adele *Goddess: Mother of Living Nature* Thames & Hudson, 1990.
Gimbutas, Marija *The Civilization of the Goddess* Harper Collins, 1991.
—*The Goddesses and Gods of Old Europe* Thames & Hudson, 1982.
—*The Language of the Goddess* Thames & Hudson, 1989.
— *Goddesses of the British Museum* Goddess Guide Group, 1988.
Gooch, Stan *Cities of Dreams – When Women Ruled the Earth* Aulis Books, 1995.
Gordon, R.K. *Anglo-Saxon Poetry* Dent, 1954.
Green, Miranda *Celtic Goddesses* British Museum Press, 1995.
— *Dictionary of Celtic Myth and Legend* Thames & Hudson, 1992.
—*The Gods of the Celts* Alan Sutton, 1986.
—*The Religions of Civilian Roman Britain* BAR, 1976.
—*The Sun-Gods of Ancient Europe* Batsford, 1991.
Grinsell, Leslie, V. *Folklore of Prehistoric Sites in Britain* David & Charles, 1976.
Harrison, Michael *The Roots of Witchcraft* Muller, 1973.
Hawkes, Jacquetta *The Shell Guide to British Archaeology* Michael Joseph, 1986.

Henig, Martin *Corpus Signorum Imperii Romani* vol 1, fasc 7, ('Roman Sculpture from the Cotswold Region') Oxford University Press, 1993.
—*Religion in Roman Britain* Batsford, 1984.
Herbert, Kathleen *Looking for the Lost Gods of England* Anglo-Saxon Books, 1994.
Hochberg, Betty *Spin Span Spun* 1979.
Hope, Robert Charles *The Legendary Lore of the Holy Wells of England* 1893.
Hudson, Paul *Mastering Herbalism* Abacus, 1977.
Hunt, Robert *Popular Romances of the West of England* 1871/1916.
Huskinson, Janet *Corpus Signorum Imperii Romani* vol 1, fasc 8, Oxford University Press, 1994.
Hutton, Ronald *The Pagan Religions of the Ancient British Isles* Blackwell, 1991.
Johns, C.M. 'A Roman Bronze statue of Epona', *British Museum Quarterly*, vol 36, part 1–2, 1971–2.
Johnson, Buffie *Lady of the Beasts* Harper Collins, 1990.
Jones, Francis *The Holy Wells of Wales* University of Wales Press, 1954.
Jones, Noragh *Power of Raven, Wisdom of Serpent* Floris Books, 1994.
Jones, Prudence, and Pennick, Nigel *A History of Pagan Europe* Routledge, 1995.
Kemm, William St John *The Story of Berrow and Brean*.
Keppie, L.J.F. and Arnold, Beverly J. *Corpus Signorum Imperii Romani* vol 1, fasc 4, Oxford University Press, 1984.
Killip, Margaret *The Folklore of the Isle of Man* Batsford, 1986.
Kinnes, Ian and Grant, J.A. *Les Fouaillages and the Megalithic Monuments of Guernsey* Ampersand Press, 1983.
Kraft, John *The Goddess in the Labyrinth* Abo, 1985.
Langstone, Alex *Bega and the Sacred Ring* The Lantern Press, 1992.
Lethbridge, T.C. *Gog Magog: the Buried Gods* Routledge & Kegan Paul, 1957.
Lewis, Shelagh *Buried around Buckingham* Friends of the Old Gaol Museum, 1992.
Logan, Patrick *The Holy Wells of Ireland* Colin Smythe, 1992.
Lynch, Frances *Prehistoric Anglesey* Anglesey Antiquarian Society, 1970.
McCrickard, Janet *Eclipse of the Sun* Gothic Image, 1990.
McCana, Proinsias *Celtic Mythology* Hamlyn, 1970.
MacNeill, Maire *The Festival of Lughnasa* Oxford University Press, 1962.
Maltwood, Katherine *A Guide to Glastonbury's Temple of the Stars* James Clarke, 1964.
Mann, Nicholas R. *Glastonbury Tor* Triskele, 1993.
Markale, Jean *Women of the Celts* Inner Traditions, 1975.
Matthews, Caitlin *Mabon and the Mysteries of Britain* Arkana, 1987.
Matthews, John *Taliesin* Aquarian Press, 1991.
Meaden, George Terence *The Goddess of the Stones* Souvenir Press, 1991.
—*The Stonehenge Solution* Souvenir Press, 1992.
Merrifield, Ralph *The Archaeology of Ritual and Magic* Batsford, 1987.
—*London – City of the Romans* Batsford, 1983.
—*Roman London* Cassell, 1969.
Michell, John *Sacred England* Harrap Columbus, 1989.
Milne, Gustav *Roman London* Batsford, 1996.
Monaghan, Patricia *The Book of Goddesses and Heroines* Llewellyn, 1990.

Newall, Venetia (ed) *The Witch Figure* Routledge & Kegan Paul, 1973.
O'Brien, Tim *Light Years Ago* Black Cat Press, 1992.
ó Catháin, Séamas *The Festival of Brigit* DBA Publications, 1995.
Pennick, Nigel *Celtic Sacred Landscapes* Thames & Hudson, 1996.
—*Mazes and Labyrinths* Robert Hale, 1990.
Phillips, E.J. *Corpus Signorum Imperii Romani* vol 1, fasc 1, Oxford University Press, 1977.
Phillips, Guy Ragland *Brigantia: A Mysteriography* Routledge & Kegan Paul, 1976.
Ponting, Gerald and Margaret *New Light on the stones of Callanish* 1984.
—*The Stones around Callanish* 1984.
Raftery, Barry *Pagan Celtic Ireland* Thames & Hudson, 1994.
Rahtz, Philip *Glastonbury* Batsford, 1993.
Rawson, P. (ed) *Primitive Erotic Art* Weidenfeld & Nicolson, 1973.
Rhys, John *Celtic Folklore: Welsh and Manx* Wildwood House, 1983.
Richards, Julian *Stonehenge* Batsford, 1991.
Ryall, Rhiannon *West Country Wicca* Phoenix, 1989.
Roberts, Jack *The Sacred Mythological Centres of Ireland* Bandia, 1996.
— *The Sheela-na-Gigs of Britain and Ireland* Key Books, 1994.
Ross, Anne and Robins, Don *Life and Death of a Druid Prince* Rider, 1989.
— *Celtic and Northern Art* from Rawson – cit above.
— *The Divine Hag of the Pagan Celts* from Newall – cit above.
— *The Folklore of the Scottish Highlands* Barnes & Noble, 1993.
— *Pagan Celtic Britain* Constable, 1992.
Rudkin, Ethel *Lincolnshire Folklore* G.W. Belton, 1936, reprinted 1973.
St Ledger Gordon, Ruth *The Witchcraft and Folklore of Dartmoor* Alan Sutton, 1982.
Sant, Jonathan *The Healing Wells of Herefordshire* Moondial, 1994.
Service, Alstair and Bradbury, Jean *The Standing Stones of Europe* Dent, 1993.
Sharkey, John *The Road through the Isles* Wildwood House, 1986.
Sharp, Mick *A Land of Gods and Giants* Alan Sutton, 1989.
Sjöö, Monica and Mor, Barbara *The Great Cosmic Mother* Harper, 1987.
Slade, Brian *The Well of the Triple Goddess* Santa Maria, 1993.
—*The Well of the Triple Goddess: What the Experts Say* Santa Maria, 1994.
Smith, Rev William *Ancient Springs and Streams of the East Riding of Yorkshire* Brown & Sons, 1923.
Spencer, Ray *A Guide to the Saints of Wales and the West Country* Llanerch, 1991.
Starhawk *The Spiral Dance* Harper Collins, 1989.
Steer, Francis W. *Guide to Burton Church* Sussex Historic Churches Trust.
Stewart, R.J. *Celtic Gods, Celtic Goddesses* Blandford, 1990.
Stone, Merlin *The Paradise Papers* Virago, 1976.
Straffon, Cheryl, *Pagan Cornwall: Land of the Goddess* Meyn Mamuro, 1993.
Streep, Peg *Sanctuaries of the Goddess* Bulfinch, 1994.
Swire, Otta F. *Skye – the Island and its Legends* Blackie, 1860.
Thomas, Charles *Celtic Britain* Thames & Hudson, 1986.
— *Explorations of a Drowned Landscape* Batsford, 1985.
—*Tintagel* Batsford, 1993.

Toynbee, J.M.C. *Art in Roman Britain* Phaidon, 1962.
Tufi, Sergio Rinaldi *Corpus Signorum Imperii Romani* vol 1, fasc 3, Oxford University Press, 1983.
Twohig, Elizabeth Shee *The Megalithic Art of Western Europe* Clarendon Press, 1981.
Walker, Barbara *The Woman's Encyclopedia of Myths and Secrets* Harper & Row, 1983.
Walker, Peter *Folk Tales from the North York Moors* Hale, 1990.
Weir, Anthony *Early Ireland: A Field Guide* Blackstaff Press, 1980.
Wheelan, Edna and Taylor, John *Yorkshire Holy Wells and Sacred Springs* Northern Lights, 1989.
Wilde, Lyn Webster *Celtic Women in Legend, Myth and History* Blandford, 1997.
Wilson, David *Anglo-Saxon Paganism* Routledge, 1982.
Wilson, Rob *Holy Wells and Spas of South Yorkshire* Northern Arts, 1991.
Wood, John Edwin *Sun, Moon and Standing Stones* Oxford University Press, 1978.
Worsley, Roger *The Pembrokeshire Explorer* 1988.

Journals and Magazines

Antiquity
Oxford Journals, Walton Street, Oxford OX2 6DP.
ASH – *Albion's Sacred Heritage*
2 Kent View Road, Vange, Basildon, Essex SS10 4LA.
Avalon
Glastonbury Experience, 2–4 High Street, Glastonbury, Somerset BA6 9DU.
The Cauldron
Contact: Mike Howard, Caemorgan Cottage, Cardigan, Dyfed, Wales SA43 IQU.
Cornish Archaeology
c/o David Donohue, 115 Longfield, Falmouth, Cornwall TR11 4SL.
Current Archaeology
9 Nassington Road, London NW3 2TX.
Dalriada – Pagan Celtic Journal
Dun-na-Beatha, 2 Brathwic Place, Brodick, Arran, Scotland KA27 8BN.
F.O.G.S – *Friends of Grampian Stones* Library House, Keith Hall, Invenarie, Aberdeenshire AB51 OLD
Gloucestershire Earth Mysteries (now replaced by *3rd Stone*)
PO Box 961, Devizes, Wiltshire SN10 2TS.
The Ley Hunter – Ancient Wisdom, Landscapes and Sacred Sites
PO Box 961, Devizes, Wiltshire, SN10 2TS
London Earth Mysteries
Contact: Rob Stephenson, PO Box 1035, London W2 6ZX.
Markstone – Lincolnshire Earth Mysteries
Formerly at Glebe Farm House, Fen Road, Owmby-by-Spital, Lincoln LN2 3DR.
Matriarchy Research and Reclaim Network Newsletter
c/o Wesley House, 4 Wild Court, London WC2B 5AU.
Mercian Mysteries (now replaced by *At The Edge*)
2 Cross Hill Close, Wymeswold, Loughborough LE12 6UJ.

Meyn Mamvro – Ancient Stones and Sacred Sites in Cornwall
51 Carn Bosavern, St.Just, Penzance, Cornwall TR19 7QX.
Northern Earth Mysteries/Northern Earth
10 Jubilee Street, Mytholmroyd, Hebden Bridge, Yorkshire HX7 5NP.
Source – Journal of Holy Wells
Pen-y-Bont, Bont Newydd, Cefn, St Asaph, Clwyd, Wales LL17 OHH.
White Dragon
103 Abbotswood Close, Winyates Green, Redditch, Worcestershire B98 0QF.
Wisht Maen – Devon Earth Mysteries
4 Victoria Cottages, North Street, North Tawton, Devon EX20 2DF.
Wood & Water – Goddess-centred Magazine
77 Parliament Hill, London NW3 2TH.

Useful Addresses

Goddess organizations

Matriachy Research and Reclaim Network
c/o Wesley House, 4 Wild Court, London WC2B 5AU (women only).
Fellowship of Isis
Clonegal Castle, Enniscorthy, County Wexford, Ireland.
International Goddess Festival, Women's Spirituality Forum
PO Box 11363, Piedmont, California 94611–0383, USA (women only).
Goddess Regenerating
PO Box 73, Sliema, Malta.
Glastonbury Goddess Conference
2-4 High Street, Glastonbury BA6 9DU

Museums

British Museum
Great Russell Street, London WC1.
Tel: 0171–636–1555
National Museum of Antiquities of Scotland
Queen Street, Edinburgh.
Tel: 0131–225–7534
Museum of Scotland (from end 1988)
Chambers Street, Edinburgh.
National Museum of Wales
Cathays Park, Cardiff.
Tel: 01222–397951

Index